WHAT PROCESS IS DUE ?

COURTS AND SCIENCE-POLICY DISPUTES

Other Books by the Author

Storm Center: The Supreme Court in American Politics

Views from The Bench: The Judiciary and Constitutional Politics
(with Mark Cannon)

The Politics of Technology Assessment:
Institutions, Processes, and Policy-Disputes
(with Donald Marchand)

The Public's Right to Know:
The First Amendment and the Supreme Court

Privacy, Law, and Public Policy

WHAT PROCESS IS DUE?

COURTS AND SCIENCE-POLICY DISPUTES

David M. O'Brien

RUSSELL SAGE FOUNDATION   NEW YORK

The Russell Sage Foundation

The Russell Sage Foundation, one of the oldest of America's general purpose foundations, was established in 1907 by Mrs. Margaret Olivia Sage for "the improvement of social and living conditions in the United States." The Foundation seeks to fulfill this mandate by fostering the development and dissemination of knowledge about the political, social, and economic problems of America. It conducts research in the social sciences and public policy, and publishes books and pamphlets that derive from this research.

The Board of Trustees is responsible for oversight and the general policies of the Foundation, while administrative direction of the program and staff is vested in the President, assisted by the officers and staff. The President bears final responsibility for the decision to publish a manuscript as a Russell Sage Foundation book. In reaching a judgment on the competence, accuracy, and objectivity of each study, the President is advised by the staff and selected expert readers. The conclusions and interpretations in Russell Sage Foundation publications are those of the authors and not of the Foundation, its Trustees, or its staff. Publication by the Foundation, therefore, does not imply endorsement of the contents of the study.

Library of Congress Cataloging-in-Publication Data

O'Brien, David M.
　What process is due?

　Bibliography: p.
　Includes index.
　1. Courts—United States.　2. Judicial process—United
States.　3. Personal injuries—United States.　4. Products
liability—United States.　5. Hazardous substances—Law
and legislation—United States.　6. Health risk
assessment—United States.　I. Title.
KF8700.O27　1987　　　346.7303'0269　　　87-43100
　　　　　　　　　　　　347.30630269
ISBN 0-87154-623-X (alk. paper)

Cover and text design: Huguette Franco

10 9 8 7 6 5 4 3 2 1

For
Benjamin and Sara

Preface

Why is it that courts are in the business of assessing the scientific basis for claims about newly discovered occupational hazards or new-found risks in consumer products? Are judges competent to decide such disputes? Is the judicial process appropriate for resolving the scientific controversies and intense value conflicts underlying disputes over toxic chemicals and hazardous wastes? Have courts gone too far in awarding damages? Do courts unreasonably limit the competitive forces of the free market, demand too much from regulatory agencies, and usurp power from elected branches of government? What process is due?

These questions are as unsettling for judges and lawyers as they are for scientists and social critics. Yet they are central to understanding what role courts and the judicial process have in the regulation of risks and how and why that role has evolved. There are no simple answers. What courts do will continue to invite criticism from either the left or the right of the political spectrum and occasionally from both at the same time. This is in part due to the remarkable degree of institutional independence courts enjoy in the United States. Also, because courts are reactive agents of social change, they respond (more or less slowly) to scientific and technological innovations no less than to social forces in the country.

Controversy over courts and science-policy disputes in regulating risk emerged in the 1970s, "the environmental decade." Emergent environmental sciences drew attention to the health-safety and environmental risks of our petrochemical and industrial society. Evolving scientific evidence led to the assertion of new legal rights in state and federal courts and to political pressure for regulatory action in the halls of state legislatures and Congress. Social forces pushed for compensation for those injured by hazardous consumer products and unsafe working conditions and also for "public goods" like clean air, water, and environmental quality.

Courts, along with Congress and state legislatures, gradually proved responsive. A new body of law—environmental law—took shape and has had profound consequences for regulatory policy. State courts applied old common law doctrines to new claims brought to light on the frontiers of science. Congress responded with unparalleled legislation. Federal agencies were given authority to promulgate a wide range of health-safety and environmental regulations. Those regulations in turn were challenged in litigation. State and federal courts thus assumed a major and controversial role in assessing new claims and forging regulatory policy, as well as in overseeing governmental regulation of health-safety and environmental risks.

The role of courts in the regulation of risks is likely to continue to draw criticism. This is precisely because the role of courts will loom larger in the wake of the movement toward deregulation, begun under Democratic President Jimmy Carter and continued under Republican President Ronald Reagan. Few advocates of deregulation adhere to strict principles of an unfettered free market in the area of health-safety and environmental risks. Yet there remains wide disagreement over how to regulate those risks and how much regulation is needed.

Although conceding that some regulation of health-safety and environmental risks may be necessary, conservatives are inclined to point out that judicial rulings, no less than federal agency regulations, are not sufficiently grounded in science. They therefore criticize recent trends toward relying on courts and tort liability to regulate risk. Without a firm scientific basis, they argue, the regulation of risk— whether by agencies or courts—goes too far and fails to be cost-effective. As a result, the private sector bears unreasonable and unfair burdens when compensating victims of unsafe working conditions and consumer products, as well as for securing "public goods" like clean air and water. For these and other reasons, they view judicial regulation through a system of tort liability no more favorably than other forms of governmental regulation.

Consumer groups, environmental advocates, and others aligned with liberals counter that self-regulation by the private sector and the free market cannot be trusted. There are too many disincentives for businesses to assume the costs of "public goods," and collective bar-gaining agreements tend to work against those injured by the pro-cesses of industrial competition. Courts may help to correct such mar-ket imperfections, though at times they have been slow to recognize new claims and new scientific data. For these critics, health-safety and environmental regulation has neither gone far enough nor been ef-fectively and vigorously enforced by courts.

However, along with advocates of deregulation, consumer and environmental advocates agree that the regulatory process has be-come more complex procedurally and is dominated by the courts. The judicialization of the politics of regulating risk indeed contributes to costly delays, as well as often uneven and ineffective regulation that overregulates some risks and underregulates others. This leads some liberals and conservatives to propose greater reliance on alternative methods of dispute resolution and to advance more radical institu-tional changes, such as the creation of a "science court."

Regardless of such criticism and normative debates, courts will continue to play a large role in the regulation of risk. Why this is so and the ways in which courts respond to the regulation of risk is the subject of this book.

Unlike other studies focusing on particular controversies and the role of courts in either private law litigation or in administrative law and politics, this volume aims to explain why disputes involving scientific uncertainty and intense value conflict over regulating risk tend to be judicialized and to find their way into the courts, at least in the United States. Beyond that, I assess recent trends and the changing role of courts in the politics of regulating health-safety and environmental risks.

What most critics of courts and the regulatory politics of science-policy disputes overlook is how deeply embedded the value of fairness—as identified with the judicial process—is in our cultural responses to dispute resolution. The argument here is that courts are drawn into science-policy disputes, and the regulatory politics of managing risk tends to be judicialized, because of the interplay of the normative cultures of science, law, and democratic politics. In other words, what process is due is culturally determined.

While the scope of this study is broad, the basic line of argument may be stated at the outset. The surge of legislation and litigation involving science-policy disputes in the last two decades reflects profound social changes—changes that evolved in accordance with basic cultural characteristics of the American way of life. Specifically, Chapter 1 argues that science-policy disputes tend to be judicialized because the regulation of risks—brought by carcinogenic and toxic substances, for example—almost uniformly poses a vexing trilemma for policymakers. That trilemma consists of accommodating competing demands for scientific certainty, political compromise, and procedural fairness in the regulation of risks.

Scientific disagreements over the basis for regulating risks makes negotiated settlements and political compromises extremely difficult, if not usually impossible. Indeed, fundamental uncertainties in scientific knowledge pose underlying normative conflicts. Science-policy disputes do not tend to be judicialized, however, primarily because of conflicts and uncertainties in the scientific basis for regulation. Rather, the judicial process and courts assume a major role because negotiations break down, agreement on regulating risks cannot be achieved, and political compromises and coalition building often prove elusive. Science-policy disputes are turned into litigation and courts are called upon not to settle scientific controversies per se but to perform their traditional role as independent tribunals for settling value conflicts and imposing social norms.

Courts actually play several roles in the regulation of risk because of the way in which science-policy litigation is channeled in our dual system of state and federal judiciaries and according to the basic allocation of judicial power between trial and appellate courts. The varied and changing roles of state and federal courts are examined in subsequent chapters.

Court critics also tend to forget that the judiciary has historically had a role in assessing and managing risks in private law litigation. Chapter 2 considers this traditional regulatory role of courts, along with recent trends in tort law that have given private law litigation a new public-law perspective and greater significance in the regulation of risk. In the discussion of state courts' recognition of toxic torts, special attention is given to DES lawsuits and to the explosion in asbestos litigation. These science-policy disputes not only illustrate the role of state courts but permit an assessment of the limitations and contributions of private law litigation and judicial regulation through the imposition of tort liability.

Chapter 3 takes up the questions of whether judges are less competent to decide science-policy disputes than other kinds of social conflict, and whether the adjudicatory process is ill-suited to resolve them. Judges are not trained in science and the adjudicatory process is an imperfect means of fact-finding, particularly from a scientific perspective. But, as the chapter shows, state and federal trial courts must decide basic normative conflicts, usually on the basis of uncertain scientific evidence, because of the failure of out-of-court negotiations and political compromise. A case study of one of the first major environmental disputes, involving the Reserve Mining Company's daily dumping of 67,000 tons of taconite tailings into Lake Superior, illuminates how scientific uncertainties combine with a breakdown of political negotiations to generate pressures for a judicial resolution of the underlying social conflict.

The relationship between federal courts and regulatory agencies in the politics of managing health-safety and environmental risks is examined in Chapters 4 and 5. A dramatic growth in federal legislation and administrative regulations propelled the federal judiciary into a new role in the resolution of science-policy disputes. More than thirty federal statutes now govern toxic and carcinogenic substances. That legislation led not only to more agency regulation but also to more litigation and a greater role for federal district and appellate courts in the regulation of risk. This is largely due to congressional mandates for health-safety and environmental regulation that ex-

panded opportunities for special interest groups to challenge regulations as well as agency failure to regulate. Congress also mandated
changes in the administrative rulemaking process that made for
greater procedural complexity and heightened judicial review of the
regulatory process. No less important was the absence of agreement
within the scientific community on carcinogenic risk assessment and
the fear (on the part of both liberal and conservative interest groups)
that agencies would be co-opted without severe procedural constraints and rigorous judicial review of their health-safety and environmental standards.

Chapter 4 discusses the evolution in the so-called judicial/admin-
istrative partnership in administrative law and regulatory politics. A
case study of the Consumer Product Safety Commission's ban on Tris,
a carcinogenic flame-retardant sprayed on children's clothing, illustrates the dynamics of court–agency interaction. We see why agencies—no less than trial courts—usually must base their regulatory
decisions on uncertain scientific evidence. Beyond that we see both
agency resistance to prolonged adversarial-type rulemaking proceedings, and what effect litigation strategies and reviewing courts have on
regulatory policymaking.

From the study of Tris, I go on to argue that the costs of judicializing regulatory politics are high in terms of delay and inefficiency in
both under- and overregulating the risks of carcinogenic substances.
There are unanticipated consequences as well. The decentralized
structure of the federal judiciary promotes litigation strategies for
competing interest groups that work against the development of
coherent and uniform regulatory policies. Still, I conclude that this is
the inescapable price of resolving disputes over the regulation of risk
in a pluralistic society in which the cultural values of science, law, and
politics collide in determining the direction of policies for managing
health-safety and environmental risks.

The case studies and discussion in Chapters 3 and 4 are largely
devoted to the role of federal district courts in adjudicating science-
policy disputes and reviewing challenges to agency regulations. Chapter 5 turns to the role of federal appellate courts in science-policy
litigation. In particular, the chapter focuses on the Court of Appeals
for the District of Columbia Circuit—which reviews the overwhelming number of challenges to federal regulations—and the Supreme

Court of the United States. This is because the problems that science-policy litigation pose for courts differ at the trial and the appellate levels. The demands for more procedural complexity and heightened judicial review of the regulatory process, discussed in Chapter 4, created a major debate within the D.C. Circuit that eventually led the Supreme Court to sanction greater judicial supervision—or what has come to be known as the "hard look" approach to reviewing agency regulations.

From the debate within the D.C. Circuit over the role of appellate courts to the Supreme Court's ruling in *Vermont Yankee,* involving the Nuclear Regulatory Commission's licensing of nuclear reactors, we turn to the problematic nature of the "hard look" doctrine and to two case studies of appellate courts reviewing the Occupational Health and Safety Administration's regulation of benzene and cotton dust. While these controversies reveal problems with heightened judicial scrutiny of agencies, I argue that the prevailing pattern of intensive judicial review will not only persist but become more crucial in the era of deregulation. Two further case studies of regulation and deregulation—involving the Environmental Protection Agency's "bubble policy" and the Department of Transportation's requirements for passive restraints in automobiles—show the persistence of the "hard look" doctrine. They also indicate why the federal judiciary will remain a key player in the politics of regulating health-safety and environmental risks.

The book concludes that, despite controversy over courts and science-policy litigation, state and federal judiciaries have an important role in the regulatory politics of managing health-safety and environmental risks. This, as we will see in Chapter 1, is due to the very nature of science-policy disputes and the ways in which science, law, and politics interact and combine to create competing expectations for conflict resolution.

Acknowledgments

This book would not have been started or completed without the support of the Russell Sage Foundation. During a year spent at the Foundation as a Visiting Postdoctoral Fellow, I benefited from conversations with Herbert Kaufman, Robert Merton, and Byron Shafer. The then-President Marshall Robinson and Vice-President Peter E. de Janosi remained patient supporters.

In the course of my research, a number of people kindly made materials available and helped me clarify my views on the issues discussed here. In particular, I am grateful to Dean Richard Merrill of the University of Virginia Law School, and Judge David Bazelon. O. E. Breviu provided trial transcripts for the Reserve Mining controversy, discussed in Chapter 3. Priscilla Martinez and Todd Stevenson expedited a request under the Freedom of Information Act for transcripts of the Consumer Product Safety Commission's executive meetings on banning Tris. Those materials and others supplied by Elizabeth Cherry of the Environmental Defense Fund proved central to my discussion in Chapter 4. Attorneys Neil J. King, George H. Cohen, Edward Warren, Robert Payne, and Gary Tobin furnished both materials and insights on the litigation over the Occupational Health and Safety Administration's regulation of benzene and cotton dust, discussed in Chapter 5. James S. Young provided a needed stimulus and Kenneth Thompson and the University of Virginia Committee on Summer Grants gave additional assistance for which I am grateful.

Portions of Chapter 2 draw on my article on "The Courts and Science-Policy Disputes" in the *Journal of Energy Law and Policy* (1983), and portions of Chapters 4 and 5 on another that appeared in the *Harvard Journal of Law and Public Policy* (1984). The book benefited from the meticulous reading of Philip Cooper and the comments of several other manuscript reviewers, including Colin Diver and Roger Kasperson. I alone, of course, bear responsibility for what is said or omitted here.

David M. O'Brien

Woodrow Wilson Department of Government and Foreign Affairs
University of Virginia

Contents

List of Figures

1

Science, Law, and American Politics

Perceptions of and responses to risk vary among societies and, as sociologist Mary Douglas and political scientist Aaron Wildavsky argue, reflect basic cultural values and choices.[1] In America, three competing ideals or cultures underlie responses to disputes over the health-safety and environmental risks. They are science, law, and democratic politics. Each prescribes different methods for dispute resolution. But together they create a trilemma for policymakers—whether legislators, administrators, or judges—in resolving science-policy disputes over the regulation of risk.

My argument is that, because of these competing cultures, science-policy disputes almost uniformly pose a trilemma in the regulation of risk. That is, policymakers must respond in ways that (1) satisfy demands for a scientific basis for regulation; while (2) arriving at politically responsive and acceptable policies; and at the same time (3)

---

[1] M. Douglas and A. Wildavsky, *Risk and Culture: An Essay on the Selection of Technical and Environmental Dangers* (Berkeley: University of California Press, 1982).

guaranteeing some measure of procedural fairness for those contesting the scientific and normative basis for regulations. The nature of this trilemma is such that science-policy disputes tend to be judicialized, or structured according to adversarial processes, if not ultimately forced into the courts.

A Cultural Trilemma

The cultures of science, law, and democratic politics are inherently at odds with each other and at times in open conflict. But before exploring the tensions, and the social changes that have exacerbated them, something more should be said about how deeply rooted these cultures are in the sources and ways of American life.

A belief in science—in rationality and empiricism—unmistakably lay at the founding of the Republic. The Founding Fathers were children of the Enlightenment, influenced by Scottish social scientists and philosophers like David Hume and Jean-Jacques Burlamaqui.[2] James Madison, for one, sought in a new "science of politics" the justifications he gave in *The Federalist Papers* for ratifying the Constitution. The Enlightenment philosophies on which the Founding Fathers and their forebears drew enabled them to do more than reject the "divine right of kings." They also rejected a public religion and relegated religious truths to matters of private opinion. At the same time, the importance of science was elevated for the first time in history to a position of authoritatively providing answers to questions of public policy.

The Founding Fathers, to be sure, were not all of one mind on the precise relationship between science and government. Thomas Jefferson favored private rewards (as exemplified in the country's first patent law, which he drafted) rather than a direct governmental role in promoting science. By contrast, Alexander Hamilton favored more direct governmental involvement in the advance of science, particularly in developing manufacturing, commerce, and the arts.

---

[2] See, generally, M. White, *The Philosophy of the American Revolution* (New York: Oxford University Press, 1978); and D. Adair, *Fame and the Founding Fathers* (New York: Norton, 1974).

But, we need not retrace the history of science in America to appreciate its pivotal role in stimulating technological advances and industrial competition, as well as in both challenging and guiding public policy. Scholars such as Don Price, Hunter Dupree, and others have described the ambivalent and changing relationship between science and government.[3] All that is important, here, is that the founding of the American Republic presupposed and established conditions for the advance of science and its utilization in resolving questions of public policy. By World War II, science itself had become a kind of secular religion, promising new frontiers and "technological fixes" for societal problems.

No less important than the cultural value of science has been the related ideal of "a government of laws, and not of men." That ideal is embodied in the bold experiment with a written constitution and lies at the heart of what has been called our "adversary culture" and litigious society.[4] In the 1830s, Alexis de Tocqueville attributed our litigious propensities to the peculiar practice of rights or, as he put it, "legal habit." A distinguishing feature of democracy in America is the celebration of individual rights. "The [very] idea of right," he claimed, "is simply that of virtue introduced into the political world. It was the idea of right that enabled men to define anarchy and tyranny, and that taught them how to be independent without arrogance and to obey without servility."[5]

Our society is litigious and our culture adversarial. In 1980–1981, for instance, there were 180,576 civil and 31,287 criminal cases filed in federal courts, more than twice the number of a decade earlier. Federal courts handle but a small percentage of the total litigation in the United States. State courts annually face over 25 million filings.

[3] See A. H. Dupree, *Science in the Federal Government: A History of Policies and Activities to 1940* (Cambridge, Mass.: Harvard University Press, 1957); D. K. Price, *Government and Science* (New York: New York University Press, 1954); and D. K. Price, *Scientific Estate* (Cambridge, Mass.: Harvard University Press, 1965).

[4] See, generally, J. Mansbridge, *Beyond Adversary Democracy* (New York: Basic Books, 1980).

[5] A. de Tocqueville, *Democracy in America*, vol. 1, ed. P. Bradley (New York: New American Library, 1945), at 280.

Litigation rates, in the view of many judges and court-watchers, reflect the "judicialization" of an ever-widening range of issues.[6]

At its best, the idea of rights and the rule of law embodied in our governmental system creates expectations of procedural fairness, if not distributive (or substantive) justice. At its worst, the premium placed on individual rights degenerates with an expansion of claims to new "rights" and "frivolous" litigation. "Rights" are indeed no longer thought to be only substantive, like the right to property or liberty. Instead, rights increasingly include more procedural claims. Procedural rights to participate in and challenge the decision-making process and final decisions of public and private sector officials have greatly expanded. And the expansion of these rights has dramatically increased the procedural complexity of public and private sector decision making.

Finally, embedded in the rejection of "the divine right of kings" is the idea of popular sovereignty—the idea that government is a trustee for and ultimately accountable to the people. "A dependence on the people," Madison insisted in *The Federalist #51*, is "the primary control on the government." The Constitution does not embody a democracy per se but rather a "mixed form of government" or representative democracy. Constitutional amendments and judicial rulings, expanding the voting rights and making elected representatives more politically accountable, however, have made the Constitution a more democratic framework for governance. And the idea of popular sovereignty has been transformed in this century into a cultural value emphasizing democratic control over public policy.

These three cultures place competing demands on policymakers. Science-policy disputes, in particular, pose the trilemma of responding to the perceived risks of industrial society in ways that (1) satisfy demands for a scientific basis for regulating those risks; (2) arrive at politically responsive and acceptable policies; while (3) ensuring procedural fairness for those disputing the scientific basis and/or normative assumptions for regulation. The trilemma is that of accommodating different cultural demands for scientific certainty, responsiveness to democratic politics, and procedural fairness in the formulation of

---

[6] This discussion draws on D. M. O'Brien, " 'The Imperial Judiciary': Of Paper Tigers and Socio-Legal Indicators," 2 *Journal of Law & Politics* 1 (1985).

public policy. The nature of this trilemma becomes clearer when we consider how these competing cultural values enter into science-policy disputes and, ultimately, promote rather judicialized responses to regulating health-safety and environmental risks.

The Politics of Science in a Democracy

Science has a distinctive culture, though it is also conditioned by societal attitudes toward science. "The belief in the value of scientific truth," as sociologist Max Weber points out, "is not derived from nature but is a product of particular cultures."[7] The normative culture of science, in other words, affects and changes with societal attitudes toward science. For much of America's history, science and democratic politics have generally progressed in a mutually reinforcing fashion. At least until the mid-twentieth century, both were viewed as sharing common social processes and values. Both, in a sense, operate by a process of self-coordination and mutual adjustment, and implicitly maintain a faith in the "hidden hand" of progress.[8]

What is crucial, however, is how the premium placed on methods of attaining scientific certainty makes the resolution of science-policy disputes exceedingly difficult. No less important are challenges from within and without the scientific community to the quest for scientific certainty. They both exacerbate the political conflict over regulating risks and contribute to the judicialization of science-policy disputes.

Essential Tensions: Irreconcilable Differences

The culture of science is largely defined by professional norms. They preserve the independence of science and historically have fostered a

[7] M. Weber, *Gesammelte Aufsätze zur Wissenschaftslehre* 213 (2d ed., Tübingen: J. C. B. Mohr, 1951), as quoted by R. Merton, *The Sociology of Science: An Episodic Memoir* (Carbondale: Southern Illinois University Press, 1977), at 109.

[8] M. Polanyi, "The Republic of Science," in *Criteria for Scientific Development*, ed. E. Shills (Boston: Massachusetts Institute of Technology Press, 1968), at 3 and 18.

kind of coexistence with democratic politics with little intrusive governmental regulation. The main professional norms, in the view of the father of the sociology of science, Robert K. Merton, are four: (1) universalism, or the established impersonal criteria of judgment, consonant with observation and previously confirmed knowledge; (2) communism, in a nontechnical sense, of results inasmuch as the "substantive findings of science are a product of social collaboration and are assigned to the community"; (3) disinterestedness in the verifiability of results, as preserved by the exacting scrutiny of fellow scientists; and (4) organized skepticism within the scientific community about theoretical interpretations and conclusions.[9]

These professional norms sharply distinguish the culture of science from that of democratic politics. In particular, the *process* of resolving disagreements within the scientific and political communities is marked. Repeated experimentation and collegial review of scientific findings, for one thing, contrast sharply with the process of coalition building in the political arena. Time is basically of little concern for scientists, whereas timing may be of the essence in resolving political disagreements. Resolving disagreements within the scientific community on the risks of an alleged toxin or carcinogen thus takes a long time—a longer period than policymakers can generally afford.[10] Because the scientific process often has not yet produced acceptable data from which to reach indisputable conclusions about risks, there are also, typically, uncertainties over the scientific basis for regulation.

Even more significant is that within the scientific community uncertainties and disagreements are to be expected. And that reflects a fundamental tension between the *goals* of science and democratic politics. Science pushes away from personal value judgments and toward a rigorous principle of scientific certainty on questions of causality. The quest for certainty, however, comes at the cost of greater scientific skepticism. Indeed, according to a dominant philosophy of science, science never "proves" anything. It only establishes the prob-

---

[9] R. K. Merton, "The Normative Structure of Science," in *The Sociology of Science*, ed. R. Merton and N. Storer (Chicago: University of Chicago Press, 1973), at 267.

[10] L. Lave, *The Strategy of Social Regulation* (Washington, D.C.: Brookings Institution, 1982), at 32.

ability that something is likely to be true—likely to occur under certain specified conditions. Scientific propositions, in other words, can only be disproved, not confirmed.[11]

By comparison, the culture of democratic politics aims at compromise in conflicts involving both values and causation. More important for policymakers than scientific certainty is reaching agreement on the means and ends of managing risks, and more generally the allocation of power. Rather than the achievement of disinterested unanimity within the scientific community on the risk of risk, policymakers are interested in what scientific evidence is available at the moment and how it can be used in supporting or attacking public policies.

These are essential tensions between science and democratic politics and in the competition for influence in determining the outcome of science-policy disputes: one pushes toward high standards of certainty, while the other aims at achieving compromise.

There are those who maintain that the cultures of science and democratic politics can be accommodated in such a way that they complement, rather than compete with, each other in determining the outcome of science-policy disputes. A former president of the National Academy of Sciences, Philip Handler, for one, insists that "the *estimation* of risk is a scientific question—and, therefore, a legitimate activity of scientists in federal agencies, in universities and in the National Research Council. The *acceptability* of a given level of risk, however, is a political question to be determined in the political arena."[12]

But, the lines—between risk assessment and management, and between science and politics—are easier to draw in theory than in practice. Obviously, as Douglas and Wildavsky note, "when someone says a risk is unacceptable, the question *ipso facto* becomes political."[13] Yet, the estimation or assessment of risk is itself political—political in the kinds of assumptions made and in their implications for regulat-

---

[11] See, generally, K. Popper, *The Logic of Scientific Discovery* (1959).

[12] P. Handler, "Some Comments on Risk Assessment," in National Research Council, *Current Issues and Studies: Annual Report* (Washington, D.C.: National Academy Press, 1979).

[13] Douglas and Wildavsky, supra note 1, at 65.

ing risk. Indeed, what makes science-policy disputes particularly difficult is the politicalization of the scientific community and the failure to appreciate the politics of science in a democracy.

Before getting too far ahead of the story, however, the obvious may bear emphasizing, namely, that while the scientific and political (regulatory) communities are defined by distinctive cultural values, they overlap, intersect, and interact. Because this is so, policymakers tend to exaggerate the scientific basis for regulation, and scientists may be enticed into abandoning scientific skepticism and the quest for certainty for normative prescriptions. As a result, the essential tensions between science and politics may be blurred, and irreconcilable differences may be overlooked. Two science-policy controversies—involving the regulation of saccharin and cyclamates—may make this point even more obvious.

The Science and Politics of Nonsugar Sweeteners

The dispute over banning saccharin, a food additive and sweetener, illustrates not only how the scientific basis for regulation may be exaggerated but also why science alone does not determine or dictate responses to risk management. The controversy also serves to underscore the premium placed on compromise in regulatory policymaking and how politics works against the establishment of a coherent scientific basis for regulation.

In 1958, when amending the Food, Drug, and Cosmetic Act of 1938, Congress added the so-called Delaney Clause, sponsored by New York Democratic Representative James J. Delaney. The amendment prohibited the Food and Drug Administration (FDA) from approving any food additive that is a suspected carcinogen based on laboratory animal tests. The Delaney Clause raised a particular scientific theory—the theory of zero tolerance or no-safe-threshold of carcinogenic exposure—to the level of public policy. The FDA could approve other foods, drugs, and cosmetics, based on a balancing of their respective risks, costs, and benefits. But it could not do so with regard to food additives. Unlike the overwhelming majority of legislation governing the regulation of health-safety and environmental risks, the Delaney Clause forbids any form of cost-benefit analysis, regardless of how small a risk is associated with a substance like saccharin.

After laboratory tests linked saccharin to cancer in rats, the FDA moved to ban the substance in 1977. In the twenty years after the enactment of the Delaney Clause, however, the study of cancer had progressed but it had also become more politicized. The view that there is no safe threshold of exposure to a carcinogen remains hotly contested within the scientific community, as well as in the regulatory arena.

Scientists who support the Delaney Clause maintain that, since the mechanisms of cancer are not fully understood, no level of carcinogenic exposure should be accepted. The no-safe-threshold theory of carcinogenesis, in short, carries with it a political bias toward regulation. For instance, Sidney P. Wolfe, the director of the Health Research Group, a consumer protection organization, opposes modification of the Delaney Clause. He maintains that the FDA should not have the discretion, enjoyed by other agencies, to ban substances based on their relative risks, costs, and benefits. "Food is different from everything else," Wolfe argues. "In the work place you can determine a risk to a hazardous or carcinogenic chemical. But you can't avoid contact with food. It is too important a topic to allow it to be arbitrarily changed at the discretion of a commissioner who may or may not be sympathetic to industry's arguments." Another scientist-turned-environmental activist, Samuel S. Epstein, likewise argues against risk/cost/benefit analysis on the ground that "[i]ts use in making regulatory decisions concerning deliberatively added carcinogenic food additives would be both premature and irresponsible." In his view, the zero-risk standard in the Delaney Clause was a "cautious and prudent societal judgment." These arguments, of course, are not scientific. They are political. Yet, they are based on a particular model of carcinogenesis—the no-safe-threshold level of carcinogenic exposure—and reflect that model's implicit political bias toward regulation.

By contrast, other scientists support the view of the food industry. They insist that the finding of a minute cancer risk from the use of saccharin is an insufficient basis for prohibiting the additive. Comparable cancer risks, they point out, can be established for "natural" foods such as caffeine, safrole in spices like nutmeg, coumarin in strawberries and cherries, and fungal contaminants like aflatoxins in a wide range of grains and rice. Hydrocarbons, nitrogen oxides, sulfur oxides, and radioactivity, along with a range of metals and other chemical compounds in the environment, are also carcinogenic at some level. Given these comparable and relative risks, the no-safe-threshold model of carcinogenesis that lies at the basis of the Delaney Clause appears unwarranted. According to Stuart E. Proctor, assistant director of the Farm Bureau Federation, an influential lobbying organization, the Delaney Clause mandates "outdated, maybe even archaic regulation."[14]

There are other problems with banning saccharin as well. The validity of the laboratory animal tests (as we will further discuss later) is open to sharp attack by some scientists. In one of the three tests, the rats had a normal lifespan, though they suffered metabolic stress. With one exception, tumors developed only in rodents whose mothers ingested large quantities of saccharin and who were exposed to similar quantities of the chemical from birth. The tumors, then, appeared only in male rodents. Scientists critical of the ban on saccharin thus raise a crucial problem with all carcinogenic risk estimation: the appropriateness of extrapolating cancer risks to humans exposed to low doses of a chemical based on the cancer rates of a rodent population that is less genetically diverse and exposed to very high levels of a suspected carcinogen, often over several generations.[15]

While rooted in science, disagreements over banning saccharin are as much political as scientific. On the one hand, scientists who embrace the no-safe-threshold model of carcinogenesis and models for extrapolating from high-dosage exposures in rodent populations to low-dosage responses in humans tend to be biased toward regulation—toward a no-risk-of-risk policy. On the other hand, scientists who reject the no-safe-threshold model of carcinogenesis are inclined toward a policy of relative-risk management based on the costs and benefits of assuming those risks.

In short, scientific models order not only research but also political agendas. They serve to sharpen political divisions among public

[14] Quoted by Karen De Witt, "Food Law and the Carcinogen Problem," *New York Times* (May 9, 1981). See also National Research Council, *Safety of Saccharin and Sodium Saccharin in the Human Diet* (1974); and General Accounting Office, *Sugar and Other Sweeteners: An Industry Assessment* (1979).

[15] For a further discussion, see W. R. Havender, "Ruminations on a Rat: Saccharin and Human Risk," *Regulation* (March/April, 1979), at 17.

interest groups (liberal and conservative), proprietary interest groups and businesses, and even unaffiliated scientists who are pressed into taking normative positions by legislators, judges, and other policy-makers.

When the saccharin dispute erupted in 1977, consumers and manufacturers of diet food and drinks successfully lobbied Congress to establish an eighteen-month moratorium on the FDA's ban. The moratorium allowed time for further study but, when it expired on May 23, 1979, there remained sharp division over the risks of saccharin. Congress extended the moratorium. Finally, a majority of scientists who participated in an Institute of Medicine study for Congress concluded that, though the Delaney Clause prohibited a risk-cost-benefit analysis and a rigorous analysis of that sort was not feasible, some balance had to be struck. They recommended that the FDA have discretion to decide whether or not to prohibit food additives like saccharin.[16] But, responding to political pressure and the public's fears of cancer, Congress voted to adhere to the scientific theory underlying the Delaney Clause. At the same time, however, Congress passed a law forbidding the FDA from enforcing the ban on saccharin, which the Delaney Clause requires.

The public's perception of the threat of cancer and the pressures of democratic politics made it politically unfeasible to rescind the Delaney Clause. The scientific community was divided. Assessments of the risks of saccharin proved inconclusive and simply buttressed the lobbying efforts of manufacturers and consumers of soft drinks. Congress was forced to override what by law it required the FDA to do.

Congress cannot resolve disputes within the scientific community any more than the latter can dictate regulatory policies. At best, Congress arrives at a compromise accommodating a range of conflicting interests, even though that often entails inconsistent public policies. At most, the scientific community informs political debate on whether and how to manage the risks of our industrial society. At worst, scientists may be coopted and serve only to exacerbate the difficulties of developing coherent and consistent regulatory policies.

[16] Institute of Medicine, National Academy of Sciences, *Food Safety Policy: Scientific and Societal Considerations* (March 1, 1979).

Another controversy over a related food additive, cyclamate, further illustrates the politics of science and how scientists may be politically coopted. In this controversy, the FDA's science advisory board issued recommendations in 1980 that were tailor-made to political pressure from the executive branch. Cyclamate, which is about thirty times sweeter than sugar (compared with saccharin which is 300 times sweeter), was thought to be carcinogenic based on laboratory tests on rodents conducted in the 1960s. The FDA sharply limited its use in 1969. The following year the Department of Health and Human Services (DHHS) removed it from the market. Five years later, a committee for the National Cancer Institute found that evidence did not in fact "establish the carcinogenity of cyclamate." But, in 1980 public fears about cancer due to the widely publicized controversy over saccharin led government officials to conclude that they should demonstrate that they were not soft on managing cancer risks. Instead of recommending a waiver of the ban on cyclamates, the FDA science advisory board reported that there was not enough evidence showing that cyclamates were linked to cancer. The dispute, however, continues. In Canada an early ban on cyclamates was lifted. In 1985 the National Academy of Science again found that cyclamate, by itself, does not appear to pose a risk of cancer.[17]

When the scientific community is divided or becomes politicized, those divisions fuel conflict among policymakers, frustrate coalition building, and invite litigation challenging regulation. The inherent tendency in democratic politics toward a fragmentation of issues and away from systematic analysis and development of comprehensive policies is reinforced. The politics of science in a democracy, in short, may contribute to the defeat of attempts at developing coherent regulations based on indisputable scientific evidence.

The Politics of Science in Risk Regulation

The controversies over saccharin and cyclamates are typical of most science-policy disputes over health-safety and environmental regulation. "In reaction to the public's often emotional response to risk,"

---

[17] C. Russell, "Cyclamate Alone Said Not Cancer-Causing," *Washington Post* A3 (June 11, 1985).

Judge David Bazelon observes after many years of reviewing challenges to regulations, "scientists are tempted to disguise controversial value decisions in the cloak of scientific objectivity, obscuring those decisions from political accountability."[18] Indeed, in the last thirty years, scientists have claimed to be "under siege" while being charged with ideological bias in their view of the risks of synthetic chemicals and new industrial processes. Scientific norms have been challenged both from within and from without the scientific community.

The politicization of the scientific community in the 1970s over the risks of cancer differs in some basic ways from the political activism of scientists thirty years earlier. Dorothy Nelkin, a historian and sociologist of science, offers this account:

> A striking feature of the new scientific activism is the public nature of its activities and the willingness of activists to engage in and, indeed, to abet political controversy. Disputes among scientists are normally resolved within the scientific community using well-established provisions of collegial review. However, recently, scientists appear willing to air grievances in a political forum—through the mass media, litigation, or appeals to citizens' groups or political representatives. Citizen participation is sought today for a different reason—as a means to increase the political accountability of science. While activists in the 1940s fought against political control over research, their recent counterparts—by calling public attention to conflicts of interest within the scientific community—seek to increase political control.[19]

The abandonment of scientific norms for political activism, historian of science Loren Graham notes, often occurs at critical periods in the development of science. In Graham's words, "the most dangerous period of the development of science is when enough is known to advance the first fruitful speculations and to try a few interventions, but not enough is known to bring discipline to these speculations or to predict the possible side effects or after effects of intervention."[20]

[18] D. Bazelon, "Risk and Responsibility," 205 *Science* 277 (1979), at 278.

[19] D. Nelkin, "Scientists in our Adversary Culture: The 1970s Program in Science, Technology and Society," paper presented to the Organization of American Historians, 1978.

[20] L. Graham, *Between Science and Values* (New York: Columbia University Press, 1981), at 379.

This is precisely what occurred with the emergence of environmental sciences devoted to assessing risks to health, safety, and the environment. Some environmental scientists became political activists and abandoned the norm of scientific skepticism. That led to heightened political conflict over the regulation of risks.

When turning to the politicization of the scientific community, and how that has made the resolution of science-policy disputes even more difficult, I argue that the methodology of science and the uncertainties of scientific knowledge necessitate choices about particular scientific models. Those choices in turn reflect implicit political biases toward or against governmental regulation. The aim of the next section is to show why science alone cannot dictate solutions to science-policy disputes and how it serves to intensify political conflict rather than help forge consensus in risk regulation.

The Uncertainties of Knowledge

Somewhat ironically, the emergence of environmental sciences, which sought to provide a basis for health-safety and environmental regulation, proved especially divisive. This was so for basically three reasons. First, as Graham suggests about scientific development more generally, environmental sciences were too young, too experimental in the 1970s, to generate wide-ranging consensus on carcinogenic risk assessment. Second, some environmental scientists became highly politicized and challenged both the traditional norms of science and democratic politics to respond to their view of the risks of industrial society. Finally, and most crucially, the premium placed on scientific certainty in the normative culture of science invites political divisions within the scientific community that carry over into the conflicts over regulating risks.

From Truth to Politics

The quest for scientific certainty comes at the price of prolonged skepticism and uncertainty. Environmental scientists still have not achieved an integrated interdisciplinary study of health and environmental risks. Differences among the discrete sciences that environmental science endeavors to incorporate have not been fully resolved. Scientists trained in different disciplines, for instance, occasionally arrive at rival interpretations of carcinogenic risks based on the same data. By training they are predisposed to disagree on fundamental models and methods of carcinogenesis. Not surprisingly, they also differ on the kinds of inferences that can be made about cancer risks and are biased in different ways toward regulation of risk.

Disciplinary divisions were intensified by the political activism of some environmentally conscious scientists. Edith Efron, in her book *The Apocalyptics: Cancer and the Big Lie*,[21] is perhaps the most critical of scientists for politicizing the risks of cancer in works like Rachel Carson's *Silent Spring* (1962) and Samuel Epstein's *The Politics of Cancer* (1979).[22] By aligning themselves with the media, environmental scientists heightened public perception of threats to health and the environment, but at the cost of misrepresenting scientific evidence. They perpetuated a "big lie," in Efron's words, in pandering to public fears about cancer.

What remains striking, however, is that environmental scientists, even though capturing media attention for their claims, succeeded only in evoking an emotional—not a cognitive—response from the general public. Whereas they tend to exaggerate carcinogenic risks, the general public tends to underestimate them. Despite widespread media attention to the concerns raised by environmental scientists, the public tends to misperceive and wrongly assess the risks of death by, for example, fireworks and smoking (see Figure 1.1).[23] The general public, of course, is not typically disposed or particularly equipped to analyze the data and conclusions of environmental scientists.

Environmental scientists nonetheless successfully pushed health and environmental concerns on to the national political agenda. And they did so by often exaggerated claims about the risks of cancer.

[21] E. Efron, *The Apocalyptics: Cancer and the Big Lie* (New York: Simon & Schuster, 1984).

[22] R. Carson, *Silent Spring* (Greenwich, Conn.: Fawcett-Crest, 1962); and S. Epstein, *The Politics of Cancer* (Garden City, N.Y.: Anchor Books, 1979).

[23] Based on *State of the Environment: An Assessment at Mid-Decade* (Washington, D. C.: Conservation Foundation, 1984), at 275.

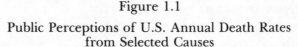

Figure 1.1

Public Perceptions of U.S. Annual Death Rates
from Selected Causes

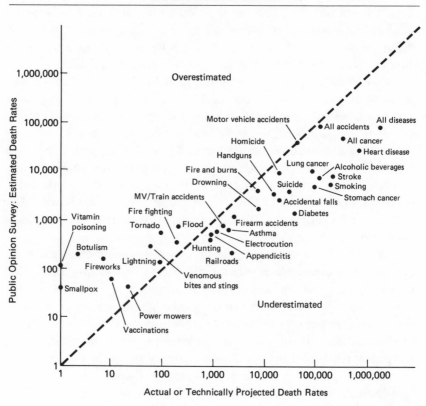

Samuel Epstein, for one, in a 1980 call for more regulation, asserts
that

> Cancer is now the only major fatal disease whose incidence is on the
> rise. Standardization of cancer death rates (i.e., adjusted for age and
> based on the total U.S. population) shows an overall and progressive
> increase of about 11 percent from 1933 to 1970. This increase has been
> even more striking over the last decade, and cannot be accounted for by
> smoking or increased longevity. At today's death rates, the probability

of a person born today getting cancer by the age of 85 is 27 percent (in contrast to about 20 percent for a person born in 1950.[24]

While it is true that cancer rates have been increasing, many scientists contend that most cancers are related to diet and smoking. "The fat-associated and smoking-derived cancers collectively account for more than half of all cancer deaths," points out Richard Petro, a leading cancer researcher at Oxford University.[25] Setting the incidence of lung cancer aside, and taking into account demographic changes (that the lifespan is increasing), another leading scientist, Gio Batta Gori, claims that there might actually be a decrease in the current cancer rate.[26] Philip Handler uses even stronger language in attacking the claims of environmental scientists like Epstein:

> [T]he United States is not suffering an "epidemic of cancer," it is experiencing an "epidemic of law"—in that an ever greater fraction of the population survives to the advanced ages at which cancer has always been prevalent. The overall, age-corrected incidence of cancer has not been increasing; it has been declining slowly for some years.[27]

In other words, cancer-related deaths may be increasing, as indicated in Figure 1.2, because of increased lifespan due to a decline in other kinds of causes of death, such as influenza, pneumonia, and heart attacks.[28]

Epstein and other environmental advocates, nonetheless, counter that "overemphasis on smoking [as a large factor in cancer incidence] is widely used to divert attention from occupational causes of lung and other cancers."[29] Basically, they refuse to abandon their view that

[24] S. Epstein, "Cancer, Inflation and the Failure to Regulate," 82 *Technology Review* 425 (Dec./Jan., 1980).

[25] R. Petro, "Distorting the Epidemiology of Cancer: The Need for a More Balanced Overview," 284 *Nature* 297 (March, 1980).

[26] G. B. Gori, "The Regulation of Carcinogenic Hazards," 208 *Science* 256 (April 18, 1980).

[27] Handler, supra note 12.

[28] *Report to the President by the Toxic Substances Strategy Committee* (1980), at 147.

[29] S. Epstein and J. Swartz, "Fallacies of Lifestyle Cancer Theories," 289 *Nature* 127 (Jan. 15, 1981).

Figure 1.2

Age-Adjusted Death Rates for Major Causes of Death in the United States, 1900–1976

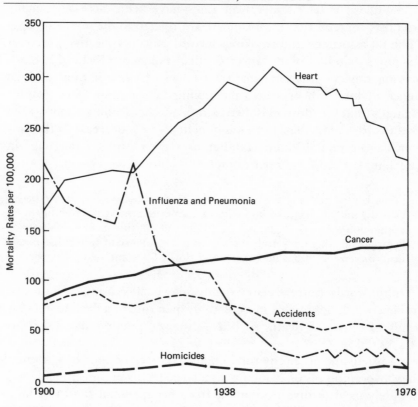

industrial pollutants significantly contribute to cancer rates. They charge that we do not (and cannot) know the full effect of industrial pollutants. "We haven't seen the effects in terms of carcinogenicity of the modern chemical world," claims Bruce Ames, a scientist at the University of California at Berkeley. "That is going to hit us in the 1980s because of the 20-to-25 year lag period. We'll pay something for it. But whether that's relatively small or relatively large, no one knows."[30] For precisely that reason, environmental scientists and law-

[30] Quoted by the Environmental Defense Fund and R. Boyle, *Malignant Neglect* (New York: Knopf, 1979).

yers like Devra Lee Davis and Brian H. Magee of the Environmental Law Institute continue to push for "[c]ontrol of the production, use, and disposal of chemical carcinogens" and against attempts at deregulation.[31]

These arguments about cancer risks, however, are based not on scientific evidence but on the very uncertainty of knowledge. The scientific community remains divided on this crucial regulatory issue. Part of the problem is that, as illustrated in Figure 1.3, there is no information available on most petrochemicals currently in production.[32] Estimates of the number of chemical carcinogens vary widely, from about 500, reported by Isaac Berenblum in 1967 in *Cancer Research Today*, to twice that number according to a report for *Science* magazine in 1976, and to over 2,000 according to estimates of the National Institute for Occupational Safety and Health.[33]

What is also clear is that the uncertainty of knowledge encourages political divisions within the scientific community. Those divisions are based on divergent views of carcinogenesis and (normative) judgments as to whether it is better to err by over- or underregulation. Disagreements about the relative influence of environmental factors on cancer rates ultimately turn as much on politics as on science. Why this is so becomes clearer if we consider, first, the general debate within the scientific community on cancer risks, and then, in the following subsection, that over models for carcinogenic risk assessment.

The Politics of Carcinogenesis

Only in the 1950s did the scientific community begin to study the links between cancer and environmental factors. John Higginson, the founding director of the World Health Organization's International Agency for Research on Cancer (IARC), over thirty years ago formulated the rather complex idea that cancer rates are linked to the

[31] See D. Davis and B. Magee, Letter, "Cancer and Industrial Chemical Production," 206 *Science* 1356 (1976).

[32] Based on the Conservation Foundation, supra note 23, at 64. For further discussion of public perceptions of risks, see R. Wilson and E. Crouch, *Risk/Benefit Analysis* (Cambridge, Mass.: Ballinger, 1982).

[33] For further discussion, see Efron, supra note 21.

Figure 1.3
Availability of Information
on the Health Effects of Selected Chemicals

Category	Number of Chemicals in Category	Estimated Percentage of Chemicals with Information Available
Pesticides and inert ingredients of pesticide formulations	3,350	
Cosmetic ingredients	3,410	
Drugs and excipients used in drug formulations	1,815	
Food additives	8,627	
Chemicals in commerce: At least 1 million pounds produced per year	12,860	
Chemicals in commerce: Less than 1 million pounds produced per year	13,911	
Chemicals in commerce: Production unknown or inaccessible	21,752	

Complete health-hazard assessment possible

Partial health-hazard assessment possible

Minimal toxicity information available

Some toxicity information available (but below minimal)

No toxicity information available

environment. He did so in order "to show that most cancers were not due to genetic factors and thus that prevention was not impossible."

Subsequently, environmental scientists and activists took an extreme view of Higginson's theory. They advanced the position that increased cancer rates are related primarily to the post-World War II growth in the production of industrial chemicals. Cancer is largely due to the "man-made" components of our environment, and is therefore controllable and preventable through regulation. That view became predominant in the 1970s, not within the scientific community but among members of the media and key policymakers.

By the end of the environmental decade, though, Higginson issued an unprecedented attack on the view advanced by Epstein and others. His prestige lent support to other scientists who had been insisting that environmentalists perpetuate a distorted view of cancer and exaggerate the effects of industrial chemical production. Higginson explains that by "environment" he meant "*total* environment, cultural as well as chemical. . . . Environment is what surrounds people and impinges on them. The air you breathe, the culture you live in, the agricultural habits of your community, the social cultural habits, the social pressures, the physical chemicals with which you come in contact, the diet, and so on." By identifying "environment" with primarily industrial chemicals, environmental scientists neglected the effect of "lifestyle" factors—diet and behavior—on cancer incidence. As a result, Higginson concludes, "overemphasis on chemical carcinogens has distorted our approach to the environmental theory for many cancers."[34]

Environmental scientists quickly countered that scientific data were misrepresented and that the new emphasis on "lifestyle" factors was politically motivated.[35] But, following Higginson, other scientists continue to rebuff the view advanced by Epstein and others. According to Howard Hiatt, dean of the Harvard School of Public Health, cancer trends in the 1970s indicate "that there isn't any epidemic of cancer in prospect, except for lung cancer attributable to smoking." The American Medical Association's Council on Scientific Affairs

[34] Research News, "Cancer and Environment: Higginson Speaks Out," 205 *Science* 1363 (September 28, 1979).

[35] Epstein and Swartz, supra note 29, at 130.

concludes further in a 1981 report that there was "as yet no convincing increase in cancer incidence that parallels the rising industrial petrochemical pollution since 1950s in the United States."[36]

In sum, scientific opinion evolved and became more politically polarized throughout the environmental decade. Initially, there was wide-ranging support for some form of regulation based on a general agreement (but by no means a consensus) that (1) environmental, versus genetic, factors induce most cancers; (2) the environment contains massive amounts of toxic and carcinogenic chemical substances; (3) no safe threshold level of exposure to a carcinogen exists, and hence any exposure creates the risk of cancer; and (4) since there are no presently available cures for cancer, preventive regulatory measures are necessary.[37] A decade later, the scientific community was more sophisticated about what environmental factors are linked to the incidence of cancer. It had become more divided over the theory of a no-safe-threshold level of carcinogenic exposure as well. The explicit political bias in the views of early environmental scientists and advocates was subjected to greater criticism. These disputes escalated in intensity and more narrowly focused on such critical issues as (1) the relative association between cancer incidence and rising petrochemical production[38]; (2) the relative importance of individual lifestyle factors and other environmental factors for understanding cancer rates; and perhaps most crucially (3) the models and methods for extrapolation from data to determine carcinogenic risks.[39]

---

[36] See P. Boffey, "Cancer Experts Lean Toward Steady Vigilance, But Less Alarm, on Environment," *New York Times* C1 (March 2, 1982).

[37] See, generally, International Trade Commission, *Synthetic Organic Chemicals: United States Production and Sales* (1977); and U.S. Department of Labor, *An Interim Report to Congress on Occupational Diseases* (1980).

[38] See, e.g., B. Ames, "Identifying Environmental Chemicals Causing Mutations and Cancer," 204 *Science* 587 (1979); M. Luppe, "Carcinogens and Regulation," 211 *Science* 332 (1981); and R. Doll, "Strategy for Detection of Cancer Hazards to Man," 265 *Nature* 589 (1977).

[39] See discussion in text below and, generally, Office of Technology Assessment, *Assessment of Technologies for Determining Cancer Risks from the Environment* (Washington, D.C.: Office of Technology Assessment, 1981); Department of Health and Human Services, National Cancer Institute, *First Annual Report on Carcinogens* (Washington, D.C.: National Cancer Institute, 1980).

Models and Modes of Carcinogenic Risk Assessment

Underlying the controversy over the relative importance of environmental versus lifestyle factors is a fundamental disagreement over models for carcinogenic risk assessments. At bottom, that disagreement is as much political as scientific. This is because models and modes of carcinogenic risk assessment order both research and political agendas. Models of carcinogenesis are a combination of scientific and social hypotheses that carry their own implicit political bias. Scientists in turn have vested interests in promoting particular models and theories that they are testing.[40]

The choice of basic models of carcinogenesis entails a political bias and predisposes the assessment and regulation of risks. Given the uncertainties of knowledge, scientists and policymakers must make normative judgments in carcinogenic risk assessment. These judgments are usually implicit, but at times are explicitly made. The *First Annual Report on Carcinogens* issued by the Department of Health and Human Services (DHHS) in 1980 is illustrative. When explaining why only a handful of carcinogens—twenty-six—had been included, based on data of human exposure, and numerous other suspected carcinogens were excluded based on laboratory animal tests, the HHS observes:

> Science and society have not arrived at a final consensus on the definition of carcinogen either in human population or in experimental animals. Scientific judgment plays an important role in the final decision on whether a substance is a carcinogen where test results are unclear. This judgment rests on a knowledge base that is fluid and evolving.[41]

Scientific knowledge is "fluid and evolving" indeed. The various kinds of data and tests used in carcinogenic risk assessment, along with their relative limitations, are shown in Figure 1.4.[42] Figure 1.5

---

[40] Petro, supra note 25.

[41] Department of Health and Human Services, supra note 39, at v.

[42] Based on A. Fisher, "An Overview and Evaluation of EPA's Guidelines for Conducting Regulatory Impact Analysis," in V. K. Smith, editor, *Environmental Policy Under Reagan's Executive Order: The Role of Benefit-Cost Analysis* (Chapel Hill: University of North Carolina Press, 1984), at 104–105.

Figure 1.4

Kinds of Data Used in Risk Assessments

I. HUMAN DATA

A. Clinical Studies

Planned research experiment, with controlled exposure levels. But, ethical considerations and legal restrictions limit utility of approach. The data generated are typically for a pollutant's impact on an index of organ function, rather than for a particular disease (but not for determining levels that cause death).

B. Cohort Studies (prospective and retrospective)

Groups with different levels of exposure to a suspect substance are followed over time to determine differences in response. Inferences are made based on large samples, long follow-up periods, and statistical analysis. Such samples are not always feasible, and it remains difficult to detect rare effects, especially for retrospective studies with poor records of exposure levels.

C. Case Control Studies

A group with a disease is compared to a control group without the disease. Such studies, often on workers, may be macroepidemiological, in which aggregate mortality and morbidity rates are related to characteristics of relevant population groups, or microepidemological, in which analyses are based on data for particular individuals. This type of study can adjust for other influences such as sex, race, smoking, income, diet, and exercise. The sample size may be smaller than for cohort studies, but finding a suitable control group is difficult. Moreover, the data usually do not consider the lag between exposure and adverse health effects, since current exposure levels are typically assumed to be the same as past exposure in estimating cumulative health effects. The results can be biased by population migration or mitigating actions that make actual exposure differ from apparent exposure. Results from occupation-related studies may not be applicable to the much lower doses expected in the environment, especially for people with varying sensitivities compared to those of workers.

D. Episodic Studies

These studies depend on accidents, so researchers are often unprepared and control groups are not readily available; therapy usually takes precedence over research.

Figure 1.4 (*continued*)

II. ANIMAL DATA

A. Animal (in vivo) Experiments

Controlled laboratory setting permits isolation of effects from a specific substance, allowing the study of the full effects of the substance—from causing disease to death. Laboratory tests, however, have certain limitations, including ambiguity of response identification and uncertainty in predicting response at much lower levels of exposure, based on high test dosages, and in extrapolating effects from a rodent population to that of a human population, due to different metabolic processes. Controlled laboratory experiments may reveal no response to an isolated substance that may in fact have a synergetic relation with other substances resulting in disease.

B. Short-Term (in vitro) Tests

Bacteria, mammalian cell cultures, or small organisms are observed (after exposure to a suspect substance) for a few days to a few weeks. The advantages of this kind of experiment are that the costs are much less than life-time animal experiments and can be completed in a short period of time. But, in vitro tests, though useful for preliminary screening of substances, imperfectly coordinate with the relatively few comparable life-time animal studies.

C. Structure Activity Analysis

Molecular structures of suspect substances are compared with substances whose toxicity and metabolic pathways are well known. The data generated, however, are weak for some classes of chemicals, and this approach is relatively new.

lists the chemicals and industrial processes that have been evaluated for human and animal carcinogenicity by the IARC.[43]

Risk assessments based on data from human exposure are the most reliable. But for both moral and practical reasons, they are virtually impossible to obtain. Clinical studies of human exposure to suspected chemicals are all but foreclosed by the cultural values of demo-

[43] Reprinted from Office of Technology Assessment, supra note 39.

Figure 1.5

Chemical and Industrial Processes
Evaluated for Human Carcinogenicity
by the International Agency for Research on Cancer

	Degree of Evidence	
	Humans	Experimental Animals
CHEMICALS AND PROCESSES JUDGED CARCINOGENIC FOR HUMANS		
4-aminobiphenyl	Sufficient	Sufficient
Arsenic and certain arsenic compounds	Sufficient	Inadequate
Asbestos	Sufficient	Sufficient
Manufacture of auramine	Sufficient	Not applicable
Benzene	Sufficient	Inadequate
Benzidine	Sufficient	Sufficient
N,N-bis (2-chloroethyl)-2-naphthylamine (chlornaphazine)	Sufficient	Limited
Bis(chloromethyl)ether and technical grade chloromethyl methyl ether	Sufficient	Sufficient
Chromium and certain chromium compounds	Sufficient	Sufficient
Diethylstilbestrol (DES)	Sufficient	Sufficient
Underground hematite mining	Sufficient	Not applicable
Manufacture of isopropyl alcohol by the strong acid process	Sufficient	Not applicable
Melphalan	Sufficient	Sufficient
Mustard gas	Sufficient	Limited
2-naphthylamine	Sufficient	Sufficient
Nickel refining	Sufficient	Not applicable
Soots, tars, and mineral oils	Sufficient	Sufficient
Vinyl chloride	Sufficient	Sufficient
CHEMICALS AND PROCESSES JUDGED PROBABLY CARCINOGENIC FOR HUMANS		
GROUP A: CHEMICALS AND PROCESSES WITH "HIGHER DEGREES OF EVIDENCE"		
Aflatoxins	Limited	Sufficient
Cadmium and certain cadmium compounds	Limited	Sufficient
Chlorambucil	Limited	Sufficient
Cyclophosphamide	Limited	Sufficient

Figure 1.5
(*continued*)

| | Degree of Evidence | |
	Humans	Experimental Animals

CHEMICALS AND PROCESSES JUDGED
PROBABLY CARCINOGENIC
FOR HUMANS (cont.)

Nickel and certain nickel compounds	Limited	Sufficient
Tris(1-aziridinyl)phosphine sulphide (thiotepa)	Limited	Sufficient

GROUP B: CHEMICALS AND PROCESSES
WITH "LOWER DEGREES OF EVIDENCE"

Acrylonitrile	Limited	Sufficient
Amitrole (aminotriazole)	Inadequate	Sufficient
Auramine	Limited	Limited
Beryllium and certain beryllium compounds	Limited	Sufficient
Carbon tetrachloride	Inadequate	Sufficient
Dimethylcarbamoyl chloride	Inadequate	Sufficient
Dimethyl sulphate	Inadequate	Sufficient
Ethylene oxide	Limited	Inadequate
Iron dextran	Inadequate	Sufficient
Oxymetholone	Limited	No data
Phenacetin	Limited	Limited
Polychlorinated biphenyls	Inadequate	Sufficient

CHEMICALS AND PROCESSES THAT COULD
NOT BE CLASSIFIED AS TO THEIR
CARCINOGENICITY FOR HUMANS

Chloramphenicol	Inadequate	No data
Chlordane/heptachlor	Inadequate	Limited
Chloroprene	Inadequate	Inadequate
Dichlorodiphenyltrichloroethane (DDT)	Inadequate	Limited
Dieldrin	Inadequate	Limited
Epichlorohydrin	Inadequate	Limited
Hematite	Inadequate	Negative

Figure 1.5

(*continued*)

	Degree of Evidence	
	Humans	Experimental Animals

CHEMICALS AND PROCESSES THAT
COULD NOT BE CLASSIFIED AS TO
THEIR CARCINOGENICITY FOR
HUMANS (cont.)

	Humans	Experimental Animals
Hexachlorocyclohexane (technical grade HCH/lindane)	Inadequate	Limited
Isoniazid	Inadequate	Limited
Isopropyl oils	Inadequate	Inadequate
Lead and certain lead compounds	Inadequate	Sufficient (for some soluble salts)
Phenobarbitone	Limited	Limited
N-phenyl-2-naphthylamine	Inadequate	Inadequate
Phenytoin	Limited	Limited
Reserpine	Inadequate	Inadequate
Styrene	Inadequate	Limited
Trichloroethylene	Inadequate	Limited
Tris(aziridinyl)-*para*-benzoquinone (triaziquone)	Inadequate	Limited

CHEMICALS AND PROCESSES FOR WHICH
HUMAN DATA ARE AVAILABLE, BUT
WHICH WERE NOT CONSIDERED BY
THE IARC WORKING GROUP

Ortho- and *para*-dichlorobenzene
Dichlorobenzidine
Phenylbutazone
2,3,7,8-tetrachlorodibenzo-*para*-dioxin
  (TCDD, the "dioxin" of Agent Orange)
Vinylidene chloride

cratic politics. For moral and political reasons, the best of all possible scientific assessments of risk—based on human experimentation—remain impossible to obtain.

General agreement within the scientific and regulatory communities thus emerged on the appropriateness of extrapolating the carcinogenic risks of a chemical that causes cancer at high doses in a rodent population to that of a human population, which is diverse and disproportionately exposed to low doses. Scientists, though, disagree about the relative degree of confidence that may be invested in studies of laboratory animals. They do so for a number of reasons, including the fact that the mechanisms of cancer are not well understood and that rodent and human metabolic structures differ. A linear no-threshold dose-response curve may therefore not always prove reliable. It, for instance, fits ionizing radiation but may not fit other toxic substances that have a range of effects on different animal organisms. Benzene thus appears to be a human, but not an animal, carcinogen. Consequently, there exists genuine disagreement over various extrapolation models, all of which fit data within the high-dose, experimental range but diverge in the untested, low-dose range that approximates human exposure.

Approximations of carcinogenic risk based on *a* model of extrapolation from the effects of high doses on rodent populations are therefore necessary for basically two reasons. First, a moral-political decision has been made not to test potential carcinogens on humans. Second, as a practical matter scientists cannot conduct so-called mega-mouse experiments that could determine carcinogenic response rates at low doses. Mega-mouse experiments are simply too costly and administratively unfeasible. To determine with 95 percent accuracy that the carcinogenic response to a substance is one in a million, over six million rodents would be required for a controlled laboratory experiment, lasting eighteen to twenty-four months. Scientists therefore must test fewer animals at significantly higher doses, and then extrapolate to approximate the low-dose rates associated with human exposure.

Risk assessments are political, moreover, for another, still more basic reason. Models of extrapolation from high to low dosage rates, and from response rates in rodent to those in human populations, bias assessments in either a conservative or a liberal direction. So, too, the tests for screening potentially hazardous chemicals involve crucial political decisions—decisions made by scientists no less than regulators. The relatively high costs of standard laboratory tests, which typically run for two years at a cost of $200,000 to $500,000, necessitate such decisions. Decisions must also be made about, among other things, the cost-effectiveness of various kinds of tests and the selection of chemical substances to be studied.[44]

The choice of models and modes of testing carcinogenicity in turn leads to disagreements on the levels of confidence appropriate for the inferences drawn from various kinds of tests and data. Even though adequate bioassays are performed, scientists may disagree in their diagnosis of lesions due to their different professional backgrounds. Disagreements over the adequacy of various methodologies for testing suspected carcinogens further exacerbate differences in interpreting the results of an experiment, and how to apply the results of animal bioassays.

Central to these disagreements is the no-safe-threshold model of carcinogenesis, underlying the Delaney Clause of the Food, Drug and Cosmetic Act and a good number of disputes over substances like saccharin. Yet, that disagreement is also instructive in highlighting, again, the inescapable political bias in carcinogenic risk assessments.

Those scientists who support the model of no-safe-threshold of carcinogenic exposure argue that cancer may start with the transformation of a (possibly mutagenic) single cell, which then triggers cancer. Cancerous cells are self-replicating, multiplying, and proliferating. They also may interact with others incrementally, synergistically, and cumulatively. This process of carcinogenesis is irreversible.

By contrast, other scientists reject some or all of these assumptions about carcinogenesis. They insist that low levels of exposure to carcinogens—even to a single molecule of a mutagen—need not necessarily pose a significant threat. This is because there is a range of biological defense mechanisms that can repair, deactivate, and detoxify a mutagen or carcinogen. A minimum number of molecules in a cell must be affected before any biological reaction, including carcinogenesis, begins to take place. Humans are constantly bombarded by

[44] For a further discussion, see Office of Technology Assessment, supra note 39, at 113–172.

many different carcinogens and yet little happens—cells die but no carcinogenesis occurs. Human cells differ from those of rodents. They are far more resistant both to radiation and to chemical carcinogenesis than are rodents. In sum, the process of carcinogenesis is neither inexorable nor necessarily irreversible, as the no-safe-threshold theory maintains.[45]

Carcinogenic risk assessments—the inferences drawn from available data and the degree of confidence invested in those inferences—largely depend on acceptance or rejection of the basic assumptions of the theory of a no-safe-threshold level of carcinogenic exposure. Depending on whether some or all of those assumptions identified with the no-safe-threshold model of carcinogenesis are accepted, risk assessments will take either a conservative or a liberal bias toward regulation of alleged health-safety or environmental risks.

Regulation of these risks is problematic because risk assessment itself is problematic and political. As a 1974 report by the World Health Organization observes, "The toxicologist must assess the risks associated with different levels of exposure. Proposed approaches for such evaluation [have been made]. All the proposals suffer from lack of sufficient data to establish their validity and/or [freedom] from arbitrary assumptions that lead to unrealistic estimates."[46] In 1976, R. L. Dixon, of the National Institute of Environmental and Health Sciences, put the matter this way, "There appears to be worldwide agreement concerning the fact that extrapolating laboratory animal toxicity data to man remains a major unsolved problem in toxicology. . . . The lack of understanding in this area makes the building of mathematical models for extrapolation unreliable at the present time."[47] And, almost a decade later, in 1984, the former head of the Environmental Protection Agency, William Ruckelshaus, again perceptively cautioned, "We should remember that risk assessment data

[45] For further discussion and additional references, see Office of Technology Assessment, supra note 39: and Efron, supra note 21.

[46] Report of World Health Organization Scientific Group, "Assessment of the Carcinogenicity and Mutagenicity of Chemicals" (Geneva: World Health Organization, 1974).

[47] R. L. Dixon, "Problems in Extrapolating Toxicity Data from Laboratory Animals to Man," 13 *Environmental Health Perspective* 43 (1976), at 45.

can be like a captured spy: if you torture it long enough, it will tell you anything you want to know."[48]

Dispute Resolution in a Jurocracy

Science cannot dictate responses to the perceived risks of industrial society; indeed, science is part of the problem. No less than the political activism of some environmental scientists, the very uncertainties and implicit political bias of models of carcinogenic risk assessment heighten the clash between special interests over whether and how to regulate health-safety and the environment.

Even if science could provide an uncontestable foundation for assessing cancer risks, our culture of democratic politics would not let it dictate regulatory responses to managing those risks (just as it forbids human experimentation that would give science a firm basis for assessing risks).

Democratic politics, however, cannot provide a solution either. In regulating the risks of an industrial society it would be irrational and imprudent to rest public policy solely on bargains struck through political compromises—compromises that do not also "rest in reasonable part upon the strength of the scientific record." As Philip Handler emphasizes, "Government regulation of technical products and processes must rest on a rational and sufficient scientific basis."[49] Yet that, of course, leads us back to the difficulties of how we determine what is a "sufficient scientific basis" for regulation.

Science-policy disputes thus pose the fundamental question: What process is due? How are the science-policy disputes underlying health-safety and environmental regulations to be settled (if not resolved)? The response has been largely one of judicializing those disputes. Like other kinds of social conflict, the disputes over the scientific basis for and the basic value conflicts in regulating risks are

[48] W. Ruckelshaus, "Risk in a Free Society," 14 *Environmental Law Reporter* 10190 (1984).

[49] P. Handler, "A Rebuttal: The Need for a Sufficient Scientific Basis for Government Regulation," 43 *George Washington Law Review* 808 (1975), at 813.

structured according to adversarial processes and forced into the courts. And this is ultimately a cultural response—the response of our uniquely adversarial culture and its relation to democratic politics.

That our legal culture largely determines responses to science-policy disputes should not be surprising. For democratic politics rests on the paradox of how a self-governing society can govern when sharply divided or fragmented by competing interests. From their own experience as much as from reading John Locke's *Two Treatises on Civil Government*, those of the founding generation understood the need for formal procedures and independent tribunals to resolve social conflict. Having justified the basis for political authority on popular sovereignty and rejected rule by the divine right of kings, Locke posed the fundamental question for modern political philosophy and experience, "[W]ho shall be the judge when [governmental] power is made right use of?" Locke concluded that "there can be no judge on earth."[50] But, for the Founding Fathers judicial review provided the solution—a solution without precedent and the unique contribution of our system of constitutional politics.[51]

Adversarial processes and the courts play a major role in the formulation and implementation of regulatory policies precisely because, as Peter Schuck observes, "in a liberal society in which there is no received or even widely shared notion of truth, they are simply indispensable for resolving sharply conflicting interests."[52] The attempt to resolve science-policy disputes by formal adversarial processes and in the courts, in other words, is a cultural response of a society that neither professes a belief in a universal truth nor sanctions the concentration of political power.

Our legal culture places a premium on adversarial processes not so much for the sake of "finding the truth" as to achieve fairness in

[50] Excerpt from J. Locke, *Two Treatises on Civil Government* (1690), reprinted in A. T. Mason and G. E. Baker, *Free Government in the Making*, 4th ed. (New York: Oxford University Press, 1985), at 36–37.

[51] For a further discussion, see D. M. O'Brien, "Judicial Review and Constitutional Politics: Theory and Practice," 48 *University of Chicago Law Review* 1052 (1981).

[52] P. Schuck, "Litigation, Bargaining, and Regulation," *Regulation* 26 (July/August, 1979), at 26.

resolving social conflicts. This is due to the premium placed on individual liberty and a corresponding distrust of the coercive powers of government. Adversary proceedings elevate fairness above truth in order to resolve conflict in a society that places great value on political compromise but in which it is not always possible.

That science-policy disputes are judicialized would seem odd were it not for our adversarial culture and litigious society. Yet, courts and judges are expected to settle them in private law litigation over, say, toxic torts and when reviewing challenges to agencies' regulatory decisions—because of our basic cultural attitudes toward science, law, and politics.

The judicialization of science-policy disputes, like other kinds of social conflict, is a uniquely American response rooted in cultural attitudes toward science, law, and democratic politics. But, it is also an imperfect response to the problems of managing risk. Consider Richard Petro's characterization of the problems of managing risks:

> There exist, both in the general environment and in certain occupations, chemical or physical agents which increase the likelihood of human cancer. Our political response to this would, in an ideal world where sufficient knowledge was available, depend on the direct and indirect costs of the various possible measures of control, and on how many cancers each such measure would prevent. In the real world, estimates of the direct financial costs of the control of particular agents can easily differ by one or two orders of magnitude, the indirect costs may be grossly exaggerated, or some major indirect costs may be completely overlooked. Worst of all, we have in general no remotely reliable estimates of the numbers of cancers which particular legislative controls would prevent. Consequently, there is wide scope for pressure groups to have considerable influence on public policy.[53]

In England, science-policy disputes are settled in a parlimentary fashion and with deference to the expertise of the civil service. By contrast, the American response has largely been the judicialization of science-policy disputes.

[53] Petro, supra note 25, at 297.

Courts and Science-Policy Disputes

Courts confront science-policy disputes in basically two ways. Trial courts serve as a forum for resolving those disputes according to common law and statutory rules. Appellate courts review lower court rulings and the scientific basis and value choices in legislative and administrative rulemaking. In both instances, judges play an important role in structuring and reviewing the regulation of risk: In the next chapter we will explore the traditional regulatory role of courts in the management of risks.

CHAPTER

2

Courts and Toxic Torts

Science-policy litigation is not new to courts. Some disputes arise over age-old problems, like that of a farmer who builds a dam to facilitate the irrigation of his land, which leads to flooding of his neighbor's pasture. Did the dam's diversion of the river cause the flooded pasture? Others arise because new technologies bring unforeseen consequences, such as when a chemical plant's deposits of waste in a company-owned lake spills over, or leaches, to a neighboring farmer's land, contaminating the water, soil, and grazing cattle. Did the chemical plant's deposits cause the contamination? Both of these cases raise similar questions of legal rights and responsibilities. But they differ in the complexity of the facts and the kinds of evidence that will stand up in establishing legal responsibility and in awarding remedies for each farmer's injury.

Courts have historically handled scientifically complex disputes over trespass, nuisance, negligence, and the like. By applying these traditional doctrines of tort law, they perform an important regulatory role. They assess risks and responsibilities, and their rulings regulate social and economic relations. Tort law, as Leon Green perceptively remarked, is simply "public law in disguise." The public and regulatory nature of private law litigation arises from providing remedies "for the every day hurts inflicted by the multitudinous activities of our society."[1]

If courts have a traditional regulatory role and respond more or less quickly to social forces and technological and industrial developments, then the central concern is, in Judge David Bazelon's words, "not *whether* but *how* the law deals with risk."[2] Are legal doctrines sufficiently pliable? Are courts efficiently and effectively responsive, or, alternatively, have they gone too far?

Since World War II, the pace of social and scientific developments has posed ever more complex science-policy disputes. Initially, courts were reluctant to apply traditional common law doctrines to new problems, but in the 1970s they responded to the pressures of private law adjudication. They thereby forged a revolution in private law litigation, which in turn propelled them into a growing range of disputes on the frontiers of science.

After discussing the traditional regulatory role of courts, and how legal doctrines have been transformed in response to the pressures of private law litigation, I will assess the limitations and contributions of judicial regulation. Controversies brought by DES and asbestos litigation illuminate how courts respond to new-found risks and how broad an impact they may have on social and economic relations. Judicial regulation, like other kinds of regulation, involves tradeoffs—exacting its own costs while conferring certain benefits. As such, it is an imperfect, though crucial, response to the regulation of risk.

The Regulatory Role of Courts

Courts are not self-starters; they must await actual cases or controversies. Yet, when deciding individual cases, their rulings may have a

[1] L. Green, "Tort Law: Public Law in Disguise," 38 *Texas Law Review* 257 (1960), at 269.

[2] Address, "The Courts and the Public: Policy Decisions about High Technology and Risk," delivered at the University of Pennsylvania (April 4, 1981). The author appreciates Judge Bazelon's making a copy of his speech available.

broad regulatory impact. Because courts make regulatory policy on an incremental, case-by-case basis, private law litigation is an often overlooked vehicle for fashioning public policy. From a political perspective, however, there are distinct advantages to bringing into courts disputes over industrial air pollution, the disposal of hazardous substances, and the like. For one thing, though the financial and informational costs of adjudication often exceed the resources of would-be litigants, they are less than the comparable social-transaction costs of mobilizing forces in legislative and regulatory arenas.[3] Another reason why litigation is often advantageous is that it focuses in a more discriminating fashion on particular claims than legislation or regulatory standards typically do. Litigation holds the potential for direct compensation, whereas other kinds of regulation need not, and a tax scheme may not even address entire categories of injuries. Sometimes Congress passes special legislation to compensate individuals, as it did in the late 1970s for those exposed to particular toxic substances.[4] But generally, private law litigation remains the primary vehicle for individuals seeking compensation for damages due to exposure to toxic chemicals and to stimulate the development of regulatory policy.

Private Law Litigation as Regulation

The role of private law litigation in regulating market decisions and technological developments has received only recent attention. Economist Arthur Pigou drew attention to the fact that business transactions have external social costs.[5] Competitive pressures for investments and innovations discourage businesses from taking into

[3] See, generally, U.S. Congress, Senate, Committee on Environment and Public Works, 96th Cong., 2d Sess., *Six Case Studies of Compensation for Toxic Substances Pollution: Alabama, California, Michigan, Missouri, New Jersey, and Texas* (Washington, D.C.: GPO, 1980).

[4] See 42 Sec. 9601–9657 (Supp. IV 1980) (permitting compensation for victims of hazardous waste disposal); and 30 U.S.C. Sec. 901 (1976) (permitting compensation for coal miners contracting pneumoconiosis).

[5] See A. Pigou, *The Economics of Welfare* (4th ed., 1932); Buchanan and Subblebine, "Externality," 29 *Economica* 371 (1963); Coase, "The Problems of Social Cost," 3 *Journal of Law & Economics* 1 (1960); Haveman and Weisbrod, "Defining Benefits of Public Programs: Some Guidance for Policy Analysis," 1 *Policy Analysis* 169 (1975).

account the "externalities" of their activities. The secondary effects and impact on parties not directly involved in economic transactions are generally not reflected in the price of goods. Air pollution, for example, is an externality accompanying the production of goods such as steel. But, the social and economic costs of air pollution are not reflected in the price of the goods determined by free market forces alone. Plants that ignore pollution have lower costs than those that treat effluents, and thus may prosper at the expense of more responsible competitors. No company, moreover, could afford indefinitely to assume—or internalize—the costs of pollution, if its competitors do not do likewise. And individuals or groups typically cannot afford to pay the cost of "public goods" like clean water and air. In addition, it would be economically unreasonable for them to do so.

Because market forces work against the internalization of the social costs of production, some form of governmental intervention is necessary to secure public goods. In economists Allen Kneese and Charles Schultze's words, "Private markets cannot make it possible for individuals to buy clean rivers, uncongested city streets, safe neighborhoods, protection from exotic chemicals, or freedom from discriminating practices."[6] If these goods are to be had, governmentally imposed regulations or incentive systems must structure the competitive forces of free markets.

Private law litigation has traditionally been one way of securing public goods. It can control some kinds of pollution by forcing individuals and industries to assume the costs of pollution. As such, private law litigation is an alternative to legislation and regulatory standards, subsidy schemes, and taxes on effluents, as well as voluntary self-regulation by industries.

Through private law litigation the judiciary assumes an important regulatory role. By extending private rights to include injuries due to pollution, courts impose liability on polluters. They thereby provide incentives to conduct activities in a safer—or, at least, more legally defensible—manner. Private law litigation is thus a vehicle for

---

[6] A. Kneese and C. Schultze, *Pollution, Prices and Public Policy* (Washington, D.C.: Brookings Institution, 1975), at 3.

correcting the failures of the marketplace, structuring technological and industrial decision making, and forging regulatory policies.

Tort Pressure on Public Law: The Case of DES

How courts may respond to new science-policy disputes and the potentially broad impact that private law litigation may have is well illustrated by *Sindell v. Abbott Laboratories* (1980). Mrs. Sindell and other women filed suits against the manufacturers of diethylstilbestrol (DES) in California courts. All suffered vaginal disorders which they claimed resulted from the use of DES by their mothers. DES, a synthetic estrogen manufactured since 1941 by approximately 200 companies, had been approved by the Food and Drug Administration in 1947 as a prescription drug for preventing miscarriages.

Mrs. Sindell and the other women argued that their disorders were attributable to the DES taken by their mothers and they demanded compensation. Like other plaintiffs in tort litigation, they had to show three things: a personal injury; negligence on the part of the defendant, Abbott Laboratories, a manufacturer of DES; and a causal connection between the injuries suffered and the defendant's action. Here, the women were able to show that they had suffered personal injuries and that DES manufacturers had been negligent in not sufficiently testing for and warning about the possible adverse effects of DES. But, they were unable to meet the last criterion. After so many years, it was impossible to identify conclusively which company manufactured the DES taken by the women's respective mothers.

The California State Supreme Court decided in favor of Mrs. Sindell under a new theory of recovery. Basically, the court held that plaintiffs who cannot identify the tort-feasor may sue all manufacturers who collectively represent a "substantial share" of a product's market. When plaintiffs show that an industry acted negligently and its product causes injury, the burden shifts to each defendant company to prove that its specific product could not have caused the injury. Liability, in other words, is assigned on the basis of each company's share of a market.

The Supreme Court of the United States let the ruling stand when it denied an appeal in 1980. But, like most watershed rulings, *Sindell* left many questions unanswered. Because courts decide only particular cases, their rulings do not usually consider the broader policy implications of their decisions, as might an agency in the process of promulgating regulatory standards. The California State Supreme Court, for instance, did not explain what factors other plaintiffs must show in similar suits over exposure to other allegedly dangerous products in order to justify reliance on *Sindell*'s market share theory of liability. The court neither defined what constitutes a "substantial share of the market" nor explained whether markets are based on local, regional, or national sales. It also was unclear whether plaintiffs must establish the market shares of particular manufacturers, or whether in a suit against all manufacturers the defendant companies simply have to fight that out among themselves.

Sindell's theory of joint liability significantly expands the liability of the pharmaceutical industry for injurious products. Claims for recovery against manufacturers of DES alone could total $40 billion. The impact of the ruling is broader than that, however. For the pharmaceutical industry, it forebodes an increase in litigation costs. Companies must defend themselves in a larger number of lawsuits, even if they have only a small share of a market. In addition, *Sindell* provides an incentive for the industry to conduct more searching assessments of the effects of new drugs, and therefore may affect future innovative drugs. At the same time, the effect of the ruling may delay or preclude the introduction of some new drugs, increase the cost of liability insurance, and raise the price of all prescription drugs.

Sindell illustrates how judicial construction of personal and proprietary rights significantly influences market forces, technological developments, and public policy. That is also to say that private rights help to define, create, and check markets. When enforcing these rights, courts may either reinforce or constrain the competitive forces of the marketplace.

A Revolution in Private Law Litigation

Throughout much of the nineteenth and early twentieth centuries, legal doctrines worked against claims like that brought by Mrs. Sindell. Property owners always had a right to compensation for damages from neighboring property owners or trespassers. Until the mid-twentieth century, though, courts almost uniformly refused compensation for other kinds of injuries, like those due to noise and gas pollution. They did so because they applied the common law of trespass only in cases involving the uninvited presence of *corporeal* objects on an individual's property.[7] Litigation over claims to other kinds of risks and damages was no less constrained by doctrines such as the contributory negligence of the plaintiff, the assumption of risk in a situation (a worker's taking a dangerous job, for instance), and the proximate cause between a plaintiff's injury and the defendant's allegedly harmful action.

In the last thirty years, however, courts have forged a revolution in private law litigation. That has greatly increased the judiciary's role in regulating risk and settling of science-policy disputes. And courts are now more responsive to claims of private injuries that actually embrace public goods, such as clean air and water.

In revolutionizing private law litigation, courts have fashioned public law responses to the regulation of risk. They have done so notably in the areas of trespass, nuisance, and strict liability for abnormally dangerous activities. Each of these doctrines relates to different kinds of interests and injuries. Actions for trespass, unlike those for nuisance, involve liability for interference with an individual's right to exclusively own and enjoy property. Yet because of the traditional common law emphasis on proprietary concepts, the law of trespass has been less amenable to disputes over pollution. By contrast, the doctrine of nuisance has proven a more flexible doctrine in environmental litigation. And courts have begun to reformulate common law theories of negligence and strict liability in response to disputes over allegedly hazardous products.

In this section, we will see how courts have refashioned each of these traditional doctrines in the light of new science-policy disputes, and have thereby pushed private law litigation in the direction of a

[7] See, e.g., *Batten v. United States*, 360 F.2d 580 (10th Cir. 1962), *cert. denied*, 371 U.S. 955 (1963) (no recovery for airport noise unless plane flies directly over plaintiff's property); *Arvidson v. Reynolds Metals Co.*, 125 F. Supp. 481 (W.D. Wash. 1954) (fluorine gas and minute particles deposited on and over plaintiff's land not a trespass). But, see *Reynolds Metal Co. v. Martin*, 337 F.2d 780 (4th Cir. 1969) (fluorine fumes constitute both trespass and nuisance).

public law of toxic torts. Then, we will turn to the impact of these changes and the policy debate over whether courts have gone too far.

Nuisance

Although the law of each state governs actions for nuisance, plaintiffs generally must show two things to win: an actual injury and that the defendant's activities were the proximate cause of that injury. Individuals may sue for "private nuisance" when substantial and material interference with their property results from, for instance, industrial dust, noise, odors, or water pollution.

But, the law of nuisance has evolved in two important ways— ways that push in the direction of a public law of nuisance. First, and most important, the law of nuisance has been expanded to include actions for "public nuisance." Courts have done so when an industry's activities unreasonably interfere with a right common to the public and when injuries are substantial and widespread. Personal injury or proprietary damage must still be shown, but the injuries may be shared by the public, and hence the source of those injuries is a public nuisance. Activities such as acid mine drainage,[8] blasting operations in limestone quarries,[9] and the disposal of hazardous wastes[10] have all been found to constitute public nuisances.

Second, even though the law of nuisance was historically adjudicated in state courts according to state law, in the early 1970s federal courts began to recognize claims to a federal common law of nuisance. In 1972, in *Illinois v. City of Milwaukee*, the Supreme Court indicated that lower federal courts had the power to create a federal common law governing the pollution of interstate and navigable waters. In this area at least, the Court recognized an overriding interest in a uniform rule and that pollution controversies touched on basic interests of federalism.

Further development of a federal common law of public nui-

[8] See, e.g., *Commonwealth v. Barnes and Tucker Co.* 9 Pa. Commw. 1, 303 A.2d 544, *rev'd*, 455 Pa. 392, 319 A.2d 871 (1974).

[9] See, e.g., *Green v. Castle Concrete Co.*, 2 Envtl. L. Rep. (Envtl. L. Inst.) 20347 (D. Colo., 1971).

[10] See, *Wilsonville v. SCA Services*, 77 Ill. App. 3d 618, 396 N.E. 2d 552 (Ill. App., 1979).

sance for water pollution was soon overshadowed, however. Just six months after *City of Milwaukee*, the Federal Water Pollution Act Amendments of 1972 were enacted.[11] The Federal Water Pollution Control Act (FWPCA) permits citizen's suits against industrial polluters. The law preempted subsequent development of a federal common law of public nuisance covering water pollution. Federal agencies concentrated on the implementation and enforcement of the statute rather than on costly and laborious actions against individual polluters.

The Court's approval of a federal common law of public nuisance, nevertheless, opened a veritable Pandora's box. Some lower federal courts not only maintained that the FWPCA did not preempt a federal common law of nuisance in cases of environmental pollution, they also held that the federal common law of nuisance could be asserted by local governments against polluting industries, and that awards for damages could be made even after industries abated their discharges of toxic substances.[12] Some went so far as to suggest that the emergent federal common law of nuisance extended to actions for air pollution and the disposal of ultrahazardous wastes, as in the Love Canal controversy.[13] In short, the holding in *City of Milwaukee* held the potential for extensive federal judicial regulation of industrial pollution.

Nine years after *City of Milwaukee*, the Burger Court reconsidered its decision in light of these lower court rulings and the consequences of an open-ended federal common law of nuisance. In *City of Milwaukee v. Illinois and Michigan* (1981), the Court stepped back from its earlier ruling. Here, it held that lower federal courts may create substantive common law only in narrowly restricted areas. Most important, the Court ruled that federal statutory law—such as the FWPCA—governs questions previously subject to federal common law. Rather than expanding federal common law, lower courts must

[11] The Federal Water Pollution Control Act is now known as the Clean Water Act of 1977, 33 U.S.C. Sec. 1251–1376 (1976 & Supp. IV 1980).

[12] *Long Beach v. New York*, 445 F. Supp. 1203 (D.N.J. 1978); and *Evansville v. Kentucky Liquid Recycl., Inc.*, 604 F. Supp. 1008 (7th Cir. 1979).

[13] See Summary & Comment, "Hazardous Waste: EPA, Justice Invoke Emergency Authority, Common Law in Litigation Campaign Against Dump Sites," 10 Envtl. L. Rep. (Envtl. L. Inst.) 10034 (1980).

assume that congressional legislation preempts common law remedies for public nuisances.

Writing for a bare majority, Justice William Rehnquist underscored that the federal judiciary, unlike state courts, possesses only limited jurisdiction. They have no general power to develop common law rules. Federal judges, he suggested, have neither expertise nor political legitimacy to fashion rules for such complex disputes as those involving environmental pollution. Finally, Rehnquist emphasized the problematic nature of allowing localities and states to challenge out-of-state dischargers in federal courts, and to seek to impose federal common law standards that are more stringent than comparable congressionally enacted standards.

The majority in *Illinois v. Milwaukee* stemmed the tide toward more judicial involvement in such environmental disputes. For the majority, lower courts' extension of a federal common law violated their notions of separation of powers and federalism. As Rehnquist indicated, an open-ended federal common law of nuisance would greatly expand the regulatory role of courts. Federal courts' development of a common law of public nuisance intrudes on the regulatory responsibilities of the legislative and executive branches and supersedes the law developed by state courts. In short, if uniform standards are necessary, then Congress and the executive branch should provide them, not the federal judiciary.

For three other dissenters, however, Justice Harry Blackmun argued that a federal common law complements congressional action and advances interests embodied in the Constitution and federal legislation. In Blackmun's view, "each State [has] the right to be free from unreasonable interference with its natural environment and resources when the interference stems from another state or its citizens." He thereby also indicates that the Justices are no less divided on how receptive federal judges should be to the values of environmental protection.

While a majority of the Burger Court stemmed further development of a federal common law of public nuisance, lower federal and state courts still continue to reach some disputes. They do so by applying the traditional doctrine of nuisance in private law litigation. In addition, they have forged changes in the doctrine of strict liability, or liability without fault for abnormally dangerous activities. And those changes remain even more significant for the future of environmental litigation.

Strict Liability

The doctrine of strict liability derives from an 1865 English common law case, *Rylands v. Fletcher*. The case involved damages caused by a reservoir, erected on an abandoned coal mine. Water from the reservoir leaked through an unused shaft and eventually flooded Rylands's coal mine. When awarding damages to Rylands, the Exchequer Chamber established the principle of strict liability when observing that "the true role of law is that the person who for his own purposes brings on his lands and collects and keeps there anything likely to do mischief if it escapes, must keep it at his peril and if he does not do so, is prima facie answerable for all the damage which is the natural consequence of its escape."[14]

The principle of strict liability for extrahazardous and abnormally dangerous activities was subsequently adopted in the United States in the first and second *Restatement of Torts* (which unifies tort law in the United States).[15] Accordingly, state courts have permitted compensation for damages resulting from smoke, dust, and noxious gases emitted from industries; fumigation with cyanide gas; crop dusting; and exposure to toxic chemicals.[16]

United States v. FMC Corporation (1978) is an intriguing example of how far courts have gone when applying the doctrine of strict liability. The FMC Corporation manufactured a highly toxic insecticide, carofuran. Residues of the toxin contaminated a company-owned pond that was also a site for migratory waterfowl. In the suit against the company for contaminating the waterfowl, federal district court Judge Curtin ruled against FMC Corporation. Reasoning from *Rylands*, he held that even though unaware of the lethal effects on the pond water, FMC Corporation was liable for the birds' death. The

[14] *Rylands v. Fletcher*, 1 L. R.-Ex.Ch. 265, 279 (1865).

[15] *Restatement (Second) of Torts*, Secs. 519–520 (1976).

[16] *Holman v. Athens Laundry Co.*, 149 Ga. 345, 100 S.E. 207 (1919); *Luthinger v. Moore*, 31 Ca. 2d 489, 190 P.2d 1 (1948); and *Gotreaux v. Gary*, 232 La. 373, 94 So.2d 293 (1957).

company was at fault for failing to prevent the toxin from reaching the pond in the first place. The Court of Appeals for the Second Circuit later upheld Judge Curtin's application of the doctrine of strict liability.

Negligence and Hazardous Products

Along with changes in the doctrines of trespass, nuisance, and strict liability, courts have also modified common law theories of negligence and strict product liability. Judges and lawyers frequently disagree about whether negligence or strict liability should be the general standard. But, all agree that both theories aim at creating incentives for enterprises to make their activities safer. Their "dominant function," in Court of Appeals Judge Richard Posner's view, is "to generate rules of liability that [would] bring about . . . the efficient . . . level of accidents and safety."[17] Both theories, moreover, greatly contribute to the expansion of private law litigation over toxic and carcinogenic substances.

Negligence actions center on whether a company fails to exercise due care in manufacturing and marketing a product. Individuals usually assert that a company is liable for failing to inspect a product properly and that lack of due care was the cause of their injuries. But what is due care? That question must be answered on a case-by-case basis and reflects both judicial and societal perceptions of the reasonableness of risk.

Efforts to win lawsuits over exposure to toxins often prove difficult because of the problems of establishing a causal connection between injuries and an alleged or known carcinogen. In this regard, the 1973 Michigan episode over polybrominated biphenyl (PBB) is illuminating.[18] The PBB controversy arose from Michigan Chemical Company's mistakenly shipping to the Farm Bureau Services, Inc., a farm feed supplier, bags of fire retardant containing PBB, instead of a cattle feed additive. The bags containing the fire retardant and the

[17] R. Posner, "A Theory of Negligence," 1 *Journal of Legal Studies* 29 (1972).

[18] See E. Chen, *PBB: An American Tragedy* (Englewood Cliffs, N. J.: Prentice-Hall, 1979); and J. Egginton, *The Poisoning of Michigan* (New York: Norton, 1980).

food additive were similar in appearance. Farmers who purchased the food additive from the supplier mixed the fire retardant with other food additives and fed it to their cattle. The result was widespread contamination of the cattle and, eventually, of the general population of Michigan.

At a trial that lasted almost a year and a half—the longest in Michigan's history—the farmers could not persuasively show that PBB caused the adverse health effects in the cattle. Although many farmers had to destroy their cattle, the decision in 1978 went against them. They failed to show a causal connection between the ingestion of the fire retardant and the contamination of the cattle. A Mount Sinai research team in 1979, though, reported that more than 90 percent of all Michigan residents have PBB in their bodies due to the consumption of contaminated dairy products.[19]

In other situations, companies may be found negligent in failing either to warn of potential hazards or known defects of their products or to properly design and test their products.[20] In *Boyl v. California Chemical Company* (1963), for instance, Mrs. Boyl won compensation for injuries suffered from exposure to sodium arsenite in a weed killer, Triox. The circumstances of this case are particularly interesting.

After spraying her patio with Triox, Mrs. Boyl dumped the residue and waste water from cleaning the spray tank on a portion of her backyard. A couple of days later she unwittingly sunbathed on the very spot where she had poured the Triox rinse. Shortly afterward, Mrs. Boyl developed a heat rash followed by dizziness, muscle tremors, and physical malfunctioning, for which she was hospitalized. Although the company printed a warning and instructions for the use of Triox on every bottle, a federal district court ruled that the California Chemical Company was negligent. The company failed to provide a reasonable warning of the health risks of the solution, and such negligence was the proximate cause of Mrs. Boyl's injuries. The court could have found that Mrs. Boyl contributed to her own injuries by

[19] See Grezech, "PBB," in R. Hader, R. Brownstein, and J. Richard, *Who's Poisoning America* (San Francisco: Sierra Club, 1981), at 63.

[20] See, e.g., *Martinez v. Dixie Carriers Co.*, 529 F.2d 457 (5th Cir. 1976).

her negligence and lack of care in sunbathing. But, the court held that she was not contributorily negligent since she "was totally ignorant of any risk or danger to herself arising from the Triox solution contaminated earth."

Boyl illustrates the potentially broad compass of the law of toxic torts and of the role of courts in balancing the risks and benefits of consumer goods. The case also highlights how amorphous the concept of unreasonable harm or risk is in private law litigation. "Unreasonable harm" is defined in the *Restatement (Second) of Torts* (1964) as any "risk that is of such magnitude as to outweigh what the law regards as the utility of the act or of the particular manner in which it was done." Yet, when determining that a product poses an unreasonable risk, judges and juries are almost completely free to base decisions on their own perceptions of risk.

Toward Strict Product Liability

The judicial balancing of risks and responsibilities and the broad socioeconomic impact of private law litigation heighten controversy over the expansion of another legal doctrine—that of strict product liability. The doctrine of strict product liability is more sweeping than that of negligence. Strict product liability does not permit defenses such as the injured party's contributory negligence. Rather, manufacturers are strictly liable for *all* defects in the design of products that later result in injuries. "Some products are so dangerous," a Texas court concluded in *Crocker v. Winthrop Laboratories* (1974), "that the manufacturer should be liable for the resulting harm though he did not and could not have known of the dangers at the time of marketing."

Strict product liability litigation has expanded rapidly since the 1970s. The doctrine has been embraced by workers seeking compensatory damages caused by exposure to asbestos as well as by approximately 2.4 million persons (including Vietnam war veterans) who make up a class of plaintiffs claiming injuries due to exposure to various phenoxy herbicides, such as 2,4,5-T, more commonly known as "Agent Orange."[21]

---

[21] *In re "Agent Orange" Product Liability Litigation*, 635 F.2d 987 (2d Cir. 1980).

Courts enlarged the doctrine primarily in response to risks associated with technological and industrial advances, but not without a great deal of controversy.[22] Many court-watchers argue that judges do not have the expertise to assess risks and that their balancing is too ad hoc. Debate also revolves around the differences between assessing product design under the traditional negligence standards (allowing for defenses, such as contributory negligence) and more recent product liability rules.

Basically, controversy about whether negligence or strict product liability should be the touchstone for tort law centers on two models of judicial risk management: whether judges should allow for some shared responsibility for injuries on the part of the plaintiff and defendant, or whether the latter should bear all the burden of assessing and managing the risks of their products.

Under either doctrine, judicial assessments of risks and responsibilities are not entirely unfettered. The *Model Uniform Product Liability Act* (MUPLA) (1979) provides some guidance:

> In order to determine that the product was unreasonably unsafe in construction, the trier of fact must find that, when the product left the control of the manufacturer, the product deviated in some material way from the manufacturer's design specifications or performance standards, or from otherwise identical units of the same product line.

When judges evaluate the social risks, costs, and benefits of a product, the MUPLA also suggests that they consider:

(a) Any warnings and instructions provided with the product;
(b) The technological and practical feasibility of a product designed and manufactured so as to have prevented claimant's harm while substantially serving the likely user's expected needs;
(c) The effect of any proposed alternative design on the usefulness of the product;
(d) The comparative costs of producing, distributing, seeking, using and maintaining the product as designed and as alternatively designed; and

[22] See, e.g., G. Calabresi and J. Hirshoff, "Toward a Test for Strict Liability in Torts," 81 *Yale Law Journal* 1055 (1972); and R. Epstein, "A Theory of Strict Liability," 2 *Journal of Legal Studies* 151 (1973); and R. Posner, "Strict Liability: A Comment," 2 *Journal of Legal Studies* 205 (1973).

(e)   The new or additional harms that might have resulted if the product had been so alternatively designed.[23]

Central to these guidelines (and indeed all judicial balancing) is
the idea of a "reasonable man." As the Court of Appeals for the Fifth
Circuit in *Reyes v. Wyeth Laboratories* (1974) put it:

> [T]he reasonable man standard becomes the fulcrum for a balanc-
> ing process in which the utility of the product properly used is weighed
> against whatever dangers of harm inhere in its introduction into com-
> merce. . . . [I]f the potential harmful effects of the product . . . outweigh
> the legitimate public interest in its availability, it will be declared un-
> reasonable per se and the person placing it on the market held liable.

But, as Justice Felix Frankfurter once commented, reasonable
men differ as to what is "reasonable." And the MUPLA guidelines
leave judges considerably free to make their own assessments of
scientific and technological developments, as well as of the feasibility
of alternative technologies.

It is easy to see why this is troubling for critics of judicial regulation if we compare, even in a preliminary way, the characteristics of
risk assessments by judges with those by administrators. Judges (and
juries) decide questions of fact presented during an adversarial proceeding. Administrators (as further discussed later) are also required
to build a record of evidence, increasingly through adversarial-type
proceedings, in support of their decisions. But, when judges and
juries assess risks, they need not articulate their values and relative
weight. Agencies are not required to do so either. Yet, they must
provide a reasoned basis for their decisions (and, under White House
mandates of the Carter and Reagan administrations, provide cost-
benefit support for their regulatory policies). Judges need not quantify the factors they consider important and can rest their decisions
solely on qualitative evaluations, whereas agencies often must quantify or at least give a reasoned elaboration for their decisions. Judges
are also generalists by training and lack the special expertise in risk
assessment and management that administrators possess. Nor do they

[23] *Model Uniform Product Liability Act*, Sec. 104 (a), 44 Fed. Reg. 62,714
(1979).

have the informational resources that agencies enjoy, nor typically the luxury of time in decision making. Finally, courts are not politically accountable for their decisions. By contrast, administrative agencies face a variety of political checks by the White House, the Congress, and the judiciary.

Development of strict product liability, even more than other tort theories, underscores the regulatory role and broad impact of courts. Imposition of strict product liability forces industries to internalize the cost of injuries to consumers. As the Eighth Circuit Court of Appeals candidly proclaimed, "the risk of personal injury has become a cost of doing business." Judges indeed frequently justify the doctrine of strict product liability, as a panel of the Court of Appeals for the Eighth Circuit in *Helene Curtis Industries v. Pruitt* (1963) concluded, "on the realization that our technological society, with its proliferation of products and mass advertising, demands judicial protection of the consumer who has neither the capacity nor opportunity to discover latent dangers in products."

The impact of the revolution forged in private law litigation is enormous and problematic, as we will see with the avalanche of asbestos litigation, before turning to the limits and contributions of public law litigation and judicial responses to the regulation of risk.

An Asbestos Nightmare

As with most toxic substances, it took a long time for the scientific community to turn its attention to the possible risks of asbestos, and then to study and document the associated diseases. A large part of the problem of determining the health risks of asbestos is the long incubation period, which may run from twenty to forty years. And that entailed a science-policy dispute which made the initial litigation so vexing.

Asbestos is one of the most dangerous of all natural materials. A generic term, "asbestos" refers to silicate mineral fibers that can be separated into silky fibers with great tensile strength and commercial value. Asbestos was not widely produced until the turn of the century. It then quickly became crucial to modern industries due to its excellent fire-retardant and binding qualities. After World War II and until 1969, production rapidly increased due to the federal government's use of asbestos products for fire-proofing and insulation when building the modern navy.

While the benefits of asbestos products grew, the health risks remained largely ignored. Although the first recognized case of asbestosis, involving a textile worker, was reported in 1906, the connection between asbestos and various diseases was not widely accepted or publicized until a 1965 paper published in the *Annals of the New York Academy of Science* by Irving J. Selikoff, head of the Mt. Sinai Hospital Environmental Sciences Laboratory in New York and the leading expert on asbestos-related diseases.[24] A number of diseases have now been shown to result from exposure to asbestos, including asbestosis, the nonmalignant scarring of the lungs; bronchogenic carcinoma, lung cancer; mesothelioma, a malignant tumor of the lungs; and cancer of the gastrointestinal tract.[25]

The potential injuries due to asbestos now appear great indeed. There are an estimated 3,000 different kinds of asbestos products and about 300 manufacturers of these goods in the country. Selikoff estimates that 8,500 people die annually from asbestos-related diseases.[26] And federal cancer researchers predict that as much as 17 percent of all cancer cases expected to occur in the United States during the rest of this century will be asbestos-related.[27] The Department of Labor estimates that 27 million workers have been exposed to asbestos since World War II.[28]

The Asbestos Litigation

Only after the risks of asbestos became widely accepted within the scientific community was it possible for individuals to successfully

[24] Selikoff, Churg, and Hammond, "The Occurrence of Asbestosis Among Industrial Insulation Workers," 132 *Annuals of the New York Academy of Sciences* 139 (1965), at 152.

[25] See Selikoff and Hammond, "Asbestos-Associated Disease in United States Shipyards," 28 *CA-A Cancer Journal for Clinicians* 87 (1978); and Mehaffy, "Asbestos Related Lung Disease," 16 *Forum* 341 (1980).

[26] Quoted in Kelly, "Manville's Bold Maneuver," *Time* 17 (Sept. 16, 1982).

[27] *Asbestos Litigation Reporter* 2 (Feb. 7, 1979).

[28] Report of I. Selikoff, *Disability Compensation for Asbestos-Related Disease in the United States, Report to the U.S. Department of Labor* (Department of Labor, Rpt. No. J-9–M-8-0165), at 99.

pursue asbestos litigation. Most of the initial litigation was brought by government workers, but the number of suits and range of litigants quickly grew. By the 1980s, "household exposure" cases were being filed against construction companies that had used asbestos as insulation in homes. As a result, courts are overwhelmed by asbestos litigation.

The most widely publicized asbestos suit involves the Johns-Manville Corporation, the largest manufacturer, producing approximately 70 percent of the world's asbestos products. By 1980 almost 10,000 persons had filed over 5,000 cases against the company. A year later that number almost doubled, and cases were being filed at a rate of 425 a month. Yet, the company had disposed of less than 3,500 cases ever brought against it, while paying almost $50 million in claims.[29] Whereas in the early 1970s awards were in the $75,000 range, a decade later juries were awarding $1.5 million to individuals who sometimes had not yet suffered any disabling effects but only exhibited the early symptoms of asbestos-related diseases. In response to the mounting liability, the Johns-Manville Corporation filed for bankruptcy in 1982. The company, with about $2 billion in assets, faced potential claims of over $16 billion.[30]

The Johns-Manville litigation came almost two decades after the initial litigation, and long after the risks of asbestos-related diseases were known to scientists and doctors. The first two cases were settled out of court for small amounts. The third case, *Borel v. Fibreboard Paper Products Corporation* (1973), was the one that opened the way for thousands of similar suits and made asbestos litigation the "mother lode" of product-liability cases.

Borel was filed in 1969 by an insulation worker against Fibreboard Paper Products Corporation, a manufacturer of insulation products. Clarence Borel had been an insulation worker for thirty-three years

[29] Affidavit under Local Rule V.XI-2, at 5, Debtor's Petition under Chapter 11, *In re Johns-Manville Corp.*, No. 82 Bankruptcy 11656 (Bankruptcy Ct., S.D. N.Y., filed August 26, 1982). See also "Manville Submits Bankruptcy Filing to Halt Lawsuits," *New York Times* A1, Col. 6 (August 27, 1982); and *In re* Asbestos Related Cases, 23 *Bankruptcy Law Reporter* (CCH) 523, 825 (N.D. Cal., 1982).

[30] For a further discussion, see Anderson, Warshauer, and Coffin, "The Asbestos Health Hazards Compensation Act: A Legislative Solution to a Litigation Crisis," 10 *Journal of Legislation* 25 (1983).

and had contracted asbestosis and mesothelioma. He claimed the company failed to warn of the dangers of handling asbestos, and a federal district court judge in the Eastern District of Texas, Joe J. Fisher, agreed.

At his trial, Borel admitted that he knew for years that inhaling asbestos dust "was bad for me," but he never realized that it could cause serious or terminal illness. Borel said that he and his fellow workers thought that the dust "dissolves as it hits your lungs." During cross-examination at the trial, he explained:

> Yes, I knew the dust was bad but we used to talk [about] it among the insulators, [about] how bad was this dust, could it give you TB, could it give you this, and everyone was saying no, that dust don't hurt you, it dissolves as it hits your lungs. That was the question you get all the time.
>
> *Question:*   Where would you have this discussion, in your Union Hall?
>
> *Answer:*   On the jobs, just among the men.
>
> *Question:*   In other words, there was some question in your mind as to whether this was dangerous and whether it was bad for your health?
>
> *Answer:*   There was always a question, you just never knew how dangerous it was. I never did know really. If I had known I would have gotten out of it.
>
> *Question:*   All right, then you did know it had some degree of danger but you didn't know how dangerous it was?
>
> *Answer:*   I knew I was working with insulation.
>
> *Question:*   Did you know that it contained asbestos?
>
> *Answer:*   Yes, sir, but I didn't know what asbestos was.[31]

Despite knowledge of the potential risks of handling asbestos products, the lower court found that Borel could not have reasonably and fully assessed the dangers of asbestos. In Judge Fisher's view, the manufacturer had a duty to do so and to warn of the dangers.

When appealing the ruling, attorneys for the manufacturer continued to contend that workers knew the health risks of working with

---

[31] *Borel v. Fibreboard Paper Products Corporation*, 493 F.2d 1076, 1081 (1973).

asbestos. Workers, they argued, assumed a risk in their occupations and were therefore contributorily negligent in not taking precautions when handling asbestos materials. But, the court of appeals upheld the lower court's ruling. Writing for the appellate court, Judge John Minor Wisdom reasoned that the risks were not sufficiently obvious to workers and that manufacturers are subject to strict liability for all asbestos-related diseases.

Borel spawned a tidal wave of litigation that increasingly gathered force. There was virtually no escape, other than bankruptcy, for asbestos manufacturers like Johns-Manville from paying compensation for all asbestos-related diseases.

The Policy Debate

Borel illustrates the potentially enormous impact of private law litigation on the marketplace. Judicial involvement in the science-policy dispute over the risks of asbestos and responsibilities for asbestos-related diseases remains problematic for those at both ends of the political spectrum. For conservatives, *Borel* exemplifies how judicial intervention can be unfair, unreasonable, and misguided in stifling economic competition. For liberals, *Borel* and other toxic tort litigation has limited utility in compensating victims and forcing the market to assess and manage future risks. Both perspectives illuminate why political compromise is so difficult and why the formulation and implementation of alternative governmental policies are often impossible to achieve. At the same time, we see why litigation and judicial intervention are often the only alternative to self-regulation by industries.

To conservatives, *Borel*, as University of Chicago Law School professor Richard Epstein argues, is unfair because the court retroactively imposed liability on the market. The court, he says, "imposes on the firm the impossible task of complying with a liability rule of which it could not have had any knowledge. The standard practices of yesterday have become the source of liability today." As Epstein quips, "Rules, like horses, should not be changed in midstream."[32] From the

[32] R. Epstein, "Manville: The Bankruptcy of Product," *Regulation* 14 (Sept./Oct., 1982).

1940s into the 1960s, manufacturers like Johns-Manville were not subject to tort liability. Any legal responsibility for personal injuries of their employees was covered under worker's compensation laws. Quite simply, it is unfair for unelected and unaccountable federal judges to change the rules of the game twenty years later.

Courts not only changed the rules of liability without prior notice, claims Epstein, they did so in an unreasonable way. In the 1940s and 1950s the scientific community maintained that there were exposure levels at which asbestos presented no health risks. Even in the 1970s leading experts, like Selikoff and others, could not agree about the relative risks of asbestos-related diseases from different kinds of exposure—exposure by textile workers, insulation workers, or homeowners. But when imposing strict liability on all asbestos manufacturers, courts held that companies have a duty to assess all the possible dangers and to warn workers and consumers. By judicial decree, the law of liability was transformed, and imposed on the market was an altogether new duty to test for all possible risks of asbestos.

As a matter of public policy, Epstein argues, rulings like *Borel* are fundamentally misguided. Although an advocate of deregulation, he somewhat ironically insists that rulings following *Borel* are misguided. They place the duty to undertake technological and industrial risk assessments on manufacturers rather than on the companies that use asbestsos products and expose workers to asbestos-related diseases. "Surely it is better," Epstein says, "to have the work done by independent parties whose findings and motives are more difficult to call into question than those of an interested party."[33] Worker's compensation laws, perhaps combined with some regulation of asbestos exposure levels, he concludes, could (and should continue to) manage risks and compensate workers.

There are, of course, those who disagree with Epstein. To the contrary, they maintain, *Borel* and similar rulings respond to the inadequacies and distributive injustice of worker's compensation laws. Studies of asbestos claims under state and federal worker's compensation programs show that most programs are inefficient and inadequate. Over a year typically passes before disabled workers begin to receive compensation for occupational diseases. By comparison, only

[33] Id. at 43.

about two months lapse before they receive compensation for injuries due to accidents in the workplace.[34] The Department of Labor's 1980 *Interim Report to Congress on Occupational Diseases* concludes that nearly 90 percent of occupational dust-disease awards were initially contested, as compared with only 10 percent of all accident awards.[35] Other studies show that worker's compensation systems on the average provide only about one-eighth of the expected lost wages. In addition, workers are usually barred from bringing claims because of the twenty- to forty-year latency period of these diseases. Worker's compensation plans also typically do not cover those who contract mesothelioma from asbestos exposure in their homes. In short, worker's compensation laws favor industries and the only recourse for those injured is private law litigation.[36]

Even those who support such judicial rulings acknowledge that private law litigation is slow, inefficient, and expensive. It also can maldistribute compensation. They therefore propose legislation that would abolish the tort system in this area and establish a fund to compensate all asbestos victims. In 1981, Colorado's Senator Gary Hart proposed such a bill to create a fund contributed to by asbestos manufacturers and the federal government. Asbestos victims would have their claims reviewed by commissions, instead of the courts, with compensation paid from the fund. Like other similar proposals, the bill never passed. Agreement on legislation was frustrated by differences over the sources and adequacy of funding, the amount of com-

---

[34] See Statement of Nik B. Edes, Deputy Under Secretary for Legislation, Department of Labor, in *Asbestos Health Hazards Compensation Act of 1980: Hearings on S. 2847 Before the Senate Committee on Labor and Human Resources*, 96th Cong., 2d Sess. (Washington, D.C.: GPO, 1980), at 90. See also P. Barth and H. Hunt, *Workers' Compensation and Work-Related Illnesses and Diseases* (Cambridge, Mass.: Massachusetts Institute of Technology, 1980); and Chamber of Commerce of the United States, *Analysis of Worker's Compensation Laws*, 1984 Edition (Washington, D.C.: U.S. Chamber of Commerce).

[35] Department of Labor, *Interim Report to Congress on Occupational Diseases* (Washington, D.C.: GPO, 1980).

[36] For further discussion, see J. Kakalik, P. Ebener, W. Felstiner, G. Haggstrom, and M. Shanley, *Variation in Asbestos Litigation Compensation and Expenses* (Santa Monica, Cal.: Rand, 1984); and Darling-Hammond and T. Kniesner, *The Law and Economics of Workers' Compensation* (Santa Monica, Cal.: Rand, 1980).

pensation possible (about $30,000 per injury, well below even early awards in asbestos cases), and the basis for claims for compensation—particularly troublesome was whether and on what basis homeowners could recover for diseases due to household exposure.

The litigation over asbestos-related diseases illustrates that judicial regulation is an imperfect policy response to the risks born of an industrial economy. In the next section we will further examine the impact, as well as the limits and contributions, of such judicial regulation.

The Impact of Private Law Litigation

Private law litigation brings science-policy disputes into the courts, and they in turn may extend common law doctrines and make substantial awards to those injured or at risk. Media coverage of large awards like that made in the Karen Ann Silkwood case highlights the role of courts. But the actual impact of tort liability is much less than that portrayed by the media and critics of the system.

Less than Meets the Eye—The Silkwood Case

The case of Karen Ann Silkwood got a great deal of public attention. A worker and union organizer at a Kerr-McGee nuclear power plant, Karen Silkwood became contaminated from plutonium and sued Kerr-McGee. She subsequently died in an unrelated automobile accident. Her father, Bill Silkwood, continued the fight against Kerr-McGee for damages for his daughter's contamination and the mental distress it caused her.

At trial, it was revealed that Kerr-McGee had not complied with regulations set down by the Nuclear Regulatory Commission (NRC) for monitoring levels of radioactive exposure. And the company's contention that Silkwood had stolen plutonium in order to embarrass it was expressly rejected. But, while there was evidence that the levels of plutonium in her apartment exceeded safe levels, it was not conclusively shown that Silkwood had been contaminated while working at the plant. The trial judge accordingly instructed the jury that an award could not be made under the Oklahoma Worker's Compensation Act, covering employment-related accidents. Instead, he instructed the jury that awards could be made under the common law of negligence and strict liability. The jury awarded Silkwood's estate $505,000 in actual damages ($500,000 for personal injuries and $5,000 for property damages) and another $10,000,000 punitive damages for Silkwood's exposure to escaped plutonium.[37]

The Court of Appeals for the Tenth Circuit later overturned the award. It did so on the grounds that any personal injuries should have been handled under Oklahoma's worker compensation law and that federal law permitted compensation only for "extraordinary nuclear occurrences." Only the judgment of $5,000 in actual property damages was upheld.

Silkwood's father subsequently appealed the decision of the Court of Appeals to the Supreme Court of the United States. In 1984 a bare majority reversed the lower court's denial of recovery for injuries beyond the $5,000 for personal property damages, and held that punitive damages were not precluded by federal law. In an opinion delivered by Justice Byron R. White, the majority sought to distinguish another ruling just a year earlier. In *Gas & Electric Co. v. State Energy Conservation and Development Commission* (1983), the Court had held that state law relating to the safety of radiological effects in the construction and operation of nuclear power plants was preempted by the Price-Anderson Atomic Energy Act. That law regulates nuclear power and permits the NRC to impose penalties for violations of federal standards. In the Court's words in *Gas & Electric Co.*, "Congress has occupied entirely the field of nuclear safety concerns." But, the majority in *Silkwood* ruled that the federal preemption did not apply here. State liability law would not seriously thwart the federal government's interests in promoting nuclear power and ensuring the safe operation of nuclear power plants. Justice White admitted that the ruling created a "tension between the conclusion that safety regulation is the exclusive concern of federal law and the conclusion that a State may nevertheless award damages based on its own law of liability."

For three dissenters (Justice Thurgood Marshall also dissented,

---

[37] *Silkwood v. Kerr-McGee Corp.*, 485 F. Supp. 566, 670 (W.D. Okla. 1979), *rev'd on appeal*, 667 F.2d 908 (10th Cir. 1981).

but on different grounds), the majority's decision was inconsistent with prior rulings and a tortured reading of congressional legislation. More than that troubled Chief Justice Burger and Justices Powell and Blackmun, however. What disturbed them was that the majority had unleashed state courts to regulate nuclear power. All three were appointed by President Richard Nixon for their advocacy of states' rights and judicial self-restraint. Here, they strongly objected to the Court's sanctioning of the regulatory use of state courts and private law litigation. As Powell put it, "The Court's decision, in effect, authorizes juries and judges in each of the states to make regulatory judgements as to whether a federally licensed nuclear facility is being operated safely."

Unrestrained judicial regulation of risks is unusual, however, just as large awards for injuries are atypical. Media coverage of cases like the Silkwood trial reveal neither the actual trends in private law adjudication nor the impact of courts in regulating the risks of our industrial society. In general, private law litigation accomplishes a lot less than suggested by media coverage of large awards in cases like *Silkwood*. Recovery for toxic torts is exceedingly difficult and compensation is usually modest. The actual impact of courts is limited, far less than suggested by their critics and well-publicized cases.

The Limited Utility of Private Law Litigation

Despite the potentially enormous economic impact of tort liability and the estimated $10 billion annual social costs of product-related injuries, fewer than 1 percent of those injured sue to recover damages.[38] No less significant, in the late 1970s and early 1980s more than one-third of all state legislatures reversed court rulings that had made it easier for individuals to gain access to courts and to prove their claims of health and environmental damages.[39] At trial, industries still win an estimated three-quarters of the cases that go to juries and the

---

[38] J. Lieberman, *The Litigious Society* (New York: Basic Books, 1981) at 49. See also J. O'Connell, *The Lawsuit Lottery* (New York: Free Press, 1979).

[39] See "The Devils in the Product Liability Laws," *Business Week*, 72 (Feb. 12, 1979).

average award is less than $4,000.[40] Selective, unsystematic imposition of tort liability appears "to maldistribute benefits by overcompensating the slightly injured person and undercompensating the seriously injured."[41] Studies of disputes over toxic and hazardous substances likewise indicate an immense disparity between the costs of injuries and the number of lawsuits filed and the amount eventually recovered.[42]

Judicial regulation tends to be disjointed, uneven, and unfair. This is inevitable given our dual system of state and federal courts, differences among the fifty state jurisdictions, and the incremental case-by-case nature of judicial policymaking. In general, private law litigation remains an inauspicious vehicle for broad public policy formulation. This is so for a number of reasons.

The utility of private law litigation for managing risks depends on how well the adversary system works in assessing the risks. Many legal scholars and social scientists argue that the system is neither appropriate for nor amenable to resolution of the scientific uncertainties underlying health and environmental litigation. There are numerous practical and procedural problems with the adversary process as a mechanism for resolving complex science-policy disputes.

Practical problems stem from the state of scientific knowledge and the art of medical diagnosis, which does not always permit conclusions about the causal link between a plaintiff's injuries and the defendant's activities. The cost of bioassays and the rigor of scientific proof often prevent generation of information adequate to support legal recoveries within the time frame of particular trials. Diseases often have multiple causes and long latencies. It therefore becomes virtually impossible to identify the exact chemical agent causing a disease or the particular pollutant responsible.[43]

[40] U.S. Cong., 97th Cong., 2d Sess., House of Representatives, Committee on Small Business, *Product Liability Insurance, H.R. No. 97* (Washington, D.C.: GPO, 1978), at 6.

[41] *California Citizens' Commission on Tort Reform* (1977), quoted in Lieberman, supra note 38, at 48.

[42] See *Six Case Studies*, supra note 3.

[43] See National Academy of Sciences, *Principles for Evaluating Chemicals in the Environment* (Washington, D.C.: National Academy of Sciences, 1975);

The problems of fact-finding and discovery are numerous. Most environmental lawsuits are far more complex than a single individual alleging that an industrial plant discharged a pollutant which caused a particular disease. Typically, many people in a community have been exposed. The disease has a latency period of twenty to thirty years. And there are numerous intervening environmental variables. While an increase in the incidence of a disease may be revealed statistically, for example, there may exist no direct evidence of the disease in humans even though there is strong or overwhelming evidence in laboratory animals. Except for some forms of cancer, when testing principles and data have been agreed upon by federal regulatory agencies, courts have been reluctant to accept carcinogenic risk assessments based on extrapolations from animal data. The problems of proving causation are even greater in environmental litigation when there are several sources of pollution. Each pollutant individually may cause the disease, but there remains the possibility that only one does, even though uncertainty persists as to which pollutant. Alternatively, one pollutant may not cause a disease itself, yet in combination with others precipitate the disease. Finally, there is frequently the problem of individuals who live part of their lives by one industrial polluter, which by itself does not pose a health hazard, then move to an area polluted by a different source, and the combined exposure leads to the disease.[44] In sum, scientific uncertainty over the risk of toxins and carcinogens is impossible to resolve within private law adjudication. At best, tort litigation presupposes a substantial body of agreement within the scientific community on the causal consequences of exposure to an alleged carcinogen.

There are many procedural barriers as well. Rules of evidence limit the introduction of some forms of scientific data and testimony. Statistical and medical evidence and testimony, for example, are

---

Office of Technology Assessment, *Assessment of Technologies for Determining Cancer Risks from the Environment* (Washington, D.C.: GPO, 1981), at 31–65, 113–175.

[44] See G. Robinson, "Multiple Causation in Tort Law: Reflections on the DES Cases," 68 *Virginia Law Review* 713 (1982); and Harley, "Proof of Causation in Environmental Litigation," in *Toxic Torts*, ed. by P. Rheingold, N. Landau, and M. Canvan (Washington, D.C.: Association of Trial Lawyers, 1977), at 403.

sometimes precluded from introduction at trial or treated as "hearsay" evidence.[45] Statutes of limitations also frequently foreclose even the possibility of claiming injuries involving diseases with long latency periods, such as cancer.[46] The threshold question thus is when the period of limitation begins—when an individual is initially exposed to an alleged carcinogen or when a disease actually becomes manifest?

In one case, *Karjala v. Johns-Manville Products Corporation* (1975) involving an asbestos worker, the Court of Appeals for the Eighth Circuit acknowledged that "there is rarely a major moment when one exposed to asbestos can be said to contract asbestosis; the exposure is more in the nature of a continuing tort." The court, furthermore, held that the statute of limitations begins to run when "the disease manifests itself in a way which supplies some evidence of causal relationship to the manufactured product."

In an earlier case involving federal law, *Urie v. Thompson* (1948), the Supreme Court ruled that it would be unreasonable to preclude individuals from suing simply because they did not or could not know of their disease. Urie was a fireman who had contracted silicosis, a disease similar to asbestosis. In order to receive compensation for his disease under the Federal Employer's Liability Act, Urie had to overcome the argument that the act's three-year statute of limitations barred recovery. In this case, and where diseases have long periods of latency, the Court held that the statute of limitations did not apply. But state statutes of limitations still generally start to run before individuals discover their diseases, and therefore make winning compensation extremely difficult.

A related problem arises, as with the Silkwood case, over whether tort actions are precluded by state worker compensation laws. Generally, workers lose their right to sue employers in exchange for a specified income (typically, two-thirds of their salary) in the event of work-related injuries, medical payments, and other services. Employ-

---

[45] See *Hazelwood School Dist. v. United States*, 433 U.S. 277 (1977) (statistics in use of employment discrimination litigation); and, generally, Phelen, "Proof of Cancer from a Legal Viewpoint," in S. Birnbaum, *Toxic Substances: Problems in Litigation* (New York: Practising Law Institute, 1981), at 155.

[46] See *Urie v. Thompson*, 337 U.S. 163 (1948) (statute of limitations does not commence until accumulated effects manifest themselves—silicosis case); but, see *Karjala v. Johns-Manville Pro. Corp.*, 523 F.d 155 (8th Cir. 1975).

ers are able to spread the risk of potentially large awards that might be given by trial judges and juries. In theory, the premium rates of a system of compensation also give employers an incentive to internalize the costs of occupational accidents and diseases.

Under worker's compensation plans, recovery for diseases due to exposure to exotic substances is often extremely difficult, much more difficult than recovery for work-related accidents. Most worker's compensation laws are causal dependent. A worker must first establish a relationship between an injury or disease and the workplace. But workers usually have a greater difficulty proving that their diseases are occupationally related than they have showing that injuries are due to accidents in the workplace under either tort law or worker's compensation schemes. This is due to several factors. First, workers face the same difficulties of showing a causal connection between diseases and the workplace that they would under tort law. Second, the fact-finding or discovery process is less elaborate under worker compensation systems than in the trial context. Finally, chronic diseases, like asbestosis, have generally not been covered by worker's compensation plans. In 1978, for instance, there were approximately 7.8 million worker's compensation awards. Yet, less than 2 percent of those were for work-related diseases.[47]

Because of the problems of establishing a link between a disease and exposure to some exotic substance, employers tend to deny or contest a higher rate of worker's compensation claims for contracting diseases than they do for work-related accidents. In a 1980 survey of worker's compensation claims, the Department of Labor found that 60 percent of all disease cases for which compensation was granted were initially contested by employers. By contrast, only 10 percent of all accident claims were similarly contested by employers. Where employers contested claims, the dispute was over a question of causality in 73 percent of the disease cases but only 21 percent of the accident cases.[48]

Common law defenses further compound the problems of litigating disputes involving scientific uncertainty. Employers generally have immunity from negligence suits by employees who were exposed

[47] Department of Labor, supra note 35, at 66.
[48] Id. at 69–70.

to chemical hazards. They also usually enjoy immunity from liability for injuries resulting from risks that were unknown or are not yet supported by scientific data.[49] Frequently, employers contend that workers assume a risk in their employment (which salaries in theory, but in practice may or may not, reflect) and should not receive compensation for occupational diseases under tort law. In *Thomas v. Kaiser Agricultural Chemicals* (1980), for instance, the Illinois state court found that a farmer's practical experience and knowledge in dealing with dangerous substances created an "assumption of risk" that undercut any compensation for injuries received when exposed to a liquid nitrogen fertilizer while filling a spray gun.

In general, private law litigation appears ill-suited for resolving massive tort claims—such as those over air and water pollution—because the pollution effects are weakly associated with existing individuals and the damages are thinly spread among those individuals. "From the standpoint of society as a whole," Julian Juergensmeyer observes, "the most that can be expected from air pollution control through assertion of private rights is the handling of some instances of air pollution which cannot be or are not yet controlled by public regulation."[50]

Private law litigation involving science-policy disputes is not only costly but also cumbersome and time-consuming. Adjudication discourages certain lawsuits and promotes out-of-court settlements. Litigation, as the Environmental Law Institute concluded in a 1980 study of compensation for toxic substance pollution, becomes practically unfeasible and economically unreasonable for those suffering, in need of reparation, and facing legal uncertainties and procedural barriers that make success unlikely.[51]

Private law adjudication also maldistributes compensation. Only a small percentage of those injured actually carry through with a

[49] See, e.g., *Restatement (Second) of Torts*, Sec. 406 A; *Dalke v. UpJohn Co.*, 555 F.2d 245, 248 (9th Cir. 1977) (limited liability); *Thomas v. Kaiser Agri. Chem.*, 74 Ill. Ap. 3d 522, 393 N.E. 2d 1141 (Ill. App.Ct. 1979), *aff'd.* 81 Ill. 2d 206, 407 N.E. 2d 32 (1980) (assumption of risk).

[50] J. Juergensmeyer, "Control of Air Pollution Through the Assertion of Private Rights," 1967 *Duke Law Journal* 1126, 1155 (1967).

[51] See *Six Case Studies*, supra note 3.

lawsuit and even fewer win recovery for damages. Inequities in compensation also arise from the fact that private adjudication, considered as a political process, fragments decision making and the management of risks. Within the fifty states, and between state and federal jurisdictions, private law litigation inevitably produces fragmented, piecemeal, and often redundant and conflicting decisions. Any actual deterrent effect on other industries generally depends on injured plaintiffs with adequate finances and interest pursuing litigation that may or may not prove successful. From a broad political perspective, tort litigation is haphazard and distributively uneven in operation.

The tort-liability system not only may prove unfair and unreasonable for victims, but it may also result in the imposition on producers of a legal responsibility for risk management that is unfair and unreasonable. Requiring industries to assume all the costs of risk—in effect, imposing a judicial policy of no risk of risk—may be unfair and unreasonable. Recent developments in the area of strict product liability, as we saw earlier, are moving in this direction.

Private law litigation can prompt other governmental responses, but by itself it cannot efficiently handle situations of widespread toxic exposure. In instances of massive tort exposure, like that involving the disposal of hazardous waste or coal miners suffering from black lung disease, an administrative-regulatory response is more efficient and effective. In both of these latter instances, Congress has responded. The enactment, in the last weeks of the Carter administration, of the Comprehensive Environmental Response, Compensation, and Liability (Superfund) Act of 1980 was designed to cover the cost of cleaning up toxic waste dump sites, and to compensate those injured by exposure to toxic wastes. Congress had previously passed the Black Lung Benefits Reform Act to administer compensation for miners suffering from black lung disease.[52]

---

[52] Comprehensive Environmental Response, Compensation, and Liability (Superfund) Act of 1980, 42 U.S.C. Secs. 9601–56 (Supp. 1984); and Black Lung Benefit Act, 33 U.S.C. Sec. 901. For further discussion, see chapter 4; and J. Trauberman, "Compensating Victims of Toxic Substances Pollution: An Analysis of Existing Federal Statutes," 5 *Harvard Environmental Law Review* 1 (1981); and S. Soble, "A Proposal for the Administrative Compensation of Victims of Toxic Substances Pollution: A Model Act," 14 *Harvard Journal on Legislation* 683 (1977).

Judicial Regulation in an Imperfect World

Courts are neither structurally nor situationally predisposed to resolve but a modest number of disputes over the impact of past technological developments. Judges lack the resources, opportunity, and training to assess the impact of advancing technologies. For these reasons, we might conclude, as does Harold Green, "that we cannot rely on the courts alone to protect society against fast-moving technological developments."[53]

But that should not unduly minimize the utility of private law litigation in managing some of the risks of toxic torts. Historically, our democratic society has relied on private law litigation to compensate victims and prevent accidents. Courts have responded and regulated the market forces of our industrial economy. Moreover, as Harvard law professor David Rosenberg points out, courts and private law litigation hold certain advantages over other forms of government regulation of the marketplace.[54] Courts—given the tradition of judicial independence and the decentralized structure of our state and federal judiciaries—are not as likely as administrative agencies to be "captured" by the special interests that they are supposed to regulate. And agencies cannot screen and regulate all of the thousands of suspected toxins, let alone manage all of the risks of our industrial society.

Courts can and do respond when injuries occur. Private law litigation is also more discriminating than regulatory standards and other forms of governmental risk management. Finally, in some ways it is a more democratic response to managing risk than administrative regulation. It allows individuals who have the most at stake to become involved and to help forge regulatory policy. In the words of Milton Katz, a member of the National Academy of Science Panel on Technology Assessment, private law litigation constitutes "a channel

---

[53] H. Green, *The New Technological Era: A View from the Law* (1967); and H. Green, "The Role of Law and Lawyers in Technology Assessment," 13 *Atomic Energy Law Journal* 246 (1971).

[54] D. Rosenberg, "The Causal Connection in Mass Exposure Cases: A 'Public Law' Vision of the Tort System," 97 *Harvard Law Review* 851 (1984).

through which the diverse interests, outlooks and moods of the general public can be given expression."[55]

At best, private law litigation is one means of forging change in public policy governing the risks of a competitive economy and industrial society. In an ideal world, the judicial imposition of tort liability might be offset by a system of administrative regulation. The inequities and administrative problems of handling mass tort actions might be addressed by legislation, as with the Black Lung Benefits and Superfund Acts, just as developments in product liability might be made more moderate and uniform. The advantages of the traditional regulatory role of courts thus might be preserved in a way that complements the role and resources of administrative agencies. But we live in an imperfect world. And in the next chapter, we will further examine the problems confronting judges and the adversary system in resolving science-policy disputes, and then turn to the judicial/administrative partnership in regulatory politics of managing health-safety and environmental risks.

[55] M. Katz, "Decision-Making in the Production of Power," 223 *Scientific American* 191 (1971), at 198.

Beleaguered and Embattled Judges?

Litigation has historically brought science-policy disputes to the courts and, as we saw in the last chapter, will continue to do so. Because judicial resolution of these disputes is often less than perfect and the impact of judicial rulings may be exceedingly broad, controversy over whether courts have gone too far or not far enough will undoubtedly continue as well. But that is not all there is to the controversy over courts and science-policy disputes.

Many lawyers, judges, and social scientists argue that judges are less competent to settle complex science-policy disputes than other subjects under dispute. They also frequently maintain that the adjudicatory process itself is ill-suited for resolving science-policy disputes. Sociologists Sheila Jasanoff and Dorothy Nelkin, for example, observe that the "surge of science-related disputes into the judicial arena has produced a set of difficult and highly visible problems for the courts, and it is widely believed that the traditional processes of adjudication are no longer capable of handling many of these disputes."[1]

[1] S. Jasanoff and D. Nelkin, "Science, Technology, and the Limits of Judicial Competence," 22 *Jurimetrics Journal* 266 (1982), at 267. The article also appears in 68 *ABA Journal* 1094 (1982), and in 214 *Science* 1211 (1981).

Are judges competent to decide science-policy disputes and is the adjudicatory process amenable to resolving them? Both of these claims are examined here. At the outset, it is important to emphasize that whatever the limitations of judicial competence and the adjudicatory process, they differ at the trial and the appellate court levels. The adjudication of science-policy disputes by trial judges is examined in this chapter. In Chapters 4 and 5, we will turn to the use of adjudicatory-type proceedings by administrative agencies and to appellate courts' review of the scientific basis for federal regulations.

In contrast to the view of many social critics, I maintain that it is not the complexity or even the uncertainties surrounding the scientific basis for such disputes that are uniquely troubling for judges. Nor is the lack of special training or professional competence in disciplines of the natural sciences the main problem. Judges decide equally complex issues involving other social policies, though they are no better trained in the social sciences, economics, or moral philosophy. What is unique about science-policy disputes is that they often involve polycentric or "many-centered" issues that make negotiation and compromise exceedingly difficult if not impossible. Indeed, it is because negotiations and political compromise fail that science-policy disputes are channeled into litigation and judges are forced to decide them.

A case study of one of the first major environmental disputes, over the dumping of taconite into Lake Superior by the Reserve Mining Company, illustrates the polycentricity of many science-policy disputes. From it we see how the overlay of scientific, economic, and social conflicts contributes to the failure of political compromise and negotiated settlements, and leads to protracted litigation. Judges, like Miles Lord in the Reserve Mining controversy, face not only lengthy litigation but also political pressures, which test their independence and impartiality. Despite the limitations of the adjudicatory process and the challenges to judicial competence, judges cannot and do not resolve the underlying scientific disagreements. What they do is resolve social conflicts and impose social norms. When doing so, they are generally no more or no less competent than when confronted with other kinds of demands for conflict resolution.

The Trials of Trial Courts

Litigation involving complex science-policy disputes frequently gives rise to the claim that courts are incompetent and ill-equipped to decide them.[2] In Columbia Law School Professor Maurice Rosenberg's words, "Courts clearly lack an institutional capacity to obtain information they need if they are to dispose wisely of complex controversies involving ramified, technical information."[3] Before embracing that conclusion, however, we need to understand whether and in what ways those disputes differ from other kinds of litigation.

The number and nature of science-policy disputes confronting courts, critics charge, push the adjudicatory process to its limits and strain judicial competence to the breaking point. The frequency of complex science-policy disputes due to changes in tort liability and federal regulation has increased, and may tax judges by increasing caseload pressures. Former federal appellate court Judge David Bazelon offers this perspective:

> When I came on the bench thirty-one years ago, a judge reviewing rate regulation, or labor law, or securities law could be expected to have some understanding of such subjects. These fields lay within the general experiences of most lawyers. Today, a court reviewing regulatory action in arcane areas of science and technology can have little real knowledge of the substantive questions.[4]

Because these suits tend to be time-consuming, federal judges have requested the Federal Judicial Center (the research and training branch of the federal judiciary) to study how to expedite the handling

---

[2] See, e.g., R. Cooper, "Scientists and Lawyers in the Legal Process," *Food/ Drug/Cosmetic Law Journal* 9 (January 1981); M. Baram, "Social Control of Science and Technology," 172 *Science* 535 (May 7, 1971); and M. Wessel, "Science, Technology and Law in America: A Plea for Credibility in Dispute Resolution," 22 *Jurimetrics Journal* 245 (1982).

[3] M. Rosenberg, "Let's Everybody Litigate," 50 *Texas Law Review* 1349 (1972), at 1354.

[4] D. Bazelon, "Science and Uncertainty: A Jurist's View," 5 *Harvard Environmental Law Review* 209 (1981), at 211–212.

of such litigation.[5] Still, these problems are not unique or primarily due to the pressures of science-policy disputes. Moreover, they may be at least partially addressed by improved court-management techniques, court-annexed arbitration, and, in some instances, special masters to assist in fact-finding. Nor does the complexity of science-policy disputes make them more difficult than other kinds of complex litigation. Disputes involving carcinogenic risk assessments differ only in degree, not in kind, from complicated tax and antitrust litigation entailing no less complex and controversial socioeconomic analysis.[6]

Whether judges are less competent—in terms of their professional training and background—to decide disputes raising issues on the frontiers of science is another matter. Bazelon and others often contend that judges face particular problems because they have "no knowledge and training to assess the merits of competing scientific arguments."[7] Judges are generalists by training and by tradition. Yet, they have no more training in the social sciences than they do in biology or chemistry, even though socioeconomic theories and data now play a greater role in a larger area of law. In America, unlike countries on the European continent, a liberal education and legal experience have always been more highly prized than technical and scientific expertise. There also historically has been overwhelming opposition to creating specialized courts in the United States.

Whatever particular difficulties science-policy disputes pose for judges, they arise not primarily from judges' professional training and competence. Instead, they stem from the ways in which judges respond to the adjudication of these disputes. The problem is one of judicial behavior, as one judge observed:

> In environmental litigation we are constantly placed in a position of choosing between the lies told by the fisherman's expert and the lies told by utility companies' experts. The overwhelming temptation for an

[5] See *The Third Branch* 1 (November, 1985).

[6] See, e.g., *Berkey Photo, Inc. v. Eastman Kodak Co.*, 603 F.2d 263 (2d Cir. 1979), *cert. denied*, 44 U.S. 1093 (1980).

[7] D. Bazelon, "Coping with Technology Through the Legal Process," 62 *Cornell Law Review* 817 (1977), at 822.

appellate court is to accept the original fact finder's conclusion as to which expert was telling the smallest lie.[8]

In other words, the problems are rooted in judges' responses to the limitations of the adjudicatory process for resolving science-policy disputes.

The adversary system has long been criticized. Judges and social critics point to the excesses of the system: its abusive treatment of witnesses, procedural delays, exclusion of pertinent information, and high financial costs. Judge Jerome Frank eloquently argued almost forty years ago that the system is defective because it is based not on a "theory of truth" but on a " 'fight' theory, a theory which derives from the origin of trials as substitutes for private out-of-court battles." In his now classic condemnation of the process, he observes,

> Many lawyers maintain that the "fight" theory and the "truth" theory coincide. They think that the best way for a court to discover the facts in a suit is to have each side strive as hard as it can, in a keenly partisan spirit, to bring to the court's attention the evidence favorable to that side. Macaulay said that we obtain the fairest decision "when two men argue, as unfairly as possible, on opposite sides," for then "it is certain that no important consideration will altogether escape notice."[9]

The spectacle of partisan justice is uniquely replayed in each trial, and inexorably influences judges' decisions and behavior. They, as Frank put it so well, "vary in their respective qualities of intelligence, perceptiveness, attentiveness—and other mental and emotional characteristics operative while they are listening to, and observing witnesses."[10] No less than other political actors, judges are vulnerable to community pressures, particularly when trials are the focus of intense clashes of competing interests.

[8] Judge Gibbons, quoted in M. Rosenberg, "Contemporary Litigation in the United States," in *Legal Institutions Today*, ed. H. Jones (Chicago: American Bar Association, 1977), at 157.

[9] J. Frank, *Courts on Trial* (Princeton, N.J.: Princeton University Press, 1949), at 80.

[10] Id. at 153.

What remains crucial, then, is how judges respond to the conflict between their prescribed role as impartial umpires and the realities of the adversary system. But, as we will see in the next section, the sources of frustration in the adversary system are not unique to complex litigation over matters on the frontiers of science and technology. The problems of fact-finding and the potential for judges to become embroiled are no less apparent in criminal trials and civil litigation involving, for example, school desegregation, busing, and reapportionment.

Adjudicating Science-Policy Disputes

A central criticism of courts confronting science-policy disputes is that judges, according to Jasanoff and Nelkin, face extraordinary factual uncertainties and tend to be overwhelmed by "the scale and complexity of the issues involved." "Disagreements," they add, "exist about the magnitude of risk, the appropriateness of measuring techniques, and the reliability of data."[11]

But this criticism is misguided in two important ways. For one thing, as we saw in the last chapter and as Judge J. Skelly Wright reminds us, assessing risk "is a normal part of judicial and administrative fact-finding."[12] Regardless of court critics, judges will continue to play a role in resolving science-policy disputes due to the way in which social forces are channeled by the cultures of science, law, and democratic politics in the United States.

For another and more crucial reason, the criticism appears ill-founded. Quite simply this is because those that demand certainty in the resolution of science-policy disputes will inevitably find the adjudicatory process unsatisfactory. This is a failing not of the judicial process but of the critics' understanding of that process.

The adjudicatory process cannot resolve scientific controversies or generate a consensus on risk assessments any more than can the political process. The adjudicatory process actually aims at highlight-

---

[11] Jasonoff and Nelkin, supra note 1, at 268.

[12] *Ethyl Corporation v. Environmental Protection Agency*, 541 F.2d 1, 28 n.5 (1976).

ing contested facts and interpretations; the uncertainties and contestability of evidence become inflated. This is because the adjudicatory process does not fundamentally aim at certainty in the first place. Instead, procedural fairness is pursued in the resolution of normative conflict and imposition of social norms.

There is an inescapable divergence in what is understood as "proven" or "certain" in legal and in scientific processes. "Certainty" bears only a family resemblance in the language games of law and science. A former general counsel of the Food and Drug Administration, Richard Cooper, makes the same point this way, "the law takes as 'true' for its purposes (and embodies in formal findings of fact) hypotheses that scientists do not necessarily accept as true for their (quite different) purposes."[13] When rebuking an attack on the scientific basis for the Environmental Protection Agency's regulation of gasoline additives, in *Ethyl Corporation v. Environmental Protection Agency* (1976), the Court of Appeals for the District of Columbia was even more emphatic:

> Petitioners demand sole reliance on *scientific* facts, on evidence that reputable scientific techniques certify as certain. Typically, a scientist will not so certify evidence unless the probability of error, by standard statistical measurement, is less than 5%. That is, scientific fact is at least 95% certain. Such certainty has never characterized the judicial or administrative process. It may be that the "beyond the reasonable doubt" standard of criminal law demands 95% certainty. . . . Since *Reserve Mining* was adjudicated in court, this standard applied to the court's fact-finding. Inherently, such a standard is flexible; inherently, it allows the fact-finder to assess risks, to measure probabilities, to make substantive judgments. Nonetheless, the ultimate finding will be treated, at law, as fact and will be affirmed if based on substantial evidence, or, if made by a judge, not clearly erroneous.[14]

Scientific uncertainties about evidence and causality thus remain after litigation, even though they are treated as legally settled. This is by no means unique or peculiar to litigation over toxic torts or challenging the basis for health, safety, and environmental regula-

[13] Cooper, supra note 2, at 25.

[14] *Ethyl Corporation v. Environmental Protection Agency*, 541 F.2d 1, 28 n.58 (1976).

tion. Profound disagreements appear no less in litigation involving historical evidence (for instance, disputes over Indian tribal lands) or social science evidence marshalled in voting rights litigation.[15]

Just as the contentiousness underlying science-policy litigation has parallels in other areas of litigation, so too the problems of fact-finding are comparable as well. The problems of dealing with statistical measurements and cross-examination of experts on carcinogenic risks are basically the same as those encountered in personal injury cases arising from automobile accidents or medical malpractice. They are rooted in the different professional standards and objectives of the legal and scientific communities. Consider the following characterization of the rival perspectives of physicians and lawyers in contesting causality in a personal injury case:

> Physicians, in forming their conclusions about the causes of an injury, put great weight on the role played by a preexisting disorder, tending to minimize the role of later events in such cases. Judges and attorneys, in contrast, see "inevitability" as legally unimportant, because legally the event can be the proximate cause of the injury so long as the injurious result occurred even a moment sooner than would have been the case in the absence of the event. Physicians emphasize that the alleged injurious result would not have occurred in the absence of the preexisting disorder; judges and lawyers, in contrast, see it as immaterial that the event in question would not have caused the injurious result had the victim been in good or average health.[16]

The point is not simply that physicians and scientists differ from lawyers in their training and understanding of causality. Rather, there is an irreconcilable difference between scientific and legal facts. That aggravates the problems in resolving disputes over personal injuries due to automobile accidents, no less than those resulting from exposure to toxic substances.

Courts do respond to social forces, and law evolves with new

[15] For further discussion, see W. E. Washburn, "The Supreme Court's Use and Abuse of History," *OAH Newsletter* 7 (August, 1983; Organization of American Historians); and D. M. O'Brien, "The Seduction of the Judiciary: Social Science and the Courts," 64 *Judicature* 8 (1981).

[16] Danner and Sagell, "Medicolegal Causation: A Source of Professional Misunderstanding," 3 *American Journal of Law and Medicine* 303 (1979).

claims of science. Thirty years ago, courts were reluctant to rely on evidence of statistical probabilities. That severely limited recoveries for injuries due to exposures to toxic substances. When rejecting the use of statistical data as a basis for establishing causality, the Washington state supreme court, in *Tonkovich v. Department of Labor and Industries* (1948), proclaimed, "It is a fact universally known that the cause of cancer is unknown."[17] More recently, as we saw in the last chapter, courts have admitted controversial scientific evidence and expanded legal doctrines.

The issue still remains whether science-policy disputes differ in any significant way from other kinds of adjudication. If they do it is because they involve what Michael Polanyi and the late Harvard Law School professor Lon Fuller called "polycentric" disputes. It is not simply the complexity of the factual disagreements, the multiplicity of the affected parties and vested interests involved, or the concern for future conduct as well as past injuries, or even that the verdicts often have broad socioeconomic implications.[18] Instead, it is the interrelation of all these dimensions and how judges respond to them.

The adjudicatory process is ill-suited for handling polycentric disputes, Fuller maintained, because there is no single solution "toward which the affected part[ies] may direct [their] proofs and arguments," or that judges may settle and justify based only on those proofs and arguments. Such disputes ultimately require legislative or contractual solutions, either by managerial direction (as with mandates for administrative regulation) or through a mutual adjustment of the affected interests (as with worker's compensation laws).

Polycentric problems are matters of degree and, Fuller noted, "are probably present [even if implicitly] in almost all problems resolved by adjudication." Science-policy disputes are not uniquely polycentric, nor do all such disputes present problems of polycentricity. Much depends on the novelty of the claims, relevant precedents, and the history and social context of the dispute. "It is not," Fuller

[17] *Tonkovich v. Department of Labor and Industries*, 195 P.2d 368, 642 (Wash. 1948).

[18] See L. Fuller, "The Forms and Limits of Adjudication," 92 *Harvard Law Review* 353 (1978), at 394; and M. Polanyi, *The Logic of Liberty* (1951), at 771.

emphasized, "a question of distinguishing black from white. It is a question of knowing when the polycentric elements have become so significant and predominant that the proper limits of adjudication have been reached."[19]

What is problematic about trying to resolve science-policy disputes through the adjudicatory process is how trial court judges respond to the polycentricity of those disputes. They may innovate procedurally, becoming active participants in the adjudicatory process, rather than detached and impartial third parties. They may be driven to find a solution by consulting parties not involved in a particular trial and, Fuller observed, "guess[ing] at facts not proved and not properly matters for anything like judicial notice." Alternatively, judges "may reformulate the problem so as to make it amenable to solution through adjudicative procedures."[20] Evidentiary rules may be interpreted to exclude contestable data and opinions in order to minimize the polycentric dimensions of the dispute. Both alternatives are unlikely to prove satisfactory. Either way, the dispute is likely to continue after a judicial decree. But there may be no other recourse for judges when, as the following case study shows, political compromise and negotiation fail.

The Reserve Mining Controversy

The Reserve Mining controversy generated one of the first major environmental lawsuits of the 1970s. Its history reveals not only the tensions between developing technology and changing social perceptions of risk but also provides a classic example of the role of courts as independent assessors of risk. Trial court judges find themselves in basically the same position as agency administrators, confronting inconclusive risk assessments, in often prolonged adjudicatory proceedings, on which they must base and rationalize their decisions.

[19] Id. at 398.
[20] Id. at 401.

A Controversy Born of Changing Times

The controversy grew out of the Reserve Mining Company's mining of taconite in the eastern Mesabi Iron Range, in northern Minnesota. Taconite is a rock formation consisting of 20 to 25 percent iron material. Discovered in 1871, such a low-grade iron ore was not then profitable to mine. A refining process was not even available until 1922, and then another twenty years passed before the processing of taconite appeared commercially viable. High-grade iron ore was rapidly being depleted, and taconite was a plentiful alternative.

In the early 1940s, the University of Minnesota Mines Experiment Station began studying how to make the mining of taconite economically feasible. E. W. Davis, an electrical engineer at the station, became the "Father of Taconite." He discovered that taconite could be smelted as small spheres of high-grade concentration, and he designed a process for extracting taconite and producing iron and steel. Rock containing taconite was crushed small enough that iron particles could be picked up with a magnet and separated from the crushed rock by using water as the handling medium. The iron particles would sink to the bottom of large containers, through which passed the crushed rock and water, and then would be plucked up by magnets and subsequently smelted. For Davis's process to be commercially viable, there were two essential requirements: a huge water supply and a way to dispose of the waste product—"tailings," the discarded mixture of crushed rock and water. The amount of water necessary and the corresponding waste were substantial. Production of one ton of taconite concentrate required more than 45 tons of water.[21]

The Reserve Mining Company began developing plans for a taconite plant on the shores of Lake Superior. A lakeside site overcame the major constraints of processing taconite: the lake provided both an unlimited water supply and a convenient disposal site for the tailings. The plant became operational in 1953, and appropriately enough was named the "E. W. Davis Works."

---

[21] E. W. Davis, *Pioneering with Taconite* (St. Paul: Minnesota Historical Society, 1964), at 128.

The environmental effects of mining taconite were uncertain and were given little consideration in the 1940s and 1950s. Davis assured Reserve that "the gray sandy tailings of magnetic taconite would not in any way pollute the lake, interfere with any domestic water supply or with navigation, and would not adversely affect the fishing industry."[22] Laboratory tests supported his conclusion, though there were no tests of the possible effects on people consuming water containing taconite tailings.

As Reserve Mining progressed with its plans for taconite mining, however, some opposition did develop. In 1947, the state's pollution control commission held nine hearings on the plant and the proposed dumping of taconite tailings into Lake Superior. The principal objection came from sportsmen and commercial fishermen, who were concerned about the effects on fish life. In response, state senator Homer Carr proposed that the company dump the tailings onto the ground, and the state reimburse it for the difference in cost from the water disposal system. But the proposal found no support in the state legislature. There was, at the time, insufficient basis for concluding that any environmental risks justified the state's assuming the financial burden of having the tailings dumped on the ground. John Moyle, an aquatic biologist in the Minnesota Department of Conservation, produced test results indicating that "the dumping of tailings into the lake would have no harmful effects upon its fish life."[23] The Minnesota commission ultimately decided to permit Reserve Mining to proceed with its plant.

Reserve Mining's taconite plant was profitable and an economic boon for the area, indeed for the state. Two company towns, Silver Bay and Babbitt, grew to house over 3,500 employees. By the mid-1960s, the plant had expanded and raised production from about 3 million tons to over 10 million tons per year. The company was pumping out of and back into Lake Superior approximately 500 million gallons of water a day; this compared to an estimated 25 million gallons pumped daily for consumption by people in the state.[24]

[22] R. Bartlett, *The Reserve Mining Controversy* (Bloomington: Indiana University Press, 1980), at 21.

[23] Davis, supra note 21, at 132.

[24] Department of the Interior, *An Appraisal of Water Pollution in the Lake Superior Basin* (Washington, D.C.: GPO, 1969), at 17.

Almost a decade after the plant was operational, the political environment gradually but radically changed. During the late 1960s, there was a profound transformation in public attitudes concerning health-safety and environmental quality. That transformation in public values, along with the emergence of environmental sciences, set the stage for confrontations between Reserve Mining and state and federal governments.

The Federal Government Takes the Lead

Environmental concerns had risen to the national political agenda and forced major changes in federal law and policy. Environmental protection was traditionally considered a matter of state jurisdiction; the federal government had almost no role in this area of regulation. But that principle of federalism broke down and changes in federal policy precipitated the controversy over Reserve Mining. In 1965 the Federal Water Pollution Control Act (FWPCA) was amended so as to provide for the development of national water quality standards. President Lyndon B. Johnson subsequently gave environmental pollution high priority, by directing all federal agencies to cooperate with the Department of the Interior in abating and preventing water pollution.[25]

As early as 1963, Wisconsin Senator Gaylord Nelson urged a study of Reserve Mining's dumping of taconite tailings. But, in Minnesota, the state government remained supportive of the company. Its economic contributions to the state made public officials reluctant to study the effects of tailings on Lake Superior. Not until environmental concerns joined with other commercial concerns did the state move (largely at the prodding of the federal government) to take some action.

In the late 1960s Lake Superior's economic value began to appear threatened by Reserve's taconite discharges. It was both the availability of water and its quality that made the lake so valuable. Commercial fishing, recreational activities, and a growing tourist trade were all directly affected by the quality of the lake's water and

[25] Executive Order 11288, 13 *Federal Register* 9261, 33 U.S.C. 466 (July 7, 1966).

Reserve Mining's operations. A number of concerned citizens and environmentalists pressed their opposition to Reserve Mining's operation, lobbying federal and state officials. Verna Mize, a resident of Washington, D.C., who for a number of years had spent her summers vacationing on Lake Superior, led a one-woman campaign against the firm.

State officials generally remained reluctant to intervene until federal officials finally decided to take action. In 1968, at the urging of Mize, Senator Nelson, and others, Stewart Udall, secretary of the Department of the Interior, called a federal conference on water pollution control in Lake Superior. That precipitated state action. In January 1968, the department's coordinator for the Great Lakes region, Charles Stoddard, began work on what was to become the first detailed environmental impact study of the effects of taconite tailings on Lake Superior. He led a Taconite Study Group, composed of representatives from five interior departments. Corporate officials cooperated, thinking that the final report would vindicate the mining operations. But, when the Stoddard Report concluded that Reserve Mining was polluting Lake Superior, it drew a quick denunciation from the company.[26]

The following spring, in May 1969, Secretary Udall convened the Federal Enforcement Conference. The Stoddard Report and other studies were discussed, but no federal action could be taken until there was evidence of interstate pollution. The Department of the Interior's National Water Quality Laboratories began studies to assess interstate impact. They initially concluded that tailings crossed state lines, and thus the federal government had jurisdiction. A year later, the studies reached the more important conclusion that there was "presumptive evidence . . . that the discharges from the Reserve Mining Company endanger the health or welfare of persons."[27]

Reserve Mining Takes the Offensive

Even before the release of the Department of the Interior's report in September 1969, the Sierra Club and the Minnesota Committee for

[26] Department of the Interior, *Summary Report on Environmental Impacts of Taconite Water Disposed in Lake Superior* (Stoddard Report, 1969).

[27] Department of the Interior, *An Appraisal of Water Pollution in the Lake Superior Basin*, revised edition (Washington, D.C.: GPO, 1970), at 49.

Environmental Information sought to compel the state's Pollution Control Agency (PCA) and Department of Conservation to revoke the 1947 permits allowing Reserve's discharges of taconite tailings. The case, *Sierra Club v. Minnesota Pollution Control Agency*, however, was settled out of court when the state agreed to hold hearings on whether Reserve Mining had violated its permits. The hearings were to be held before May 20, 1970, but they never took place due to intervening litigation.

Reserve Mining took the offensive. In December 1969, the company challenged the validity of the state's water pollution control regulations. Under the FWPCA, states were required to establish water quality standards for interstate waters before June 10, 1967. Minnesota complied but the Department of the Interior found its standards failing to meet federal guidelines. The state redrafted its standards, and in November 1969 Interior Secretary Walter Hickel finally approved them. Under the new state and federal standards, the level of pollutants in Reserve's discharges would become illegal. The company therefore sought an exemption from the regulations.

Reserve argued that the state had not followed proper procedures in developing its new standards and that those standards were unreasonable. Moreover, company attorneys contended that the regulations were inapplicable since the state had earlier approved its disposal system. The company also claimed that enforcement of the new standards would cause undue economic hardship. In their trial brief, attorneys for Reserve Mining underscored the economic importance of its operations for the state:

> As of June 30, 1970, Reserve had 3,367 employees. During the calendar year 1969 its total payroll was approximately $31,700,000; it expended the sum of $27,400,000 for the purchase of supplies and paid state and local taxes amounting to $4,259,000. . . . [Moreover,] between four and six people are supported by each job in the mining industry. . . . Thus, workers including those at Reserve whose jobs are directly dependent upon Reserve's continued operation are estimated to number between 16,835 and 23,569.[28]

At trial, Charles Fride for the firm also attacked the methodology of the state's studies. Experts testified that the taconite tailings did not

[28] Brief for Reserve Mining, at 9.

increase the turbidity of the lake's waters, or harm water supplies or fish life. An entire month of the trial was devoted to the defense of the company's operations.

The state PCA counterclaimed that the company violated water pollution control regulations and contributed to a public nuisance under state common law. The PCA sought a court-ordered time schedule under which Reserve Mining would have to comply with pollution standards. Over thirty witnesses and 300 exhibits were produced. Charles Goldman, a University of California professor of biology, for instance, testified that taconite acted like a mild fertilizer for phytoplankton, promoting the growth of algae in the lake. An accounting professor at the University of Minnesota, R. Glen Berryman, disputed company claims that pollution control standards were financially unreasonable. He testified that the company could spend as much as $74 million in capital investment on an alternative disposal site.

The State Court's Indecision and Court-Ordered Negotiations

The state district court judge, C. Luther Eckman, in *Reserve Mining Co. v. Minnesota Pollution Control Agency* (1970), was overwhelmed by the conflicting evidence and the wide-ranging ramifications of whatever he decided. In the end, he ruled that the state's pollution control standards did not violate the company's rights under state law or the due process clause of the Fourteenth Amendment. However, Eckman also concluded that the standards were not applicable against Reserve Mining. In his view, they applied only prospectively. As to the PCA's counterclaim that Reserve was polluting Lake Superior, Eckman held that the PCA failed to meet the burden of proof of pollution. But he added that there was sufficient concern to require Reserve Mining to modify its method of discharging taconite tailings. Accordingly, Eckman ordered Reserve and the PCA to negotiate a solution, allowing the company until May 15, 1971, to submit alternative discharge plans to the PCA for approval.

Eckman avoided any conclusion about whether Reserve's dumping of taconite tailings was polluting Lake Superior. Indeed, in a memorandum accompanying his decision, he justified his failure to do so on the complexities and conflicting expert testimony on the effects of Reserve's operations. His explanation merits the following quotation:

> Probably no other trial in the history of this state has produced a more impressive array of scientists and experts expounding on their particular fields of expertise. . . . In view of this profound assistance, it would appear that the court should have had little difficulty in arriving at a logical and determinative solution. Unfortunately, however, this was not so. Contradictions in findings and opinions in varying degrees became the rule. Appellant reminded the court by inference that Respondent's witnesses were brought into the case as "Johnny-come-latelys" to render opinions based on other scientists' disqualified tests and conclusions and were propounded by pressure exerted by government superiors. Respondent inferred that Appellant's experts testified and reached conclusions expected of them as paid employees of Reserve. . . . And so the Court, completely lacking in personal expertise, found itself in the impossible position of being required to analyze, weigh, and choose between these controversial points of view.[29]

More than conflicting scientific testimony made the case vexing for Eckman. The dispute, in his view, was "in fact a socio-legal problem" that emerged as much from the scientific and technological advances as from fundamental changes in social values. Again, in the judge's words:

> It seems highly unlikely that a similar application by Reserve today for the permit issued in 1947 would be granted. The public, in only a few short years, has been alerted and alarmed over the disastrous effects upon our environment from what appears to have been a careless and callous disregard in the past of our ecological future.

Like some other state and federal trial judges confronting science-policy disputes, Eckman felt overwhelmed by the polycentricity of the controversy and the fundamental value conflicts brought by changing social forces.

Judge Eckman's ruling reflects the general tendency of state trial courts to try to accommodate local economic interests, when those interests are threatened by adverse assessments of environmental

[29] *Reserve Mining Company v. Minnesota PCA*, 2 E.L.R. 1140, 1142, 1144 (1970).

risks. Unlike appellate courts, trial courts tend to be more responsive to local community interests. They tend to place greater weight on economic and social costs in striking a balance with environmental values. They are less likely to give priority to ecological concerns when, as here, the risks are uncertain and unclear. Risk, in other words, tends to be defined in terms of the probability of imminent hazards rather than in terms of the severity of the possible consequences. No less important, Eckman tried to get the controversy out of the courts and to encourage the company and state agencies to negotiate a compromise.

The Failure of Negotiation and the Move into Federal Courts

The controversy continued to grow. By mid-1971, the Environmental Protection Agency (EPA) was under pressure to halt disposal of taconite tailings. At the time, the company's production had increased to the point that it was dumping approximately 67,000 tons of taconite tailings daily into Lake Superior. Environmental groups, senators, representatives, and governors lobbied for federal intervention. But, there was resistance from the White House. The Democrats lost the 1968 presidential election and the idea of suing a major corporation did not sit well with the Republican administration of Richard Nixon. Reserve Mining mounted its own lobbying campaign and found support among White House aides. Unlike the Johnson administration, the view of those in the Nixon administration was that industry should not be "the whipping boy of environmentalists."[30]

Environmental coalitions nevertheless had influence in Congress at the time, and the White House was forced to respond to that pressure. In his 1972 State of the Union address, Nixon called attention to the need to respond to our "threatened environment." The head of the EPA, William Ruckelshaus, subsequently received approval from Attorney General John Mitchell to challenge Reserve Mining's disposal operations in federal court. Ruckelshaus had asked the company to negotiate an acceptable abatement plan, but it balked, as it had done before with state agencies. So, on February 17, 1972, the government filed suit in federal district court against Reserve

[30] For further discussion, see Bartlett, supra note 22, at 109–110.

Mining for violating a number of federal and state water pollution laws.

When hearing the case, *United States v. Reserve Mining Company* (1974), Judge Miles Lord allowed various special interests to intervene and join the two parties in the dispute. Lord recognized the wide-ranging and conflicting interests involved, but he also set the stage for prolonged and complicated trial proceedings. The federal government was joined by Wisconsin, Michigan, and several environmental groups. Reserve Mining was joined by eleven other organizations, including the local governments for the mining towns of Babbitt, Silver Bay, and Beaver Bay.

Attorneys for the federal government wanted an injunction to stop Reserve's disposal operations. They argued that Reserve violated the 1899 Rivers and Harbors Act prohibition of discarding refuse matter in navigable waters of the United States. And they claimed that the firm's discharges were subject to abatement proceedings under the FWPCA and Minnesota's water pollution regulations. In addition, the government insisted that the tailings constituted interstate pollution. In an amended brief, the government further asserted that Reserve Mining's operations were a public nuisance under federal common law.

Attorneys for Reserve Mining made two counterclaims. Since the company had valid permits from Minnesota, it reasoned that any new restrictions constituted a taking of property without just compensation in violation of both the United States and the Minnesota constitutions. For the same reason, company lawyers contended that any new restrictions also impaired its contractual rights.

As the lengthy pretrial hearings got underway in the fall of 1972, the Minnesota State Supreme Court handed down a decision on an appeal of Judge Eckman's ruling. In *Reserve Mining Company v. Minnesota PCA* (1972), it upheld the judge's finding that the WPC regulation was valid. However, the court went on to rule that Eckman exceeded his jurisdiction in directing Reserve and the PCA to negotiate a settlement. This ruling permitted Reserve Mining to continue its operations and to resist efforts to get it to control its water pollution. The state PCA, though, also became free to begin new hearings, simultaneous with the federal trial, aimed at revoking the company's 1947 operating permits.

As the conflict shifted to Judge Lord's courtroom, two other major developments intensified the controversy.

First, the PCA began enforcement proceedings against Reserve Mining for air quality violations as well as water pollution. The controversy for the first time appeared to involve more than just an ecological dispute over the pollution of Lake Superior.

Then, in June 1973, the EPA and Minnesota's PCA announced that new studies indicated that the company's discharges were similar to asbestos, a known carcinogen. The release of these studies completed the transformation of the controversy from that revolving around the ecological risks to Lake Superior to one over public health and safety. Though the studies were preliminary, they effectively broadened the scientific uncertainties and intensified the political conflict. For, while taconite bears a resemblance to asbestos, and asbestos fibers pose a health risk when inhaled, taconite fibers were being ingested through drinking water. There were no available studies establishing the carcinogenic effects of ingesting, versus inhaling, taconite fibers.

The Uncertainties and Complexity of the Trial

After more than a year of pretrial hearings, on August 1, 1973, the trial finally began. It lasted 139 days, with testimony from over 100 witnesses and scientific experts, and more than 1,600 exhibits entered into evidence. The trial transcript eventually exceeded 18,000 pages.

The first issue considered was that of the public health risks of exposure to taconite fibers. Even though the controversy years earlier had centered on environmental risks, no evidence or testimony on ecological issues was ever formally introduced at the trial. Instead, the first five months were devoted to public health issues. Thereafter, both sides contested the need for and the economic feasibility of alternative methods of disposing of taconite tailings.

Scientific uncertainties and differing normative views dominated the trial. The pivotal issue was whether taconite discharges pose a "substantial endangerment" to public health. That issue actually turned on several interrelated questions. First, there was the question of whether the taconite fibers in Reserve's discharges of tailings and air emissions were sufficiently similar to asbestos fibers to justify conclusions about their possible effects on human health. Government scientists at the National Water Quality Laboratory and other medical experts testified that the fibers in taconite tailings had the same structure and composition as asbestos. They also reported that a small number of fibers found in Duluth's water supply were identical to asbestos fibers.[31] Reserve Mining's attorneys, however, had several other university scientists contradict that evidence. They argued that the mineral formation of taconite was different from that of asbestos, and that there were no asbestos fibers in the ore mined by the company.[32]

Estimates of the health risks of taconite fibers were further complicated by the absence of hard evidence on whether the fibers were pathological for humans. Most studies of asbestos-related diseases were conducted among workers in asbestos mills and mines. There, the levels of exposure are much higher than those facing the residents of the communities surrounding Reserve. A few studies indicated that low levels of exposure to asbestos fibers might result in mesothelioma, but the levels of exposure had not been quantified and the concentration of particles in the air around Reserve's processing plant could not be precisely measured. Lord found it impossible to draw any firm conclusions from these studies.[33]

The view that all asbestos-like fibers pose the same health risks was also vigorously attacked. Although taconite and asbestos fibers have a similar structure, the former are less than five microns in length, considerably shorter than asbestos fibers. Attorneys for the mining company advanced the theory offered by some scientists that short fibers are less carcinogenic than long fibers. Moreover, they pointed out that the federal standard for asbestos-like fibers covered only those longer than five microns. According to counsel for Reserve Mining, this represented a legal determination that occupational exposure to fibers less than five microns was not medically or legally significant.

[31] Trial Transcript, at 500–501, 2828, 2959, 3793–3808; and Plaintiff's Proposed Statement of Facts, at 23–24 (February 28, 1974).

[32] See Defendant's Proposed Statement of Facts (Second Set), at 31–34 (April 18, 1974).

[33] *Reserve Mining Company v. Environmental Protection Agency*, 514 F.2d 492, 510–512 (8th Cir. 1975) (en banc).

They also produced studies showing that exposure to short fibers was not linked to cancer, though none of these had examined the effects of low levels of human exposure solely to short fibers.

Witnesses appearing for the government conceded that studies of the effects of short, versus long, fibers were inconclusive. Yet, they maintained that no fiber length could be regarded as risk-free. The government's leading expert on asbestos-related diseases was none other than Irving Selikoff. He disputed the view that small fibers were not medically significant. The government's standards for occupational exposure to fibers longer than five microns, he testified, had been adopted for practical, not health, reasons. Most agencies could reliably detect with optical microscopes only fibers longer than five microns. It was for that reason that asbestos standards were set at five microns. In his opinion, short fibers, such as those at issue here, had the same or even greater pathological potential as long fibers.

The problems of assessing the risks were compounded by still other scientific uncertainties. Whether Reserve's discharges were actually polluting the water was hotly contested. Witnesses for the EPA maintained that taconite tailings could be traced because they consisted in large part of cummingtonite-grunerite, a mineral that would otherwise not be found in significant amounts in Lake Superior. Attorneys for Reserve Mining, however, introduced geologists and geophysicists who testified that the mineral was igneous and could be found in the lake's basin, before the beginning of the company's discharges.

No less disagreement raged over studies of air samples. The government sought to show that the company was emitting large quantities of amphibole fibers into the air. Attorneys for Reserve Mining rejected its studies as "worst case" samples, taken too close to the plant's stacks. They produced others showing that fiber levels in the air were substantially lower than indicated by the government's witnesses. Independent studies commissioned by Lord supported the firm's claims.

Even more vexing were two other sources of scientific and legal contention. First, there was the issue of whether there was a threshold level for exposure to taconite fibers at which there was no health hazard. Second, there was the related controversy over what kinds of inferences could be drawn from studies of the pathological effects of inhaling asbestos fibers to the ingestion of the smaller taconite fibers in drinking water.

Even if the company was emitting asbestos-like fibers, attorneys for Reserve Mining argued that the levels of emission were too low to pose a significant risk. Not surprisingly, the government's witnesses disputed this interpretation of available data. Selikoff testified that present studies of asbestos were insufficient to establish a level at which asbestos fibers would not cause cancer. In other words, scientists for the government and environmental groups maintained that there is no safe threshold of exposure: any level of emission places people at risk.

The related controversy over the methods of exposure involved even greater scientific uncertainty. Virtually all prior studies of asbestos-related diseases involved the inhalation, rather than ingestion, of asbestos fibers. The government's star witness, Selikoff, again testified that in his opinion there was a high probability that ingestion of asbestos-like fibers increased health risks. But, there were no epidemiological studies of populations exposed only to ingested fibers. Attorneys for Reserve Mining accordingly demanded concrete evidence linking ingestion of asbestos-like fibers to any form of cancer.

The government's case thus turned almost entirely on a series of inferences from studies of asbestos-related diseases linked to exposure to similar, though nonetheless different, kinds of fibers and with very different methods and levels of exposure. In addition, government and court-commissioned studies of cancer incidence proved inconclusive. There was simply no hard evidence linking exposure to the fibers in taconite tailings to cancer or other diseases.

Most revealing was the testimony of Arnold Brown, a court-appointed expert who reviewed the scientific evidence and reported it to Lord. Brown concluded there was no credible evidence associating the taconite tailings in Lake Superior to human diseases, nor was there clear evidence of increased cancer rates among residents of the north shore communities. Moreover, there was inadequate scientific information on which to assess the risks of ingesting short asbestos-like fibers. However, Brown also drew a distinction between his view of the uncertainties and limitations of available data as a court-appointed expert and as a practicing physician. He thereby suggested to Lord the appropriateness of different scientific and legal-policy judgments about available evidence:

> As a physician, I take the view that I cannot consider, with equanimity, the fact that a known human carcinogen is in the environment. If I knew more about that human carcinogen, if I knew what a safe level was in the water, then I could draw some firm conclusions and advise you in precise terms. That information is not available to me and I submit, sir, it's not available to anyone else. But the presence of a known human carcinogen, sir, is in my view cause for concern, and if there are means for removing the human carcinogen from the environment, that should be done.[34]

Lord ultimately drew a similar distinction when handing down his ruling. But as the trial lumbered to a close on the morning of April 20, 1974, the chairman of Reserve Mining, C. William Verity, took the witness stand one last time to present a plan for an alternative on-land disposal site. Over the preceding two years, attorneys for Reserve Mining and various state and federal government officials had tried but failed to reach a settlement. Verity's plan was a final attempt at compromise, but it did not concede enough. Instead, the company demanded assurances that it would receive operating permits for the life of the mine, that state and federal governments would assist it in obtaining low-interest financing for building an on-land disposal site, and that the court would rule favorably on the health issues.

Lord's Ruling and Higher Appeals

The company's proposed settlement was not given serious consideration by Judge Lord. In the afternoon of April 20, he ordered Reserve Mining to cease all discharges by one minute after midnight. Since it would be some weeks before he could complete his final written opinion, Lord explained his basic findings in a brief memorandum. Basically, Lord concluded that the fibers posed a health risk when ingested as well as inhaled, and that the risk was significant. Reserve

[34] Quoted in *United States v. Reserve Mining Company*, 380 F.Supp. 11 (D. Minn. 1974).

Mining was found in violation of the FWPCA; its discharges to create a common law nuisance; and its air emissions in violation of Minnesota's air pollution regulations.

Announcement of the ruling brought widespread media coverage and an immediate response from Reserve Mining. National and local newspapers devoted considerable attention to the social and economic impact of the ruling. Lord had ordered the closure of a major company that produced almost 15 percent of the ore used by the country's iron and steel industries, and forced the layoff of over 3,500 employees.

Company attorneys immediately appealed the ruling and asked for a stay of the injunction pending the appeal. When Lord denied the motion, attorneys applied for a stay from the Court of Appeals for the Eighth Circuit. After an emergency session, a three-judge panel granted a temporary stay, pending a hearing by the entire appellate court.

The Court of Appeals subsequently granted a seventy-day stay on the injunction, subject to the submission of an acceptable on-land abatement plan. The plan was to be submitted to Lord for approval, but the appellate court would continue to monitor the process and progress.

When granting the stay, the Eighth Circuit did not reach a conclusion about the health risks of Reserve's operations, though it noted that the "evidence does not support a finding of substantial danger and that, indeed, the testimony indicates that such a finding should not be made." The appellate court's response to the scientific uncertainties underlying the dispute was basically the opposite of that of Lord.

Lord had discarded the traditional legal standard for granting injunctions, based on a showing of "imminent injury," in favor of a "risk-benefit" standard of proof. But, as the appellate court observed in remanding the case,

In order to draw the conclusion that environmental exposure to Reserve's discharges presents a health threat . . . , it must be shown either that the circumstances of exposure are at least comparable to those in occupational settings, or, alternatively, that the occupational studies established certain principles of asbestos-disease pathology which may be applied to predicting the occurrences of such a disease in altered circumstances.[35]

Here, there was no hard evidence of imminent injury. Predictions of health risks, based on available data on asbestos-related diseases, were inappropriate because there were no data on the actual level of exposure to taconite fibers. And it was unknown even whether there was a safe level of exposure.

Lord had made a legal-policy judgment based on the possibility of health risk. In the appellate court's view that was neither appropriate nor justified based on available scientific evidence:

> We do not think that a bare risk of the unknown can amount to proof in this case. Plaintiffs have failed to prove that a demonstrable health hazard exists. This failure, we hasten to add, is not reflective of any weakness which it is within their power to cure, but rather, given the current state of medical and scientific knowledge, plaintiffs' case is based only on medical hypothesis and is simply beyond proof. We believe that Judge Lord carried his analysis one step beyond the evidence. Since testimony clearly established that an assessment of the risk was made impossible by the absence of medical knowledge, Judge Lord apparently took the position that all uncertainties should be resolved in favor of health safety. . . . If we are correct in our conclusion that evidence does not exist in the record on which to find Reserve's discharges to be unsafe the district court's determination to resolve all doubts in favor of health safety represents a legislative policy judgment, not a judicial one.[36]

After the appellate court's decision, the EPA asked the Department of Justice to appeal the seventy-day stay, but it declined to do so. Attorneys for Minnesota appealed to the Supreme Court of the United States, which denied its petition. Reserve Mining continued to develop an on-land disposal site, even though Minnesota's Depart-

---

[35] *Reserve Mining Company v. Environmental Protection Agency,* 514 F.2d 492, at 510–512 (8th Cir. 1975).

[36] *Reserve Mining Company v. Environmental Protection Agency,* 514 F.2d 492, 519 (8th Cir. 1975), quoting *Industrial Union Department, AFL-CIO v. Hodgson,* 499 F.2d 467, 474 (D.C. Cir. 1974).

ment of Natural Resources opposed the plan. On June 29, the company presented its plans to Lord, who held several days of hearings on the proposal. In August, he rejected the plans as technologically unsound and he recommended that the appellate court not extend the stay. The appellate court, in turn, directed Lord to dispose of all remaining unresolved issues so that it could review the entire record on appeal.

In September 1974, Minnesota again appealed to the Supreme Court of the United States to vacate the appellate court's stay of the order closing Reserve's plant. This time the federal government joined the petition, in *United States v. Reserve Mining Company* (1974), but it was again denied. However, four Justices—the number that it takes to grant a case review—indicated that they would reconsider an appeal if the appellate court did not render a final judgment by January 31, 1975. The Eighth Circuit thus came under pressure from the Supreme Court, as well as from state and federal governments and the media, to issue a ruling.

One Justice, William O. Douglas, a westerner and an environmentalist, saw no reason for further delays. He fully embraced Lord's ruling and rejected the appellate court's analysis. Douglas made clear his view of how judges should rule when uncertain scientific evidence presents a fundamental value choice:

> If, as the Court of Appeals indicates, there is doubt, it should be resolved in favor of humanity, lest in the end our judicial system be part and parcel of a regime that makes people, the sovereign power in this Nation, the victims of the great God Progress which is behind the stay permitting this vast pollution of Lake Superior and its environs.[37]

When the Eighth Circuit Court of Appeals still had not handed down its final opinion by early 1975, the federal government again asked the Supreme Court to grant review. Before the court could act, however, the appellate court handed down its ruling—a ruling that basically reversed its earlier decision. The appellate court also vindicated Lord's "risk-benefit" approach to resolving the conflict.

---

[37] *Reserve Mining Company v. United States*, 419 U.S. 287 (1974).

The Appellate Court: Vindicating Lord and the Judicial Process

Judge Myron Bright delivered the unanimous opinion in *Reserve Mining Company v. Environmental Protection Agency* (1975). After reviewing the factual disputes and scientific uncertainties, he observed that "the evidence demonstrates that the medical and scientific conclusions here at dispute clearly lie 'on the frontiers of scientific knowledge'." When confronted with disputes where there is no proof of actual harm, Bright noted, judges are "faced with a consideration of 1) the probabilities of any health harm and 2) the consequences, if any, should the harm actually occur." When appellate courts review trial judges' assessments of health risks, Bright reasoned, they have essentially the same role as when reviewing agency regulations based on the same kind of evidence of health-safety and environmental risks. The standard that other appellate courts had evolved when reviewing the decisions of trial courts or administrative agencies is whether the scientific evidence (inconclusive as it may be) supports a conclusion that there is an "endangerment" to public health that justifies preventive regulation. Here, Bright observed:

> In assessing probabilities in this case, it cannot be said that the probability of harm is more likely than not. Moreover, the level of probability does not readily convert into a prediction of consequences. On this record it cannot be forecast that the rates of cancer will increase from drinking Lake Superior water or breathing Silver Bay air. The best that can be said is that the existence of this asbestos contaminant in air and water gives rise to a reasonable medical concern for the public health. The public's exposure to asbestos fibers in air and water creates some health risk. Such a contaminant should be removed.[38]

Even though the government's claims about the hazards of Reserve Mining's operations were not based on proven scientific evidence but rather on a particular set of theories and opinions about carcinogenesis, Bright maintained that the consequences that could result if those theories and opinions were true would be especially severe. The possible risks were so great as to justify abatement "as a precautionary and preventive measure to protect the public health."

The appellate court now accepted Lord's "risk-benefit" analysis,

[38] Id. at 520.

which a year earlier it had rejected as a "legislative policy judgment." The court still disagreed with his immediate closing of Reserve's plant. It held that judicial remedies should be fashioned upon a risk-benefit analysis but be no more severe than the actual hazards. When overturning Lord's injunction, Bright explained that "an immediate injunction cannot be justified in striking a balance between unpredictable health effects and the clearly predictable social and economic consequences that would follow the plant closing."

> We believe that on this record the district court abused its discretion by immediately closing this major industrial plant. In this case, the risk of harm to the public is potential, not imminent or certain, and Reserve says it earnestly seeks a practical way to abate the pollution. A remedy should be fashioned which will serve the ultimate public weal by insuring clean air, clean water, and continued jobs in an industry vital to the nation's welfare.[39]

Reserve Mining, Bright concluded, should be given a reasonable period to end its discharges into the lake and to find an acceptable on-land disposal site. If the company and Minnesota could not agree on a site, then it would have to phase out its plant within a year. Since the air emissions were seen as more serious than the water discharges, the court also ordered the company to immediately control emissions in compliance with the state air pollution regulations. The case was remanded to Lord for further proceedings in light of the ruling of the appellate court.

Returning the Case to Lord: The Judge Embattled

The controversy appeared to have finally come to an end, except for reaching agreement on an on-land disposal site. But it did not end for Lord. He became ever more impatient with the delays of the adversary process and the politics of the controversy.

Although Lord's later actions would result in the Eighth Circuit Court of Appeals removing him from the case, he was on his way to being recused on March 15, 1975, one day after the appellate court rendered its decision. Lord called together all the parties as well as

[39] Id. at 536–537.

local government officials and members of the media. At the hearing, he issued various orders; gave directions to the company's officers; and offered his own suggestions to members of the city council, the governor of the state, congressmen, and even the state legislature. The proceeding was indeed "irregular," as the court of appeals later observed, and it set the stage for Lord's assumption of the role of a judicial power broker and policymaker.

The scientific uncertainties underlying the controversy only partially contributed to Lord's actions. A vigorous fifty-two-year-old, outspoken self-described populist, appointed by President Johnson in 1966, Lord became embroiled due to the delays and abuse of the adversary system by attorneys for Reserve Mining. In his view, the adjudicatory process had worked against a final solution. It had allowed the company to delay proceedings and misrepresent evidence. The company, for instance, had originally attempted to defend its taconite dumpings as having a purifying effect on the lake. It later withheld information about alternative dumping sites and continually tried to sway public opinion by emphasizing the economic impact of its operations. The adjudicatory process appeared to be a very imperfect method not only for fact-finding but also for resolving the basic value conflicts here.

Weary of diversionary legal tactics, Lord explained at the hearing on November 14, 1975:

> I had nine months of hearings and two and a half years of discovery before that, Reserve Mining Company was involved in two or three years of proceedings before the Lake Superior conference, they were involved in a proceeding before a [state] judge up at Silver Bay who said they had to come out of the lake. In every instance and under every circumstance Reserve Mining Company hid the evidence, misrepresented, delayed and frustrated the ultimate conclusions which had to be arrived at. . . . I have dispensed with the usual adversary proceeding here, because I simply do not have time to spend, as I did, nine months in hearing, six months of which was wasted by what I find now, and did find in my opinions, to be misrepresentations by Reserve Mining Company. Six out of nine months.[40]

---

[40] Trial Transcript, at 4 and 26 (November 14, 1975).

"It may appear that in reviewing this evidence the Court is going beyond the traditional role of a court, and this is the exact truth," he proclaimed the next day to a crowded courtroom filled with company officials, members of the city council, and officers of various state and local government agencies that he had ordered to attend. Abuse of the system, however, was not all that ired Lord. He attacked Reserve Mining for coopting city officials and placing economic interests above those of health and the environment. The reluctance of local officials to intervene, even after the appellate court's ruling, because of fear of economic loss, angered Lord. In his words, "So far in the political, social and economic climate of Duluth, the result of the pressure on the Duluth officials has been such that the people of Duluth have been invited to drink poisoned water. That will no longer go on." Accordingly, Lord ordered Reserve Mining to pay $100,000 to the City of Duluth for the cost of a water filtration system. He underscored his frustration by adding, "And there will be no stay on that. That is a firm and final order. That may be appealed, but I do not certify it for appeal because I am not at all in doubt about its propriety."[41]

The Case Against Lord and the Weary Resolution of the Dispute

Lord's order and his handling of the proceedings were promptly appealed. Attorneys for the company argued that Lord was biased and should be recused from the case. In *Reserve Mining Company v. Lord* (1976), the Eighth Circuit Court of Appeals agreed. Lord had "shed the robe of the judge and assumed the mantle of the advocate. The court thus becomes lawyer, witness, and judge in the same proceeding, and abandons the greatest virtue of a fair conscientious judge—impartiality."[42]

Lord was removed from the litigation, but the controversy continued. Chief Judge Edward Devitt for the federal district court assumed responsibility for the case. In February 1976, he reached essentially the same conclusions as had Lord. Reserve Mining was liable for the costs of furnishing drinking water for the north shore com-

[41] Id. at 137.
[42] *Reserve Mining Company v. Lord*, 529 F.2d 181, 186 (1976).

munities. Later that spring, in May 1976, Devitt ruled that the company was in violation of its discharge permits and fined the company $837,500 and levied a $200,000 fine for the company's conduct during the trial. On a motion by attorneys for the federal government, Devitt ordered Reserve Mining to immediately stop its discharges into Lake Superior. But, he subsequently stayed his order on the condition that it begin construction of an on-land disposal site with the goal of ceasing discharges by the spring of 1980. Litigation in state and federal courts, and negotiations between the company and state and federal agencies, continued for the next two years. Finally, in July 1978, Reserve Mining announced that it would stop discharges into Lake Superior by April 15, 1980.[43]

Judging Judges

Although one of the first major environmental controversies, the Reserve Mining dispute remains instructive about trial courts' involvement in science-policy disputes.

When trial courts confront novel issues of scientific complexity and uncertainty that involve large value conflicts as well, they tend to adopt one of two responses. Like Judge Eckman, some feel overwhelmed. They try to avoid a judicial resolution by finding an insufficient basis for resolving the underlying social conflict. They may try to force the conflicting interests to negotiate a compromise. However, negotiations often fail, and political compromises are impossible to achieve. In such circumstances, the continuing social conflict will be channeled back into the courts through litigation. The persistence of social conflict and unresolvable scientific controversies may then force judges like Miles Lord to innovate procedurally, to move in a managerial direction, and ultimately to make the hard policy choices that structure, if not resolve, the continuing controversy.

Judges and the adjudicatory process, of course, cannot resolve the underlying scientific controversies. Like administrative agencies,

---

[43] See *Reserve Mining Company v. Robert L. Herbst,* 256 N.W. 2d 808 (1977); and *Reserve Mining Company v. Minnesota PCA,* 267 N.W. 2d 720 (1978) (involving on-land disposal site and state permits).

trial courts must make fundamental value choices based on inconclusive scientific evidence and opinion. When making those judgments, they likewise face political pressure and may be more or less responsive to community interests.

The political pressures may be especially great on trial court judges, more so than on those on appellate courts. In general, those on trial courts, like Judge Eckman, tend to give more weight to local economic and political interests when confronted with uncertain risks.

Lord, a federal district court judge, felt the political pressures too. But he responded differently, out of frustration with the failure of state and local officials to take control of the dispute. At one point, he likened himself to "Moses in the wilderness" and expressed his frustration both at the pressures brought to bear on him and at the failure of governmental agencies to resolve the conflict:

> Now it's very difficult to be a lone and lonesome federal judge at a time like this, because it affects the lives of many people. Many people who are working versus many people who may be dying. . . . I have had less than what I conceive to be an adequate response by the local officials who seem in large part to be dependent in one way or another on Reserve Mining Company. And these pollution problems are not things that can be handled locally, they are of national scope. I personally question the wisdom, and I make this observation to you, of even having a Minnesota judge sit on this [case], and particularly question the wisdom of having a local judge . . . sit on such a case, because the pressures are just too much.[44]

Appellate courts, like the Court of Appeals for the Eighth Circuit that recused Lord, are more removed from local political pressures. Even so, the decentralized structure of the federal judiciary encourages them to apply federal law in ways that accommodate regional and local interests. Federal courts of appeals fashion a law of the circuit and thereby mediate conflicts between national and regional values. The Eighth Circuit Court of Appeals delayed in response to regional interests. It finally went along with Lord's risk-benefit analysis due to similar rulings by other courts of appeals and to the pressure from the Supreme Court.

[44] Trial Transcript (November 15, 1975) at 21–22.

When there is a high degree of uncertainty over questions of causality and wide differences over the nature of the risks, costs, and benefits of regulatory changes, negotiated settlements are often elusive. In the Reserve Mining controversy, the local political process could not resolve the basic conflicts. Lord took unusual actions because of the failure of negotiations. Still, an equally important lesson of the Reserve Mining controversy is that there are opportunities for parties to negotiate and compromise. And judicial decrees usually come after the failure of public administrators and representatives of industry to resolve their differences.

Whether judges are coopted by political pressures or become embattled depends on their own values and role perceptions. Lord's involvement was unusual and extraordinary. He was a crusading judge, who thought that his "job as a judge [was] to see that justice is done."[45] A decade later, his self-righteousness again brought him charges of judicial misconduct. This time, he denounced the corporate executives of A. H. Robins Company when holding the company liable for manufacturing and marketing the defective Dalkon Shield intrauterine device (IUD). The Dalkon Shield was found to cause infections, sterility, miscarriages, and other health problems.

Although Lord's actions were extraordinary, his approach to the underlying social conflict exemplifies the general trend and value orientation of the federal judiciary, at least in the late 1960s and 1970s. (As the composition of the federal bench gradually changes, with President Ronald Reagan expected to appoint more than half of all federal judges before he leaves the Oval Office, the direction of judicial rulings in determining the costs and benefits of regulating risks may well change yet again.)

Lord's risk-benefit approach to the possible health and environmental hazards, moreover, was ultimately upheld. After the Reserve Mining controversy, the kind of risk-benefit approach pioneered by Lord became widely accepted in federal courts. Courts are no longer willing to confine their analysis to imminent or actual hazards. Instead, they look to the severity and probability of hazards and to the

---

[45] Quoted by B. Siegel, "Judge Seeking Product Accountability Faces Misconduct Charges," *The Washington Post* A2 (July 7, 1984).

benefits of preventive regulation. And courts no longer demand the impossible—complete scientific certainty.

In *United States v. Vertac Chemical Corporation* (1980), decided by the federal district court for the Eastern District of Arkansas, similar problems of scientific proof were in dispute over another toxic substance, dioxin. Here, the government sought injunctive relief under the Resource Conservation and Recovery Act and the Federal Water Pollution Control Act. The Vertac Chemical Corporation was discharging toxic chemicals, including dioxin, into the air, water, and soil surrounding its chemical manufacturing plant. Unlike Reserve Mining, Vertac had cooperated with federal and state agencies to control discharges. Yet, at the time the suit was filed, dioxin persisted in the soil surrounding the plant, in a cooling pond, and in the Jacksonville sewage treatment plant.

The question for the court was whether the presence of such quantities of dioxin constituted an "imminent and substantial endangerment" to human health. As in *Reserve Mining*, the twin elements of endangerment—the severity of possible harm and the probability of its occurrence—were difficult to quantify. The dioxin concentrations present at Vertac's plant were far below the threshold for acute or single-dose toxic effects of dioxin. Still, the government maintained that the long-term effects could be severe. Studies indicated that harmful effects could be produced in animals exposed to dioxin at low levels, and scientists testified that there was no known threshold of safe exposure.[46]

When requiring Vertac to undertake abatement procedures, the court acknowledged that "while there may be low probability of harm from dioxin as defendants contend, there is a serious and dire risk from exposure to dioxin should the hypothesis advanced by the plaintiff prove to be valid." Following *Reserve Mining*, the court held that endangerment need not be proved with scientific certainty but merely as a probability. Because of what was known and unknown about dioxin, there was a "reasonable medical concern for public health." The court thus found an "imminent and substantial endangerment" to public health and the environment.

[46] *United States v. Vertac Chemical Corporation*, 489 F.Supp. 870, 881–889 (E.D. Ark. 1980).

Adjudication of science-policy disputes does not and cannot resolve the underlying scientific uncertainties. But, judges cannot escape the responsibility of making hard value judgments. They are often forced to do so because of the failure of political processes to arrive at compromises on the underlying social values in disputes. Moreover, they are no more nor less competent to make those judgments than when they decide equally vexing disputes over social policy involving, for example, abortion, school desegregation, reapportionment, and the like.

The Allure of a
Judicial/Administrative Partnership

"Scientific and technological developments," Judge David Bazelon observes, "outstripped the common law and thrust [the judiciary] into a new role."[1] In the last two chapters we saw how state and federal trial courts have dealt with science-policy disputes and responded to the pressures of private law litigation. Here, we turn to the role of federal appellate courts in the administrative law and politics of managing health-safety and environmental risks. The federal judiciary has a larger role in the regulatory politics of managing risks due to unprecedented congressional legislation and a surge of litigation over health-safety and environmental regulation. Underlying these trends have been profound legal and political changes. Interest-group pluralism and the absence of scientific consensus have promoted a judicialization of the administrative process and have transformed the role of federal courts in regulatory politics.

Congress led the way by enacting major health-safety and envi-

---

[1] D. Bazelon, "Science and Uncertainty: A Jurist's View," 5 *Harvard Environmental Law Review* 209 (1982), at 211.

ronmental legislation in the 1970s. It did so in response to the warnings of environmental scientists and because of political pressure brought by concerns that neither the private sector nor private law litigation effectively deals with the social costs of technological and industrial processes. In some instances, as with the Clean Air Act, Congress also mandated "technology-forcing" requirements. Within certain time limits, agencies had to set standards for pollution control commensurate with available or feasible technology. Congress and federal agencies, as one federal court put it, forced regulated industries "to develop pollution control devices that might at the time appear to be economically or technologically infeasible."[2]

Congressional legislation did not solve the problems of assessing and managing risks, nor could it have. For the most part, it delegated broad powers to federal agencies, and they in turn promulgated an unprecedented range of regulations. That only served to focus political conflict at the level of regulatory agencies and reviewing courts. This is so both because political opinion remains divided on whether and what kinds of regulations are necessary and because federal regulations rest on scientific data that typically remain subject to considerable disagreement within the scientific community itself. Moreover, regulations themselves, even in situations of greater scientific certainty, generate political conflict. That conflict typically finds its way into litigation and leads to greater judicial supervision of regulatory politics.

The dramatic growth in health-safety and environmental regulation transformed regulatory politics. Litigation not only became a crucial part of regulatory politics but substantially altered the traditional relationship between courts and agencies. Federal judges proclaimed their new role to be "that of a constructive cooperation with the agency involved in the furtherance of the public interest."[3] But, the partnership was tenuous from the outset. Actually, the relationship between courts and agencies evolved in stages: from a posture of limited judicial oversight—which characterized the pattern of admin-

[2] *Union Electric Co. v. Environmental Protection Agency*, 427 U.S. 246, 257 (1976). See also *Train v. Natural Resources Defense Council*, 421 U.S. 60 (1975).

[3] *International Harvester Co. v. Ruckelshaus*, 478 F.2d 615, 647 (D.C. Cir. 1973).

istrative law for much of the nineteenth century—to the Supreme Court's clash with New Deal agencies in the 1930s, out of which eventually emerged a uniform code for administrative procedures, the Administrative Procedure Act of 1946. That act set the stage for recent developments which have judicialized the regulation of health-safety and environmental risks.

After briefly examining the evolution of the judicial/administrative partnership, I turn to recent trends in the judicialization of regulatory politics. A case study of the ban on Tris illustrates the dynamics of court–agency interaction in risk regulation. From it, we see why agencies usually base their regulations on uncertain and contested scientific evidence. But more than that we see both why agencies are reluctant to engage in prolonged adversarial-type rule-making proceedings and how litigation strategies have become central to regulatory policymaking. From this study, I go on to argue that the costs of judicializing regulatory politics are high: they involve less reliance on agency expertise, greater procedural complexity in the regulatory process, and delay and inefficiency in both under- and overregulating the risks of toxic and carcinogenic substances. But, I conclude that this may be the inescapable price of resolving science-policy disputes in a pluralistic society characterized by our unique blend of scientific, legal, and political cultures.

Patterns of Administrative Law and Politics

Administrative discretion and expertise have always been subject to some form of judicial oversight. But the scope of judicial review has expanded enormously. In addition, the administrative process itself has become increasingly judicialized. How and why that has occurred is important to understand if we are to assess the judiciary's role in the regulatory politics of managing risks.

In the Beginning:
Limited Judicial Oversight and Political Deference

Judicial oversight of policymaking by Congress and the executive branch was first asserted in *Marbury v. Madison* (1803). That landmark case grew out of the failure to deliver a letter commissioning William Marbury as a federal judge. Marbury claimed he had a right to the commission and that under the Judiciary Act of 1789 Congress gave the Court the power to compel the delivery of the commission by issuing a writ of mandamus. Chief Justice John Marshall held that Marbury indeed had a right to the commission, but the Court could not provide a remedy by ordering Secretary of State James Madison to deliver the commission. The section of the Judiciary Act of 1789 giving the Court the power to issue writs of mandamus was held unconstitutional. In Marshall's view, Congress had enlarged the Court's powers under its original jurisdiction in Article III of the Constitution. The Court for the first time struck down an act of Congress as a violation of the Constitution, and asserted its supremacy over the actions of other governmental branches.

What remains important about *Marbury*, here, is that Chief Justice Marshall claimed control over officials when necessary to protect individuals' "vested rights." Judicial deference to administrative officials would seem almost foreclosed by *Marbury*'s assertion of judicial supremacy in declaring the law. But, Chief Justice Marshall emphasized the limited scope of review and special competence claimed by the judiciary. Judicial review is limited, he said, and turns on the unique role and competence of courts "to decide on the rights of individuals."[4]

Despite *Marbury*'s assertion of judicial supremacy, then, the Marshall Court (1800–1835) established a posture of limited judicial review of decisions by the executive and legislative branches. Congressional delegation of power to agencies and their discretionary lawmaking was sanctioned as necessary "to fill in the details" and implement the general provisions of legislation.[5]

The Marshall Court's posture of limited judicial review of administrative decisions eventually characterized the pattern of administrative law throughout the nineteenth century. As the century drew to a close, regulation assumed a larger role in the governmental process. Courts nonetheless continued to acquiesce in broad delegations of

[4] *Marbury v. Madison*, 5 U.S. 137, 168–173 (1803).

[5] *Wayman v. Southard*, 23 U.S. 1, 41 (1825); and *United States v. Vowell*, 9 U.S. 368 (1809).

power to agencies, until the Supreme Court confronted the massive delegation of power to agencies during the New Deal.

The Confrontation over the New Deal and the Rise of Administrative Expertise

In the twentieth century, the Court endeavored to counter the growth and expanding lawmaking role of federal agencies with the "substantive due process" and "nondelegation" doctrines. It did so by fashioning a "liberty of contract," under the Fourteenth Amendment's due process clause, in order to strike down progressive economic legislation. But, the Court was widely attacked for becoming a "superlegislature" and reading substance (its own economic philosophy) into the due process clause. During the 1937 Court-packing battle with FDR, the Court finally abandoned the doctrine of substantive due process.[6] In that confrontation, the Court also employed what is called the "nondelegation" doctrine to strike down congressional statutes—statutes that delegate broad powers to federal agencies, but without discernible standards for the exercise of that power. The nondelegation doctrine also became a casualty of the Court's confrontation with FDR.[7]

After the demise of these doctrines, the Court for the most part returned to its earlier deferential posture toward federal agencies. But the Court's attack on the New Deal left an indelible imprint on

[6] See *Munn v. Illinois*, 94 U.S. 113 (1877); *Chicago, M. & St. R. R. Co. v. Minnesota*, 134 U.S. 418 (1890); and *Lochner v. New York*, 198 U.S. 45 (1905). The battle between FDR and the Court is further discussed in D. M. O'Brien, *Storm Center: The Supreme Court in American Politics*, chap. 2 (New York: Norton, 1986).

[7] On the development of the doctrine, see *Panama Refining Co. v. Ryan*, 296 U.S. 383, 440 (1935); and *Schechter Poultry Corp. v. United States*, 295 U.S. 495 (1935); and also *National Cable Television Association v. United States*, 415 U.S. 336, 342 (1976) (standards required for agency action). But see also *FPC v. New England Power Co.*, 415 U.S. 345, 355 (1974) (Marshall, J., con. op.) (characterizing the nondelegation doctrine as "moribund"); and compare *Industrial Union Dept., AFL-CIO v. American Petroleum Institute*, 448 U.S. 607, 671–688 (1980) (Rehnquist, J., con. op.). The Burger Court has also suggested that the doctrine may not be passé. See *City of Eastlake v. Forest City Enterprises*, 426 U.S. 668, 675 (1976); and *Federal Energy Administrator v. Algonquin SNG, Inc.*, 426 U.S. 548 (1976).

regulators. Judicial deference to administrative discretion could no longer be presumed. Administrative discretion in regulatory policy-making was expanding and needed its own justification.

Administrative expertise became the *sine qua non* of regulatory politics and as important a justification for judicial deference to agencies as *Marbury*'s rationale of limited judicial competence. James Landis, the father of New Deal regulation, equated judicial review of administrative regulations with that of legislation. In his view, administrative judgment should be given "weight because of its assumed expertise."[8] Indeed, agencies were considered superior to Congress or the courts because of their expertise in technical and scientific matters.

Judicial oversight of the administrative process prior to World War II thus remained limited. Federal courts basically confined themselves to enforcing general principles of administrative law, fashioned from traditional common law notions of "fair play" and constitutional due process requirements.[9]

The Court, for example, sharpened the line distinguishing agencies' activities in setting public policy—a quasi-legislative or rulemaking activity—from those implementing or enforcing established policies against private citizens, which are more adversarial and verge on a quasi-judicial activity. Legislative-type decisions associated with rulemaking or standard-setting were accorded deference, whereas those enforcing regulatory policy and affecting the proprietary interests of an individual or a small number of people were deemed to necessitate close judicial supervision.[10]

[8] J. Landis, "Administrative Politics and the Courts," 47 *Yale Law Journal* 519, 533 (1938).

[9] See *Londover v. City and County of Denver*, 210 U.S. 373 (1908); *FCC v. Pottsville Broadcasting Co.*, 309 U.S. 134, 143–144 (1940). For cases discussing and extending the due process/"fair play" concept, see *United States v. Morgan (Morgan IV)*, 313 U.S. 409, 422 (1941); *Wong Yang Sung v. McGrath*, 339 U.S. 33 (1950) (*dicta* that the Administrative Procedure Act's requirements for public hearings are due process-based); *Joint Anti-Fascist Committee v. McGrath*, 341 U.S. 123 (1951); and *United States v. Florida East Coast Railway Co.*, 410 U.S. 224 (1973).

[10] See *Bi-Metallic Investment Co. v. State Board of Equalization*, 239 U.S. 441 (1915); *The Assigned Car Cases*, 274 U.S. 564, 583 (1927); and *FCC v. WJR*, 337 U.S. 265 (1949) (establishing that there is no across-the-board right to oral arguments in every administrative proceeding).

Prior to 1946 and the adoption of the Administrative Procedure Act,[11] courts for the most part thus deferred to agencies' quasi-legislative decisions and rulemaking, while supervising agency adjudicatory proceedings directed at particular individuals or groups. They respected claims of administrative expertise and their own limited role in supervising the executive branch. But the judiciary's confrontation with New Deal agencies led to the creation of a uniform code that would define the scope of judicial oversight and bring uniformity to agencies' regulatory activities.

The APA and a New Era

The Administrative Procedure Act (APA) remains the basic code for modern administrative procedure and regulatory policymaking. Its passage marked "the beginning of a new era in administrative law."[12] With it Congress aimed to curb agency reliance on adjudicatory proceedings when setting regulatory policy, and to curb judicial review of agencies. Congress did so by encouraging agencies to use rulemaking proceedings—instead of adjudicatory proceedings or relying on the courts to enforce their decisions—when establishing regulatory policies.

The APA established a detailed set of requirements for adjudicatory proceedings conducted by agencies. The requirements include (1) a hearing by an administrative law judge; (2) presentation of evidence *viva voce*; (3) cross-examination by affected parties; (4) exclusivity of the hearing record as the basis for the final agency decision; and (5) an initial decision by the presiding judge, with the opportunity for review within the agency. These requirements aimed to discourage agencies from fashioning policy through adjudication, as well as to cut back on what was then perceived as increasing judicial oversight of regulatory politics.

By comparison, requirements for agency rulemaking were few and rudimentary: (1) publication of a notice of a proposed rule or description of the subjects and issues involved; (2) receipt and consid-

[11] 60 Stat. 237 (1947), 5 U.S.C. Sec. 551 (1982).

[12] J. Wright, "Courts and the Rulemaking Process: The Limits of Judicial Review," 59 *Cornell Law Review* 375 (1974).

eration of written comments on the proposed rule from interested individuals; and (3) promulgation of a rule with "a concise general statement" of its "basis and purpose." In addition to these requirements for what is known as "informal rulemaking," Congress provided for "formal rulemaking" by requiring a separate statute "to be made on the record after the opportunity for an agency hearing." Congress also prescribed, with a few exceptions, procedural requirements identical to those for formal adjudication. But, rulemaking was understood to be legislative in character and to be given judicial deference. As the Attorney General's Committee on Administrative Procedure observed, "the whole field of rule-making . . . is outside the constitutional competence of the courts, for rules do not determine the rights of specific litigants but, like statutes, are addressed to people generally."[13]

With the APA, Congress inaugurated a new era in administrative law—an era of expanding administrative rulemaking. In the four decades following enactment of the APA, agency rulemaking has become central to regulatory politics. This is precisely because rulemaking is legislation on the administrative level. As the Supreme Court, in *Chrysler Corporation v. Brown* (1979), put it, "substantive agency regulations have the 'force and effect of law.' This doctrine is so well established that agency regulations implementing federal statutes have been held to preempt state law under the Supremacy Clause."[14] The number of rules and regulations grew exponentially, as Congress delegated more responsibilities to federal agencies. By the mid-1970s, agency rules outnumbered congressional statutes by an 8–1 ratio.[15]

What Congress accomplished with the APA had unanticipated

---

[13] Attorney General's Committee on Administrative Procedure, *Final Report*, S. Doc. 8, 77th Cong. 1st Sess. (Washington, D.C.: GPO, 1946), at 12. [Hereafter cited as *Attorney General's Final Report*.] U.S. Congress, Senate, Committee on the Judiciary, *Administrative Procedure Act, Legislative History*, S. Doc. 248, S. Rep. No. 752, 79th Cong., 2d Sess. (Washington, D.C.: GPO, 1946), at 39. [Hereafter cited as *Legislative History*.] See also *Morton v. Ruiz*, 415 U.S. 199, 231–232 (1973).

[14] *Chrysler Corporation v. Brown*, 441 U.S. 281, 295 (1979).

[15] Commission on Federal Paperwork, *Rulemaking: A Report of the Commission on Federal Paperwork* (Washington, D.C.: GPO, 1977), at 6.

consequences as well. For one thing, the APA essentially reversed the traditional relationship between reviewing courts and federal agencies. In doing so the act relieved the judiciary both of its traditional role and of the necessity for supervising the fairness of adjudicatory proceedings enforcing regulatory policies. By contrast, the relatively vague requirements for agency rulemaking invited judicial oversight. These provisions "which seem to confer discretion on the agency," political scientist Herbert Kaufman observed shortly after passage of the act, "actually constitute invitations to litigation."[16] Since 1946 judicial oversight has indeed occurred almost exclusively in the area of informal rulemaking. Courts converted the notice requirement for a proposed rule into one requiring agencies to disclose in advance all of the data on which they rely, and the requirement of a statement of the basis and purpose of a final rule has been construed to entail an agency rebuttal of major criticisms of its regulatory rules.[17]

Congress and the judiciary, moreover, subsequently imposed still more procedural requirements on regulatory rulemaking. Traditionally, judicial review of informal rulemaking took place in a collateral proceeding. The individual challenging a regulation bore the burden of showing that it was not appropriate to furthering statutory goals. A record of the dispute was prepared in a district court during such collateral attacks, whereas judicial review of formal rulemaking proceedings is based on the record of the original administrative proceeding. But, in the 1970s Congress enacted so-called hybrid rulemaking procedures, providing for judicial review based on a detailed record of agencies' informal rulemaking proceedings. Congress thereby imposed on agencies the burden of making a verbatim transcript of any oral presentation pursuant to its informal rulemaking.[18]

Congress also enlarged the scope of judicial review of agencies'

[16] H. Kaufman, "The Federal Administrative Procedure Act," 25 *Boston University Law Review* 479, 491 (1946).

[17] *Portland Cement Ass'n. v. Ruckelshaus*, 486 F.2d 375 (D.C. Cir. 1973); *United States v. Nova Scotia Food Products Corporation*, 568 F.2d 240, 251–252 (2d Cir. 1977); and *Automotive Parts & Accessories Ass'n., Inc. v. Boyd*, 407 F.2d 330, 338 (D.C. Cir. 1968).

[18] *Attorney General's Final Report*, supra note 13, at 115–117. See also Federal Trade Commission Improvement Act, 15 U.S.C. Sec. 57a(e)(1983 Supp.); and Consumer Product Safety Act, 15 U.S.C. Sec. 2060 (a)(1982).

rules and regulations. Congress authorized courts to invalidate agency rules, made via informal rulemaking procedures, based on the "substantial evidence" standard set forth in the APA, even though that standard had previously applied only to judicial review of agencies' adjudicatory proceedings. Under the Consumer Product Safety Act, for instance, courts may not affirm a product-safety rule unless the statutorily required findings "are supported by substantial evidence on the record taken as a whole." Similarly, the Occupational Safety and Health Act authorizes extensive judicial review of agency rules in providing that the "determinations of the Secretary [of Labor] shall be conclusive if supported by substantial evidence in the record considered as a whole."[19]

In sum, during the last two decades the administrative process became judicialized in two ways. On the one hand, agency rulemaking became less informal and subject to greater procedural complexity, epitomized by the congressional enactment of "hybrid rulemaking" procedures.[20] On the other hand, courts gradually adopted a "hard look" approach to reviewing the substance of agency decisions. The "hard look" approach to judicial review (as further discussed later in this and the next chapter) requires agencies to undertake a reasoned elaboration of their decisions and to submit the factual basis, methodology, and logic of those decisions to exacting judicial scrutiny.[21]

[19] See Consumer Product Safety Act, 15 U.S.C. Sec. 2060(c)(1982); Occupational Safety and Health Act, 29 U.S.C. Sec. 655(f)(1982); and Department of Labor, *Rules of Procedure for Promulgating, Modifying, or Revoking Occupational Safety or Health Standards*, 29 C.F.R. Sec. 1911.15(a)(2)(1976).

[20] See, e.g., *Vermont Yankee Nuclear Power Corp. v. Natural Resources Defense Council, Inc.*, 435 U.S. 519 (1978); *Natural Resources Defense Council, Inc. v. United States Nuclear Regulatory Commission*, 547 F.2d 633 (D.C. Cir. 1976); *Environmental Defense Fund v. Environmental Protection Agency*, 598 F.2d 62 (D.C. Cir. 1978); *Aqua Slide 'N' Dive Corp. v. Consumer Product Safety Commission*, 569 F.2d 831, 838 (5th Cir. 1978); *American Petroleum Institute v. OSHA*, 581 F.2d 493 (5th Cir. 1978), discussed in chapter 5.

[21] See *Vermont Yankee Nuclear Power Corp. v. Natural Resources Defense Council, Inc.*, 435 U.S. 519 (1978); *Greater Boston Television Corporation v. FCC.*, 444 F.2d 841 (D.C. Cir. 1970), *cert. denied*, 403 U.S. 923 (1971); *Ethyl Corporation v. Environmental Protection Agency*, 541 F.2d 1, 34–37 (D.C. Cir. 1976). The "hard look" approach is discussed further in this and the next chapter.

Judicial Review and Agency Regulations

Although both Congress and the courts have invited heightened judicial review of agency decisions, judicial scrutiny remains no less problematic. In historical perspective, *Marbury* limited judicial supervision to that area in which the courts arguably possess special expertise, namely, policing the boundaries of constitutionally limited government and ensuring the rights of individuals. But, the trend in the last twenty years has been toward more judicial scrutiny of regulatory agencies. This trend runs counter not only to *Marbury*'s defense of judicial review but also to the more recent regulatory philosophy calling for deference to administrative expertise.

Judicializing the Regulatory Process

The ways in which the regulatory process has become judicialized merit closer attention. This is so because each of two trends—the increasing procedural complexity of agency rulemaking and the heightened judicial scrutiny of regulatory decisions—is frequently examined separately. Yet, both are intimately related to social forces. Both reflect an underlying political disenchantment with administrative discretion and expertise, due to the rise of interest group pluralism and to scientific uncertainties over health-safety and environmental regulation. Before turning to the problems of regulating health-safety and environmental risks, something more should be said about how these factors are related to trends toward greater procedural complexity and heightened judicial oversight of regulatory politics.

Increasing Procedural Complexity

In the 1970s interest-group political theorists criticized deference to agency expertise as undemocratic and unaccountable. Broad delegation of power and judicial deference to agencies, as earlier noted, had been rationalized on two grounds. Administrators possess special expertise in technical and scientific areas, such as risk assessment, shared neither by Congress nor by the courts. And agencies are relatively isolated (hence, immune) from the coopting influence of special interests.[22] But, both of these assumptions were challenged by inter-est-group political theorists. They showed that agencies were fre-quently captured by the very interests they were intended to regu-late.[23]

In order to ensure against the coopting of agencies by special interests, Congress imposed adjudicatory-type requirements on agency rulemaking. And courts were urged to adopt a more interven-tionist posture when overseeing the administrative process. The aim was to ensure a fair representation of competing interests in the regu-latory process. The "due process revolution" forged by the courts, initially in the area of criminal justice, gradually extended to virtually every area of public affairs.[24]

---

[22] See *Greater Boston Television Corp. v. FCC*, 444 F.2d 841, 851–852 (D.C. Cir. 1970).

[23] See, e.g., L. Jaffe, "The Administrative Agency and Environmental Control," 20 *Buffalo Law Review* 231 (1970); S. Lazarus and J. Onek, "The Regulators and the People," 57 *Virginia Law Review* 1069 (1971); and R. Cramton, "The Why, Where and How of Broadened Public Participation in the Administrative Process," 60 *Georgetown Law Review* 525 (1972).

[24] In the area of nonregulatory decisions affecting individual entitle-ments, the Supreme Court in the 1970s expanded the protection of the due process clause of the Fifth and Fourteenth Amendments to require trial-type hearings prior to the infringement of individual rights and entitlements. Notably, in *Goldberg v. Kelly*, 397 U.S. 254 (1970), the Supreme Court held that the due process clause of the Fourteenth Amendment requires a preter-mination hearing for recipients of Aid to Families with Dependent Children. The Court subsequently extended due process-based requirements in *Wheeler v. Montgomery*, 397 U.S. 280 (1970) (termination of old age benefits); *Rowan v. United States Post Office Department*, 397 U.S. 728 (1970) (procedural irregu-larities in scheme of hearings concerning mail violations); *Wisconsin v. Con-stantineau*, 400 U.S. 208 (1971) (lack of hearing prior to public posting of names of people deemed unfit to consume alcoholic beverages); *Richardson v. Wright*, 405 U.S. 208 (1972) (lack of opportunity to offer oral evidence and to cross-examine witnesses in hearing over termination of disability benefits); *Morrissey v. Brewer*, 408 U.S. 471 (1972) (lack of hearing in parole revocation); *Board of Regents v. Roth*, 408 U.S. 564 (1972) (lack of hearing prior to employ-ment termination of state employee); *Perry v. Sinderman*, 408 U.S. 593 (1972) (lack of hearing prior to state employee's termination); *Gibson v. Berryhill*, 411 U.S. 609 (1973) (lack of impartial hearing officers in state optometry board); *Weinberger v. Hynson, Westcott & Dunning, Inc.*, 412 U.S. 609 (1973) (lack of hearing prior to Food and Drug Administration withdrawal of a new drug application); *Arnett v. Kennedy*, 416 U.S. 134 (1974) (lack of hearing prior to termination of government employee); and *Goss v. Lopez*, 419 U.S. 565 (1975)

This judicialization of regulatory politics reflected changes in the political and legal culture. The cultural premium placed on procedural fairness was elevated, as it were, above that of technical and scientific expertise. The basic assumptions of administrative law and politics shifted; or, as Harvard Law School Professor Richard Stewart argues, moved toward a "model of interest representation."[25] Whereas courts once deferred to agencies, they gradually assumed responsibility for ensuring public participation in regulatory politics. They no longer sought merely to safeguard individuals' substantive rights and "vested interests." Instead, procedural rights were created and expanded so that individuals and groups could gain access to and participate in the regulatory process.

Congress, more than the Supreme Court, led the way in increasing the procedural complexity of regulatory politics. The APA had preserved the basic presumption of judicial review, but the scope of review was limited. To challenge administrative actions individuals must show that they have standing to sue, that they have exhausted the possibility of administrative appeals, and that they have demonstrable personal interests recognized within the "zone of interests" protected by a statute.[26]

Congress went even further when enacting health-safety and environmental legislation. It typically provided for both a statutory right

---

(hearing prior to ten-day suspension from school). During the latter part of the 1970s, however, the Burger Court evidenced a more restrictive, less expansionistic view of due process requirements. See, e.g., *Meachum v. Fano*, 96 S.Ct. 2532 (1976) (due process does not entitle prisoner to a fact-finding hearing on prison transfer); *Paul v. Davis*, 424 U.S. 693 (1976) no due process violation by circulation of photograph with caption "Active Shoplifters"); *Ingraham v. Wright*, 430 U.S. 651 (1977) (due process does not require notice and hearing prior to imposition of corporal punishment in schools); and *Barry v. Barchi*, 443 U.S. 55 (1979) (summary dismissal of harness racing trainers).

[25] R. Stewart, "The Reformation of American Administrative Law," 88 *Harvard Law Review* 1669 (1975).

[26] 5 U.S.C. Secs. 551–559, 702 (1976 & Supp. IV 1980); and *Duke Power Co. v. Carolina Environmental Study Group, Inc.*, 438 U.S. 59 (1978); *Schlesinger v. Reservists Committee to Stop the War*, 418 U.S. 208 (1974); *United States v. Richardson*, 418 U.S. 166 (1974); *Association of Data Processing v. Camp*, 397 U.S. 150 (1970); *Scenic Hudson Preservation Conf. v. FPC*, 354 F.2d 608 (2d Cir. 1965), *cert. denied*, 384 U.S. 941 (1966).

of review of regulatory action and for "citizen suits" as a means of enforcing legislative mandates. By enlarging citizens' standing to challenge administrative policymaking, public participation in regulatory politics was expanded. Yet, the price of increased public participation was diminished administrative legitimacy and greater judicial supervision. Even when legislation does not provide for citizen suits, individuals may claim a "private cause of action" under a statute to gain access to the courts and to force compliance with congressional objectives.[27]

The Supreme Court also contributed. It did so by liberalizing the law of standing—the law governing access to courts and the range of interests that may be asserted in challenging agencies. Historically, individuals had access to the courts only by demonstrating personal or proprietary damage. The requirement of a personal or proprietary damage limited access to so-called pocketbook plaintiffs—those with monetary damages.[28]

Beginning in the late 1960s, the Court held that judicial review of agency decisions was a presumption of congressional legislation and enlarged the permissible range of taxpayer suits. Individuals could challenge regulatory policies for infringing not only on economic interests but also on "aesthetic, conservational, and recreational" interests.[29]

In *United States v. Students Challenging Regulatory Agency Procedures (SCRAP)* (1973), for instance, the Court signaled approval for lower federal courts to take lawsuits involving claims to other than economic damages. Here, a group of law students (SCRAP) challenged a proposed surcharge on railroad freight approved by the Interstate Commerce Commission (ICC). They argued that the effect of the regulation would be damage to the environment since the surcharge would

---

[27] See, e.g., *Cannon v. University of Chicago*, 441 U.S. 677 (1979); *Evansville v. Kentucky Liquid Recycling, Inc.*, 604 F.2d 1008 (7th Cir. 1979) (denial of private cause of action under Rivers and Harbor Act, 33 U.S.C. Sec. 1365, in challenge to the dumping of toxic chemicals into rivers).

[28] See, e.g., *Frothingham v. Mellon*, 262 U.S. 447 (1923), and compare *Flast v. Cohen*, 392 U.S. 83 (1969). See also L. Jaffe, "The Citizen as Litigant in Public Actions: The Non-Hohfeldian or Ideological Plaintiff," 116 *University of Pennsylvania Law Review* 1033 (1968).

[29] *Association of Data Processing v. Camp*, 397 U.S. 150, 153–154 (1970).

discourage the transportation of recycled materials. In granting SCRAP standing, the Court observed:

> Aesthetic and environmental well-being, like economic well-being, are important ingredients of the quality of life in our society, and the fact that particular environmental interests are shared by the many rather than the few does not make them less deserving of legal protection through the judicial process.[30]

Although retaining the requirement that individuals demonstrate a personal injury, the Court remolded the law of standing. Plaintiffs came to function as surrogates for special interest groups. They still must demonstrate a personal stake in an actual case or controversy, yet the personal injury claimed may actually embrace a public injury.[31]

Both because of congressional legislation and the Court's rulings on the law of standing, lower federal courts became a forum for more challenges to regulatory action and inaction. Agencies encountered attacks for failing to comply with the National Environmental Policy Act,[32] for example, and for making summary judgments,[33] as well as for not allowing interest groups to participate in agency rulemaking.[34] Even when afforded opportunities to participate in rulemaking pro-

[30] *United States v. Students Challenging Regulatory Agency Procedures (SCRAP)*, 412 U.S. 669, 686 (1973).

[31] *Duke Power Co. v. Carolina Environmental Study Group, Inc.*, 438 U.S. 59 (1978); *Arlington Heights v. Metropolitan Housing Development Corp.*, 429 U.S. 252, 261 (1971); *Simon v. East Kentucky Welfare Rights Organization*, 426 U.S. 26, 41–42 (1976); and *Warth v. Selden*, 422 U.S. 490 (1975).

[32] See, e.g., *Environmental Defense Fund, Inc., v. Hardin*, 325 F. Supp. 1401 (1971) (attacking the secretary of agriculture's prohibition of the use of Mirex to control infestation of fire ants under the Federal Insecticide, Fungicide and Rodenticide Act).

[33] See, e.g., *Weinberger v. Hynson, Westcott & Dunning*, 412 U.S. 609 (1973) (upholding the Food and Drug Administration's refusal of a hearing to a petitioner challenging withdrawal of a new drug application on efficacy grounds).

[34] See, e.g., *Public Citizen v. Foreman*, 631 F.2d 969 (D.C. Cir. 1980) (challenge of Food and Drug Administration's ruling on nitrate).

ceedings, interest groups may still challenge regulations on procedural and substantive grounds.[35]

Health-safety and environmental regulation was fertile ground for greater regulatory litigation and judicial oversight. Once access to the courts was broadened, the incomplete scientific data, conflicting private interests, and fundamental policy choices on which such regulation rests inevitably invited litigation. Agencies inexorably had to defend their regulations in the courts.

In sum, with the liberalization of the law of standing, the range of interests that trigger judicial review grew. They now extend well beyond those substantive rights recognized in *Marbury*. Procedural rights and guarantees now justify more judicial supervision of the administrative process. The primary function of administrative law became not merely, as Stewart concludes, "the provision of a surrogate political process to ensure the fair representation of a wide range of affected interests in the process of administrative decisions."[36] Rather, *Marbury*'s claim of limited judicial review based on special judicial competence gave way to a more activist, policy-oriented-participatory judicial posture.

The policy-oriented-participatory judicial posture that emerged is well illustrated in an early ruling on the scope of judicial review of environmental regulations. In *Calvert Cliffs Coordinating Committee v. AEC* (1971), the Court of Appeals for the District of Columbia Circuit observed:

> These cases are only the beginning of what promises to become a flood of new litigation—litigation seeking judicial assistance in protecting our national environment. Several recently enacted statutes attest to the commitment of the Government to control, at long last, the destructive engine of material "progress." But it remains to be seen whether the promise of this legislation will become a reality. Therein lies the judicial role. . . . *Our duty, in short, is to see that important legislative purposes, heralded in the halls of Congress, are not lost or misdirected in the vast hallways of the federal bureaucracy.*[37]

[35] See, e.g., *Scenic Hudson Preservation Conference v. FPC*, 354 F.2d 608 (2d Cir. 1965) (challenging agency action for failing to support decisions with relevant data and permit public access to records).

[36] Stewart, supra note 25, at 1670.

[37] *Calvert Cliffs Coordinating Committee v. AEC*, 449 F.2d 1109, 1111 (D.C. Cir. 1971) (emphasis added).

This activist-participatory role in regulatory politics deprived courts of their traditional justification for the exercise of judicial review, and led to greater substantive review of administrative decision making in areas in which judges neither possess nor may claim special competence.

Heightened Substantive Review

As agency rulemaking became central to regulatory politics, judicial review came to structure and constrain rulemaking in more significant ways. Historically, judicial review was not thought to guarantee the correctness of rulemaking. Instead, courts basically served to ensure that agencies did not exceed their delegated authority or deny individuals' rights. Accordingly, agencies enjoyed flexibility in their rulemaking procedures. They were largely free to adopt either informal (notice and comment) procedures or formal, adjudicatory-type procedures under the APA. Depending on which they used, judicial review would be more or less rigorous. Regulations based on informal rulemaking could be set aside only when agency action was "arbitrary, capricious, an abuse of discretion, or otherwise not in accordance with law." Those based on formal rulemaking procedures were subject to more rigorous judicial review, requiring a demonstration of "substantial evidence" based on the record of the agencies' rulemaking.[38]

Given the greater procedural complexity and heightened judicial review of formal adjudicatory-type rulemaking, agencies prefer more informal procedures. They are less costly, less time-consuming, and ostensibly more efficient and productive. More formal procedures also appear no more beneficial for resolving science-policy disputes in agencies than in courts with private law litigation. Adversarial processes (as we saw earlier) cannot resolve the irreducible factual uncertainties *cum* scientific controversies, or fully accommodate the numerous and diverse interests in the dispute without prolonging the

[38] 5. U.S.C. Secs. 551–559, 701–706 (1976). See *Environmental Defense Fund, Inc., v. Blum,* 458 F. Supp. 650 (1978) (arbitrary and capricious standard); *Dunlop v. Bachowski,* 421 U.S. 560 (1975); *Weinberger v. Hynson, Wescott & Dunning,* 412 U.S. 609 (1973); *Citizens to Preserve Overton Park, Inc. v. Volpe,* 401 U.S. 402 (1971).

rulemaking process. The same kinds of problems confronting trial courts not surprisingly reappear in administrative adjudications.

In the 1970s, Congress and federal courts rebuffed agency preference not only for informal rulemaking but also for lenient judicial review. Under the Occupational Safety and Health Act (OSHA), for example, Congress delegated broad authority to OSHA but at the same time provided for close judicial scrutiny of regulations based on the substantial evidence standard. Courts, then, extended the substantial evidence test to informal rulemaking as well. The distinction between judicial review under the "arbitrary and capricious" and under the "substantial evidence" standards eventually broke down. By the 1980s there had developed an "emerging consensus of the Courts of Appeals that the distinction between the arbitrary and capricious standard and substantive evidence review is largely semantic."[39]

This trend toward heightened judicial review further transformed regulatory politics. Law professor Colin Diver, for one, argues that transformation amounts to a "paradigm" reform. In his view, a "comprehensive rationality" paradigm for regulatory politics replaced that of "incremental policymaking."[40] These two "paradigms" are instructive for understanding how profoundly regulatory politics changed.

Broadly speaking, incremental policymaking characterizes the pattern of administrative law and regulation prior to the APA's reform of the administrative process.[41] Agencies' limited consideration of policy alternatives in adjudicatory proceedings was reinforced by lenient judicial review of the factual basis for regulation. Courts required an almost trivial "rationality" requirement for agency decisions. The presumption of administrative rationality was forcefully stated in *Pacific States Box & Basket Co. v. White* (1935):

[39] *Pacific Legal Foundation v. Department of Transportation*, 593 F.2d 1358, 1366 n. 35 (D.C. Cir. 1979).

[40] C. Diver, "Policymaking Paradigms in Administrative Law," 95 *Harvard Law Review* 393 (1981).

[41] See C. Lindbloom, "The Science of 'Muddling Through,' " 19 *Public Administration Review* 79 (1959).

When such legislative action is called in question, if any state of facts reasonably can be conceived that would sustain it, there is a presumption of the existence of that state of facts, and one who assails the classification must carry the burden of showing by a resort to common knowledge or other matters which may be judicially noticed, or to other legitimate proof, that the action is arbitrary.

By contrast, the comprehensive rationality paradigm of policy-making requires agencies to clearly specify policy goals, identify all possible alternatives for implementing those goals, and then undertake an evaluation of the effectiveness of each policy option. These features, Diver claims, figure prominently in the pattern of administrative law that emerged with the ascendance of agency rulemaking as the preferred method of settling regulatory standards. With the National Environmental Policy Act—and particularly its requirement of an "environmental impact statement" for agency action affecting the environment—Congress initially revealed a general expectation that agencies clarify policy goals and systematically evaluate alternative options and their consequences. Congress subsequently created "single purpose" agencies, notably, the Environmental Protection Agency (EPA), the OSHA, and the Consumer Product Safety Commission. While conferring extensive rulemaking authority on these agencies, Congress imposed requirements forcing regulatory action on certain matters within specified time periods and in accordance with prescribed standards. The Toxic Substances Control Act (TSCA), for instance, required the EPA to promulgate within six months, after the effective date of the TSCA, rules governing the disposal and distribution of polychlorinated biphenyls, PCBs.[42]

[42] See, e.g., Clean Air Act, 42 U.S.C. Secs. 7401–7642 (1983) (EPA directed to approve state implementation plans for achievement of national primary ambient air quality standards "as expeditiously as practicable but . . . in no case later than three years from the data of [EPA] approval of such plan"); Federal Water Pollution Control Act, 33 U.S.C. Sec. 1311(b)(A)(2)(A)(1978) (requiring setting of effluent liminations by July 1, 1977, and July 1, 1983, based on, respectively, "the best practicable control technology currently available" and the "best available technology economically achievable"); Toxic Substances Control Act, 15 U.S.C. Sec. 2605(e)(1982) (requiring the EPA to promulgate within six months, after the effective date of the TSCA, rules governing the disposal and distribution of polychlorinated biphenyls, PCB's); Safe Drinking Water Act, 42 U.S.C. Sec. 300g-(a)(1)-(2) (time limitation on establishment of national interim primary drinking water regulations).

Administrative law and regulatory politics shifted as Congress required agencies to base their decisions on more detailed identification and evaluation of policy objectives and consequences, and mandated more rigorous judicial review to ensure the reasoned elaboration of those decisions. Some federal courts followed the congressional lead by also demanding that agencies provide qualitative comparisons of alternative policy options and their consequences.[43]

Science-Policy Disputes and Regulatory Complexity

By the 1980s, regulatory rulemaking was well established. It had also become more procedurally complex and subject to more intrusive judicial review. But what remains crucial, here, is that these trends developed out of Congress's broad mandates for regulating health-safety and environmental risks. The judicialization of regulatory politics occurred not primarily because of a judicial usurpation of power. Rather, it was due to three factors: the enormous growth in federal regulation dealing with health-safety and the environment; the lack of consensus on the scientific basis for that regulation; and the dominance of interest group pluralism, which ostensibly posed the danger of overregulation of regulated interests and outside control of agency expertise.

More Legislative Mandates and Specification of Agency Action

The sheer growth in the number of agencies devoted to health-safety and environmental regulation was phenomenal. Congress created new agencies and greatly increased the number, range, and complexity of the regulatory responsibilities of "older" agencies—such as the Food and Drug Administration—for regulating health, safety, and environmental concerns.

---

[43] See, e.g., *Natural Resources Defense Council, Inc., v. U.S. Nuclear Regulatory Commission,* 547 F.2d 633, 645 n. 34 (D.C. Cir. 1976), *rev'd. sub. nom. Vermont Yankee Nuclear Power Corporation v. Natural Resources Defense Council,* 435 U.S. 519 (1978); *Scientists' Institute for Public Information, Inc. v. Atomic Energy Commission,* 481 F.2d 1079, 1092 (D.C. Cir. 1973); and discussion in chapter 5.

Prior to the mid-1960s there were only five agencies concerned with health-safety and environmental regulation. Chronologically, they are: the Packers and Stockyards Administration in the Department of Agriculture (DOA) (1916); the Food and Drug Administration in the Department of Health and Human Services (DHHS) (1931); the Agricultural Marketing Service in the DOA (1937); the Federal Aviation Administration in the Department of Transportation (DOT) (1948); and the Animal and Plant Inspection Service in the DOA (1953).

In the following decade, Congress established no less than nine new agencies devoted to regulating health-safety and the environment. The new agencies and independent commissions are: the Federal Highway Administration (1966); the National Highway Traffic Safety Administration (1970); the Federal Railroad Administration (1972); the Environmental Protection Agency (1972); the Consumer Product Safety Commission (1972); the Mining Enforcement and Safety Administration, in the Department of the Interior (1973); the Drug Enforcement Administration, in the Department of Justice (1973); the Occupational Safety and Health Administration, Department of Labor (1973); and the Nuclear Regulatory Commission, based on the old Atomic Energy Commission (1975).

No less dramatic was the simultaneous expansion of congressionally delegated responsibilities for regulating health-safety and environmental risks. Eight major federal laws on health and environmental quality had been enacted prior to 1960. Eleven were passed between 1960 and 1970, and twenty-three from 1971 to 1980. Figure 4.1 shows the cumulative increase. Appendix A provides a chronological list of legislation authorizing health-safety and environmental regulation.

Congress did not rest with increasing the number of agencies or statutory bases for health-safety and environmental regulation. It also increased the complexity of the criteria for regulating risks. Congressional mandates, though, were less than a systematic attempt to secure what Diver identifies as "comprehensive rationality" in regulatory politics. Instead, they provided agencies with disparate, cross-cutting, and overlapping criteria for setting regulatory standards. Appendix B categorizes the various requirements for agency risk assessment and management.

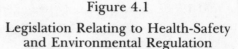

Figure 4.1

Legislation Relating to Health-Safety
and Environmental Regulation

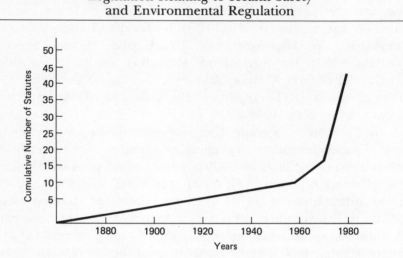

Most statutes require some sort of balancing of the risks and the costs and/or benefits of alternative standards, though they do not require rigorous cost/risk/benefit assessments per se.[44] Yet, the statutory criteria are by no means uniform. Under some statutes—the Consumer Product Safety Act; the Federal Insecticide, Fungicide and Rodenticide Act; and the Toxic Substances Control Act—agency action is contingent on a threshold determination of "unreasonable risk." The vast majority of statutes require less structured assessments and balancing. In other instances—such as with provisions of the Occupational Safety and Health Act, and those of the Clean Air and Clean Water Act—Congress constrained agency discretion by requiring a showing of the "technological feasibility" of the standard adopted by an agency. By contrast, under the Delaney Clause of the Food, Drug and Cosmetic Act, no degree of carcinogenic risk is acceptable; no cost-risk-benefit analysis permitted.

[44] For a further discussion of cost-risk-benefit analysis, see Office of Technology Assessment, *Assessment of Technologies for Determining Cancer Risks from the Environment* (Washington, D.C.: GPO, 1981), and discussion in chapter 6.

Increased Agency Rulemaking and Litigation

Congressional expansion of agency responsibilities for health-safety and environmental regulation vastly increased agency rulemaking and the number of challenges in the federal courts. The number of civil suits against the Environmental Protection Agency, for instance, rose from less than 20 in 1973 to almost 500 in 1978. Challenges to all administrative actions, moreover, rose 28.8 percent in 1980 from the previous year and constituted 14.4 percent of the total federal apellate caseload. Approximately 22 percent of all administrative appeals in 1980 involved regulatory action by the Environmental Protection Agency (10%), the Federal Regulatory Commission (8.3%), the Occupational Safety and Health Administration (2.9%), and the Nuclear Regulatory Commission (.6%).[45]

Cures Worse Than Diseases, Diseases Worse Than Cures: Tris

The controversy surrounding Tris, a fire-retardant sprayed on babies' clothing and a suspected carcinogen, illustrates some of the problems of judicializing regulatory politics. In some respects, the controversy is unique, even extreme. Yet, in many ways it reflects broad trends in regulatory politics and the changing relationship between courts and agencies.

Government regulation of risk sometimes creates new and even greater risks. In this regard, the Tris controversy is perhaps a classic example. But, the controversy also reveals the reluctance of agencies to engage in adversarial-type rulemaking proceedings and the ways in which litigation strategies have become central to regulatory policy-making. The controversy, moreover, shows that the judicialization of the regulatory process does not guarantee against agency capture. To the contrary, the threat of litigation may be used to coopt agencies

[45] See Council on Environmental Quality, *Report of the Council on Environmental Quality* (Washington, D.C.: GPO, 1980); and National Research Council, *Forecasting the Impact of Legislation on Courts* (1980); Administrative Office of the U.S. Courts, *Management Statistics for United States Courts 1980* (Washington, D.C.: GPO, 1981), at 45–46.

and produce a kind of regulatory blackmail. The threat of litigation pushes agencies to establish standards that appear defensible legally, but not necessarily scientifically.

Creating Controversy: The Risks of Governmental Regulation

Until the early 1970s, about 85 percent of all children's sleepwear was made of cotton. After the Federal Flammable Fabrics Act was passed in 1953, the Department of Commerce developed national flammability standards for a variety of consumer products. In 1971, the department established standards for children's sleepwear sizes 0 to 6x. Three years later, the Consumer Product Safety Commission (CPSC), having assumed jurisdiction over the area, followed with regulations for sizes 7 to 14. Under these standards, children's sleepwear had to pass a retardancy test developed by the National Bureau of Standards.

These standards aimed at reducing the risks of burns due to the flammability of garments. Cotton failed to meet the standards and chemically treated cotton garments were not well received by consumers. Manufacturers were forced to find other fabrics or chemical treatments of fabrics that would meet the new standards. They quickly developed garments made of polyester, acetate, triacetate, and mixtures of manmade fibers treated with chemicals. The standards thus created a large market for flame-retardant chemicals like Tris. Tris became the chemical most widely used because it was relatively inexpensive and there were no ready alternatives until late 1976, when a new product, Antiblaze 19, became available. The production of Tris in 1971, estimated at almost 3 million pounds, quadrupled within three years and was promoted for use in children's sleepwear.

Neither immediately before nor after promulgation of the standards did agencies or the chemical industry conduct toxicity tests on chemicals like Tris. In 1973, Dr. E. P. Mazzola of the CPSC's Bureau of Biomedical Sciences (the bureau responsible for determining whether consumer products pose unreasonable toxicological hazards) proposed a study but it was not funded. In that same year, the Chemical Selection Work Group of the National Cancer Institute (NCI) suggested Tris as a candidate for long-term animal laboratory tests. It did so because of the chemical structure of Tris, its increased use as a flame-retardant, and its growing exposure to humans. Still, the CPSC did not investigate why Tris was placed on the NCI's list, or even how much Tris was used in consumer products. The following year, the NCI began its two-year study of laboratory rodents fed quantities of Tris.

Scientific Initiative and Bureaucratic Delay

By late 1975, other evidence indicated that Tris was a mutagen and carcinogen. On October 29, the EPA's director of the Office of Toxic Substances informed the acting director of the CPSC that Tris had been found mutagenic in a new short-term test developed by Dr. Bruce Ames. Five months later, Dr. Robert Hehir, director of the CPSC Bureau of Biomedical Sciences, received a telephone call from Ames, who advised him that he considered Tris to be a carcinogen. Ames urged the CPSC to ban Tris in consumer products, especially children's sleepwear. Children were especially susceptible because of their wearing Tris-treated garments, and due to the sucking of their fingers and clothing. The communications were noted, yet the CPSC took no action.

Less than a week after Ames's telephone call, on March 24, 1976, the Environmental Defense Fund (EDF), a private nonprofit environmental and health-safety interest group, filed a petition requesting the CPSC to promulgate a rule "requiring a label on sleepwear [containing Tris] warning consumers of the potential hazard and recommending that sleepwear be prewashed three times prior to use, a practice which would reduce, although not eliminate the exposure" to the risks of Tris (while also reducing the flame-retardancy of the clothing).[46] The petition cited preliminary studies showing that Tris

[46] See Environmental Defense Fund, *Petition Pursuant to 15 U.S.C. Sec. 2059, To Commence a Proceeding for the Issuance of a Consumer Product Safety Rule* (March 24, 1976); Brief of Springs Mills, Inc., *Springs Mills, Inc. v. CPSC*, Nos. 77-1969, 77-1970, 4th Cir. Court of Appeals, 1978, at 5; and U.S. Congress, House of Representatives, Committee on Interstate and Foreign Commerce, 95th Cong., 2d Sess., *Consumer Product Safety Commission's Regulation of Tris: The Need for an Effective Chronic Hazards Program* (Washington, D.C.: GPO, 1978) [hereafter cited as *Regulation of Tris*].

was absorbed through the skin of rodents and that large amounts of Tris could be found on fabrics and ingested by children chewing on their sleepwear.

Staff at the CPSC evaluated the EDF petition during the summer and fall of 1976. In July, the commission received a memorandum from the principal Tris manufacturer, the Michigan Chemical Company, challenging the EDF's view of the potential hazards of Tris-treated garments. Although the CPSC did not publicly respond to the Michigan Chemical Company, an internal staff review rejected as "scientifically unmerited" the company's claim that "Tris does not pose a mutagenic or carcinogenic hazard."[47]

Because the CPSC did not publicly indicate that it doubted the industry's data and safety claims for Tris, manufacturers were unaware of the possibility of a ban on Tris. The EDF was unaware that the commission had begun to seriously consider banning Tris. And, most important, the public was unaware of the potential health risks of Tris-treated sleepwear.

Litigation Blackmail and the Ban on Tris

Six months after filing its petition, the EDF requested expedited consideration of its petition. Almost three months more passed before the CPSC secretary, Sadye E. Dunn, responded. She informed the EDF that Chairman S. John Byington had requested early reports on the NCI studies and that there would be no action until they were available. In October, the CPSC also received information from the FDA that other short-term tests suggested that Tris was a possible carcinogen. A month later, after reviewing these studies, Dr. Joseph McLaughlin of the CPSC Bureau of Biomedical Sciences wrote his director that "children's sleepwear containing Tris cannot be considered safe based on all the data now available." Director Robert Hehir, however, rejected the recommendation, apparently because the NCI studies had not yet been completed. He asked McLaughlin to revise his Tris evaluation.

The controversy over Tris grew and attracted publicity. In the January 1977 issue of *Science* magazine, Arlene Blum and Bruce

[47] Quoted, Congress, *Regulation of Tris*, id., at 10.

Ames published an article concluding that Tris was a mutagen and that "the risk of cancer [due to exposure to flame-retardants on sleepwear] might be very much higher than the risk from being burned."[48] The CPSC was also under political attack both for having promulgated too many safety standards and for failing to move quickly to regulate products under the Flammable Fabrics Act.[49]

A month after the Blum and Ames article was published, the CPSC received the preliminary data from the NCI two-year study. It indicated that Tris was a carcinogen in rodents. Four days later, Dr. Robert Harris and the EDF filed another petition. This time, based on the NCI study and Ames's research, they asked the CPSC to ban Tris-treated sleepwear as an "imminent hazard to the public health" under the Federal Hazardous Substances Act.[50] The EDF pointed out that the CPSC had at least two alternatives in banning Tris. The CPSC could file lawsuits against the manufacturers of Tris-treated garments in federal courts upon its finding that such garments pose an "imminently hazardous consumer product," or it could undertake rulemaking proceedings and promulgate a rule banning Tris-treated products.

Sadye Dunn received another letter from the EDF eight days later, on February 16, 1977. The EDF meant to show that it meant business, but it also wanted to advise the CPSC how to move expeditiously in banning Tris. The letter emphasized that there was already a sufficient basis for finding Tris to be an "imminent hazard to public health." The EDF pointed out that courts had held "that chemicals that are shown to be carcinogenic in animals can be presumed to be carcinogenic in humans." To buttress its position, the letter quoted at length from another EDF case, *Environmental Defense Fund v. Environmental Protection Agency* (1975). There, the Court of Appeals for the District of Columbia Circuit had held that "although extrapolation of data from mice to men may be quantitatively imprecise, it is sufficient

[48] A. Blum and B. Ames, "Flame-Retardant Additives as Possible Cancer Hazards," 195 *Science* 17 (January 7, 1977), at 21.

[49] See Government Accounting Office, *Improvements Needed in Administering the Flammable Fabrics Act* (Washington, D.C.: GAO, 1978).

[50] Environmental Defense Fund, *Petition to Ban the Sale of Tris-treated Wearing Apparel*, February 8, 1977.

to establish a 'substantial likelihood' that harm will result and justify an agency's regulation."[51]

The EDF then laid out the procedural avenues that the CPSC might take (and the basic choice that the commission ultimately had to make). If the CPSC agreed that Tris was a "hazardous substance," it could immediately ban all Tris-treated products under a section of the Federal Hazardous Substances Act that governs products intended for use by or accessible to children. Alternatively, under another section of the act, governing "hazardous substances" intended for the household, the CPSC would have to give manufacturers and other interested parties the opportunity to file objections to the ban, as well as to request a public hearing. The latter option was procedurally more complex and possibly more fair. But, it also entailed greater delay.

The EDF sent another letter on March 3, 1977, reaffirming its position that the CPSC should immediately ban Tris. The letter ended with the not-so-subtle threat of lawsuit to force the action:

> Because of the short time frame now facing the Commission and the extensive delay which has already taken place, EDF now feels it is essential that deadlines be established for Commission action on this issue. . . . EDF must be prepared to take additional legal action if immediate action is not taken by the Commission on our petitions. Consequently, we are hereby notifying the Commission that if no decision is reached on the question of whether Tris is a "hazardous substance" by March 15, 1977, EDF will be forced to conclude that no action to act constitutes a denial of our petition. Should no action be forthcoming by this date, EDF intends to pursue whatever legal remedies may be available to it to require the Commission to assume its statutory responsibility. . . . [W]e are fully prepared to press our case before the courts.[52]

Members of the CPSC and its staff subsequently met several times with EDF personnel, including Robert J. Rauch, EDF's chief

---

[51] Letter to Sadye Dunn, February 16, 1977, quoting at page 3 *Environmental Defense Fund v. Environmental Protection Agency*, 510 F.2d 1292, 1299 (1975). (Obtained by the author through the Freedom of Information Act.)

[52] Letter to Sadye Dunn, March 3, 1977, at page 5. (Obtained by the author through the Freedom of Information Act.)

counsel. At one meeting on March 8, Harris and Rauch admitted that "there is no correct way of extrapolating from high doses to low doses or from animals to humans." The scientific basis for banning Tris, like other health-safety and environmental regulations, was far from clear and open to attack.

"What the issue boils down to," they insisted, "is balancing the need for additional information and therefore additional certainty against the potential risk. . . ." Commissioner R. David Pittle agreed. In his view, the CPSC must "take regulatory action that is precautionary in nature . . . [even] on the basis of a record that is not entirely conclusive as to the causality" of a substance. He concluded that "where a substance has been demonstrated to be carcinogenic in test animals, we must assume it will be carcinogenic in humans." Commissioner Lawrence Kushner, however, was alive to the burdens on manufacturers and those that the commission would carry in defending its decision in the courts. He favored obtaining more information—information that "is likely to withstand or will help us withstand whatever challenge I am sure will come." Chairman Byington agreed, though he was less sanguine about the threat of litigation. The commission needed time. The EDF's attorney Rauch would not back down. He was not trying to be "arbitrary . . . [but] to protect ourselves and the public we have to begin to move."[53]

Less than two weeks later, on March 23, the EDF filed a lawsuit in district court seeking an immediate ban on the sale of all Tris-treated garments.[54] A few days later, the CPSC received a letter from the American Apparel Manufacturers Association. They wanted an opportunity to discuss possible action relating to Tris-treated garments. At an informal meeting on March 31, without advance notice to other interested parties, representatives met with the CPSC and discussed the possible ramifications of a ban.

The CPSC took no formal action on the EDF's February 9 petition until April 7, 1977. It then decided to promulgate a ruling that

---

[53] Transcript of meeting on March 8, 1977, at pages 6, 14, 21–22, 24, and 49–50. (Obtained by the author through the Freedom of Information Act.)

[54] *Environmental Defense Fund et al. v. Consumer Product Safety Commission*, Civil No. 77-517 (D.D.C. filed March 23, 1977).

banned children's sleepwear containing Tris as hazardous substances under the Federal Hazardous Substances Act.[55]

Due to the mounting pressure from the EDF, the CPSC resolved to move as quickly as possible with an interpretative ruling, rather than undertaking rulemaking procedures. The ban on Tris was neither complete nor absolute, however. It did not apply to unfinished fabric in mills or to that not yet delivered to cutters and sewers, though it covered uncut fabric for sale in retail stores directly to consumers. The CPSC also exempted children's garments that had already been washed. It did so on the theory that washing substantially reduced the risks, despite reports to the contrary by Harris and Ames.

The CPSC anticipated legal challenges. It had failed to afford interested parties any opportunity for a hearing and to rebut the scientific basis for banning Tris. Perhaps more important, the commission did not allow interested parties to present their views on the kind of ban that should be issued and the economic consequences for the clothing industry.

The issue of access was discussed extensively on April 4 at a closed meeting of the CPSC. It arose out of the problem of how far the commission should go with a ban—to the producers of Tris, textile manufacturers, cutters and sewers of garments, distributors, retailers, or simply the consumers. Some group along that line of commerce had to assume the economic losses of the ban. If they were not afforded an opportunity to present their views, they would surely challenge the ban. Commissioner Barbara Franklin put the matter bluntly:

> It is just an unfairness, John [Byington], in this whole situation that is inherent in it. You've got an apparel manufacturer who simply made sleepwear [with Tris-treated fabric] and is going to end up having to eat the whole thing when, in fact, it goes back to a chemical that was used, that wasn't tested because nobody thought of testing chemicals then.

[55] Consumer Product Safety Commission, "Children's Wearing Apparel Containing Tris: Interpretation as Banned Hazardous Substances," 42 *Federal Register* 18850 (April 8, 1977).

However, Byington countered that they should not "start mucking around in where the economic burden is going to get picked up." Anyway, he added, "the courts are going to end up deciding at what point in time or at what place in the chain this burden is going to get placed." The staff agreed and pressed for an interpretative ruling, along the lines earlier suggested by the EDF.[56]

What is striking about this penultimate meeting is how little concern there was for the scientific basis for the ban on Tris. Indeed, there was little understanding of the actual risks, particularly of those garments that had already been washed. If the risk of Tris was as great as Ames and the EDF claimed, the CPSC should have recalled all sleepwear in use. Estimates of the risks by CPSC staff, however, varied by a factor of 100 to 200 times lower than that reported by Ames and the EDF. Commissioner Pittle expressed his frustration quite frankly: "I read [Ames's report] and I can't decide whether it makes any sense or not."[57]

The scientific basis for regulation was far from clear and the degree of risk almost completely a matter of guesswork. The main issue had become one of legal strategy. "There is [sic] going to be two types of lawsuits," Byington observed, "one against us if we bend [and delay in order to get additional information on the risks of Tris and the economic costs of different kinds of bans], and then the lawsuits [from manufacturers, cutters and sewers, and others] are going to be against us to try to stop or slow down or limit what we do."[58]

Defending and Changing Regulatory Strategies

The same day that the CPSC announced its decision, the EDF amended its March 23 lawsuit to force "the repurchase of Tris-treated products sold to consumers prior to April 8 and already washed, and also seeking Commission action on adult Tris-treated wearing apparel." EDF's action was only the first of numerous challenges in the following months.

[56] Transcript of meeting on April 4, 1977, at pages 21–22. (Obtained by the author through the Freedom of Information Act.)

[57] Id. at 71.

[58] Id. at 27.

The American Manufacturing Association (AMA) filed a suit contending that the ban improperly placed the entire economic burden for repurchase of Tris-treated garments on manufacturers. It argued that the ban should extend to all Tris-treated fabric, fiber, and yarn used in or intended for use in children's clothing. On May 3, a federal district court held that the CPSC acted arbitrarily and capriciously in too narrowly defining "banned hazardous substances" in its ruling on Tris-treated clothing. The CPSC had placed the entire economic burden on manufacturers, and the court ruled that the ban had to include all fabric, yarn, or fiber containing Tris that was used or intended for use in children's apparel.

In response to the court's ruling (and indeed on the basis of it, rather than on its own authority), the CPSC amended its original ruling on May 5, 1977. It now ordered an extention of the ban to include all Tris-treated fabric, yarn, or fiber used in children's apparel.[59]

The CPSC's action generated more controversy. The Court of Appeals for the District of Columbia Circuit subsequently vacated the lower court's decision. That court also ordered the commission to promptly explain its own authority and basis for banning Tris. Not until June 1, 1977, did the CPSC publish its explanation for expanding the ban to all uncut Tris-treated fabric. Then, the commission offered this justification for its earlier ban:

> There were other important reasons, besides washing by consumers, why the Commission framed its ban in the manner it did. These include the massive marketplace disruption that such a ban would undoubtedly involve; the increased and needless anguish that the parents of children who have been exposed to the washed clothing and fabric would feel; and the practical difficulties associated with tracing and repurchasing approximately 120 million items that are years old and often lacking identifying labels.

It went on to explain why it had not engaged in rulemaking proceedings that would have allowed interested parties to contest the scientific evidence and comment on the scope of any ban:

[59] 42 *Federal Register* 22878 (1977).

If the Commission had any uncertainty about whether the TRIS products were hazardous substances, it would have conducted a rule-making procedure. . . . The Commission found, however, that the evidence supporting the risk of illness presented by TRIS products is overwhelming. The two-year NCI feeding study shows the potency of TRIS as a carcinogen in animals. The strong link between animal carcinogens and human carcinogens is supported by numerous authorities.[60]

The CPSC had again sought a legally defensible position, and one that bore little relation to the scientific evidence or the commission's understanding of that evidence at the time it issued its original ban. Less than a month later, Philip Abelson, editor of *Science* magazine, published an editorial supporting the Tris ban yet pointing out that its scientific basis remained far from established.

On the basis of the data available in May 1977, the hazards for humans of wearing Tris-treated garments are unknown. The hazards could be quite negligible. They might be enormous. Narrowing such a gap quickly will not be easy. There are too many unknown factors, such as the carcinogenicity of Tris for humans. We may have to wait the passage of years to observe whether the incidence of kidney cancer remains unchanged or increases. And if there is an increase, we could not be certain of its causes, for other agents might be responsible.[61]

The extension of the ban invited litigation that ultimately undercut the CPSC's legal justification for its action. A principal supplier of children's sleepwear, Springs Mills, Inc., attacked the commission on both substantive and procedural grounds. The main argument, however, was that the commission's failure to undertake rulemaking proceedings was a denial of due process under the Fourteenth Amendment of the Constitution. A federal district court agreed, in *Springs Mills, Inc. v. Consumer Product Safety Commission* (1977). The commission should have undertaken rulemaking proceedings rather than simply announce its ban as an interpretative rule.[62] After quoting

[60] 42 *Federal Register* 28059 (1977).

[61] Editorial, "The Tris Controversy," 197 *Science* (July 8, 1977).

[62] *Springs Mills, Inc. v. Consumer Product Safety Commission,* 434 F. Supp. 416 (1977).

from an earlier ruling in *Pactra Industries v. Consumer Product Safety Commission* (1977), in which the CPSC had also "attempted to avoid due process by bypassing the rule-making provisions of the Food, Drug and Cosmetic Act,"[63] the court overturned the ban and forbade the commission from enforcing it against "any party, any article, fabric, yarn, or fiber."

The CPSC formally withdrew its ban on December 6, 1977.[64] At the same time, however, it substituted a policy statement reiterating its original position and asserting that it did not interpret *Springs Mills* to preclude enforcement proceedings in federal courts in order to get companies to comply with its view of Tris as a hazardous substance.

In the following year, the CPSC initiated eight such lawsuits.[65] In one of these, *United States v. Articles of Hazardous Substances* (1978), the owner of seized garments challenged the commission's actions on basically the same grounds as those accepted by the district court in *Springs Mills*. This time, the Court of Appeals for the Fourth Circuit was more sympathetic to the CPSC. It held that the commission had alternative ways of regulating hazardous substances under its authorizing legislation. In the appellate court's view:

> From our examination of the statutory structure, it appears that the Commission may proceed against a substance by regulation pursuant to its rule-making authority, or may go directly to court upon its allegation that the goods or substances meet the statutory definition [of a hazardous substance] under Section 1261(q)(1)(A).[66]

After *Articles of Hazardous Substances*, the CPSC continued to enforce its position in litigation against those few companies that persisted in selling Tris-treated garments. Despite congressional criticism of its delay in regulating Tris and related hazardous substances, the CPSC never engaged in rulemaking proceedings to meet the objec-

---

[63] *Pactra Industries, Inc. v. Consumer Product Safety Commission*, 555 F.2d 677 (9th Cir. 1977).

[64] 42 *Federal Register* 61593 (1977).

[65] See U.S. Product Safety Commission, *Annual Report, Fiscal Year 1977* (Washington, D.C.: GPO, 1978), at 36.

[66] *United States v. Articles of Hazardous Substances*, 588 F.2d 39, 42 (1978).

tions in *Springs Mills*. In 1981 the CPSC released a study concluding that "the risk of contracting cancer from wearing children's pajamas treated with Tris is seven times greater than previously thought."[67] But, again, like its other studies, this one was not subject to scientific or public review and comment. Many of the legal and scientific issues underlying the Tris ban thus remain unresolved.

Beyond CPSC's Ban

The handling of Tris was typical of the CPSC and in some respects atypical of that of other agencies. After the Tris controversy, the CPSC remained under attack from Congress and, later, the Reagan administration, which wanted to eliminate it. In its regulation of Tris and other suspected carcinogens, the commission invited criticism by assuming a reactive posture to hazards identified by others. It is fair to say, along with former FDA general counsel Richard Merrill, that "the CPSC has not played a decisive role in regulating potential carcinogens."[68]

Unlike other agencies, the CPSC rarely systematically analyzed the costs and benefits of its regulations. It infrequently developed adequate risk assessments, and generally tried to find ways to get around formal rulemaking proceedings; this in turn contributed to its vulnerability to litigation and political attack. When in 1981 Congress decided to reauthorize the CPSC, it addressed some of these problems by amending the Consumer Product Safety Act. The commission now must give advance notice of any proposed rulemaking to ban hazardous substances. It must obtain an advisory report from a Chronic Hazard Advisory Panel (composed of scientists nominated by the National Academy of Sciences) on the carcinogenic risks of any substance it plans to regulate. It must also conclude that voluntary industry standards will not eliminate the risks posed by hazardous substances and that its rules have a "reasonable relationship" to the costs of regulation. Finally, it must impose the least burdensome requirements necessary to manage the risks.

[67] See 5 Chem. Reg. Rep. (BNA) 300 (1981).

[68] R. Merrill, "CPSC Regulation of Cancer Risks in Consumer Products: 1972–1981," 67 *Virginia Law Review* 1261 (1981), 1360.

The Tris controversy illustrates some broad trends in the regulatory politics of managing health-safety and environmental risks. Like most agencies, the CPSC faced large scientific uncertainties in regulating suspected carcinogens. To a great degree, agencies must base their regulations on unfolding (and uncertain) scientific evidence. Because of the threat of legal challenges, they therefore adopt legally defensible strategies. Indeed, legal strategies often become more important than the scientific basis for regulation.

The office of legal counsel in agencies has inexorably come to have more influence than scientific experts on the final formulation of regulations. That is to say that technical experts within an agency may still have the first word, but legal staff now more often than not have the last word on regulations.

The CPSC's ban on Tris also shows how agencies can be coopted by special interest groups threatening lawsuits over regulatory action and inaction. The relationship between the EDF and the CPSC and the later attack by manufacturers of Tris-treated products reveal other trends as well. They are rooted in our decentralized judicial and political system.

The decentralized structure of the federal judiciary promotes the disjointed development of regulatory policy. Political scientist Shep Melnick has shown this in a study of the interaction of federal courts and the EPA under the Clean Air Act.[69] As in disputes over the Clean Air Act and in the Tris controversy, the EDF and other environmental groups focus on lobbying (and threatening litigation against) agencies in order to get favorable regulatory standards. By contrast, regulated industries, like Springs Mills and the AMA, tend to take a defense posture. They tend to challenge the enforcement of those standards in federal district courts.

These litigation strategies tend to pay off for interest groups. In *Springs Mills*, and as Melnick found more generally under the Clean Air Act, federal district courts tend to be more responsive to regulated interests and to limit enforcement of agency standards. By con-

---

[69] R. S. Melnick, *Regulation and the Courts: The Case of the Clean Air Act* (Washington, D.C.: Brookings Institution, 1983); and "The Politics of Partnership," in C. Wise and D. M. O'Brien, *Law and Public Affairs, Special Issue,* 45 *Public Administration Review* 641 (1985).

trast, appellate courts, as in the Fourth Circuit Court of Appeals decision in *Hazardous Products*, tend to be more supportive of agency regulations.

As a result, although courts provide a forum for the representation of interest groups in regulatory politics, the decentralized structure of the judiciary promotes delay and inefficiency, as well as works against the development of a coherent and unified regulatory policy.

The Costs of Judicializing Regulatory Politics

The Tris controversy underscores the central concern of what process is due. The episode makes clear the importance of opportunities for parties to contest the basis for and scope of proposed regulations. On the one hand, the CPSC's failure to engage in a formal rulemaking process invited invalidation of its regulation. On the other hand, the CPSC's decision to announce an interpretative ban reflects agency opposition to the judicialization of the administrative process and their increasing vulnerability to judicial review. The CPSC paid the price of trying to avoid the delays encountered by other agencies when undertaking more formal rulemaking proceedings. But, perhaps, the ultimate lesson of the Tris controversy is that there are considerable costs to judicializing regulatory politics, regardless of whether agencies undertake an end run around formal rulemaking proceedings.

The costs are threefold: diminishing reliance on administrative discretion and expertise; undermining agency legitimacy; and regulatory inefficiency.

Agency Discretion and Expertise in Rulemaking

Agencies are so far down the road toward judicialized rulemaking proceedings that the history and purposes of administrative rulemaking have been all but lost sight of. When reporting on the enactment of the APA, the Senate Committee on the Judiciary endorsed rulemaking as an *efficient* mechanism for establishing regulatory policy. Rulemaking was desirable "because [it] involve[s] subject matter demanding judgment based on technical knowledge and experience."

The rulemaking process was basically "for the education of the administrator." Public participation was deemed "essential [not to the fairness of a regulation per se but rather] in order to permit administrative agencies to inform themselves."[70]

The rulemaking process was designed to broaden the information base, and thereby enhance the *accuracy* of the factual basis for regulations. By comparison, administrative adjudications were deemed necessary for ensuring *fairness* in the application of regulatory standards. Under the APA, agencies were to enjoy flexibility in conducting rulemaking proceedings—the process for *setting* rather than *applying* regulatory standards. Agencies were also to be accorded judicial deference—"undetailed review"—due to their technical expertise and because in the "realms of economic, environmental and energy regulation, the policy disputes are too sharp, the technological considerations too complex, the interests affected too numerous, and the missions too urgent for agencies to rely on the ponderous workings of adjudication."[71]

The judicialization of the rulemaking process thus registers both a distrust of administrative expertise and an acknowledgment of the uncertainties underlying the regulation of risk. In other words, as the factual basis for regulatory policy was judicially and politically perceived to become more complex and controversial, Congress and the courts imposed more adjudicatory requirements on agency rulemaking. They did so in order to ensure the ventilation—if not resolution—of those disputes prior to the promulgation of regulatory standards.

But that, of course, undercuts the APA's basic dichotomy between the function of rulemaking and that of administrative adjudication. Even if agencies follow more formal rulemaking procedures, there is now a greater possibility that some dissatisfied interest group will challenge regulations in the courts. If agencies try to avoid more procedurally complex rulemaking, as in the Tris controversy, then they face certain litigation and possible judicial invalidation of their

[70] Congress, *Legislative History of the APA*, supra note 13, at 20 and 39; and *Attorney General's Final Report*, supra note 13, at 26–35.

[71] *Attorney General's Final Report*, supra note 13, at 116–117.

regulations. Administrative discretion and expertise are diminished in either event.

Judicial Oversight and Administrative Legitimacy

Heightened judicial review undercuts the legitimacy of agency decisions in the sense that they are not considered final until one or more courts have passed muster. Reviewing courts now demand agencies to establish a "framework for principled decisionmaking" so as to facilitate a "hard look" at the scientific assumptions and evidence supporting regulatory standards.[72] The demand for principled administrative decision making requires agencies to establish a coherent and usable (that is, judicially reviewable) record of their decision-making processes. All relevant materials must be placed in a rulemaking record, and agencies must give interested parties the opportunity to respond to the factual, technical, and theoretical bases for their regulations. The administrative record, in short, must evidence "a thorough ventilation of the [scientific and normative] issues" so that judges may scrutinize and assess the rationality of administrative decisions.[73]

Just as the APA's dichotomy between administrative rulemaking and adjudication collapsed, so has its distinction between undetailed judicial review of agency rulemaking—based on the "arbitrary and capricious" standard—and the more rigorous review under the "substantial evidence" standard.[74] The Court of Appeals for the District of Columbia Circuit thus has proclaimed an "emerging consensus of the

[72] See *Environmental Defense Fund, Inc. v. Ruckelshaus*, 439 F.2d 584, 598 (D.C. Cir. 1971); and *Portland Cement Association v. Ruckelshaus*, 486 F.2d 375, 394 (D.C. Cir. 1973), *cert. denied*, 417 U.S. 921 (1974).

[73] *Natural Resources Defense Council v. U.S. Nuclear Regulatory Commission*, 547 F.2d 633, 644 (D.C. Cir. 1976). See also *Aqua Slide 'N' Dive Corp. v. Consumer Product Safety Commission*, 569 F.2d 831, 837–838 (5th Cir. 1978); *Texas v. EPA*, 499 F.2d 289, 297 (5th Cir. 1974). Some courts have suggested that the use of nonrecord material may be grounds for remanding an agency's decision. See *Dry Color Manufacturers' Ass'n v. Department of Labor*, 486 F.2d 98, 103–105 (3d Cir. 1978). They have also limited agencies' ex parte communications, see *Home Box Office, Inc. v. FCC*, 567 F.2d 9, 51–57 (D.C. Cir. 1977). But, see also *Sierra Club v. Costle*, 657 F.2d 298, 396–410 (D.C. Cir. 1981).

[74] See 5 U.S.C. Sec. 706(2)(A)(E)(1982).

Courts of Appeals that the distinction between the arbitrary and capricious standard and substantial evidence review is largely semantic."[75]

Agencies now carry the burden of a reasoned elaboration of the basis for their regulatory decisions. That at a minimum requires them to state clearly their scientific and technological assumptions; reveal the data, methodology, and literature on which they relied; explain their rejection of alternative theories and technological options; and, finally, articulate their rationales for setting particular regulatory standards in a manner that permits public comment and judicial scrutiny.[76]

But, by rendering the APA anachronistic, agencies are confined and checked at the expense of their own legitimacy in regulatory politics. As litigation plays a more critical role in regulatory politics, agencies must defend all major regulatory (and deregulatory) actions in the courts. Judicial supervision increases the vulnerability of agency rules, and the legitimacy of agencies inexorably wanes when their regulations are contingent on the judicial imprimatur.

Agency Delay and Inefficiency

The judicialization of the administrative process also contributes to inordinate delays and inefficiencies. These problems have been well documented.[77] Under the hybrid rulemaking procedures specified in the Magnuson-Moss Warranty-Federal Trade Commission Improvement Act, for instance, the FTC completed by 1980 only four of the nineteen rulemaking proceedings initiated during the previous five

[75] *Pacific Legal Foundation v. Department of Transportation*, 593 F.2d 1358, 1343 n. 35 (1979).

[76] See *Portland Cement Association v. Ruckelshaus*, 486 F.2d 375 (D.C. Cir. 1973); *Amoco Oil Co. v. EPA*, 501 F.2d 722, 738–739 (D.C. Cir. 1974); *American Petroleum Institute v. Costle*, 609 F.2d 20 (D.C. Cir. 1981); *Lead Industries, Association v. EPA*, 627 F.2d 416 (D.C. Cir. 1980); *National Lime Ass'n v. EPA*, 627 F.2d 416 (D.C. Cir. 1980).

[77] See, e.g., Administrative Conference of the United States, *Time Limits on Agency Actions*, 1 C.F.R. Sec. 305.78-3; Congress, House of Representatives, Committee on Interstate and Foreign Commerce, 94th Cong., 2d Sess, *Federal Regulation and Regulatory Reform* (Washington, D.C.: GPO, 1976), at 195–242.

years, and estimates that future regulations will "take four to five years to complete" at a cost in excess of $1 million each. Likewise, the CPSC found its hybrid rulemaking procedures cumbersome and its final rules still subject to judicial attack.[78]

Regulatory delay and inefficiency are particularly acute in the regulation of carcinogenic substances. The OSHA, despite promulgating extensive (if not also excessive) safety regulations in its initial seven years, completed standards for only fifteen relatively rare carcinogens by 1980. Similarly, under both the Clean Air Act and the Toxic Substances Control Act, authorizing regulation of some 55,000 potentially hazardous substances, the EPA was slow to regulate carcinogenic substances. Appendix C shows the substances that have been regulated as carcinogens under federal legislation.[79]

Inefficiency, to be sure, arises from the interplay of many factors both internal and external to particular agencies; such as organizational structure, fiscal and technical resources, and the shifting political environment. Some agencies had start-up difficulties and continue to have problems in locating, maintaining, and funding key personnel for conducting risk assessments. All agencies experience some delay in regulating suspected carcinogens because of difficulties in generating the information base for such regulation. Scientific data are rarely readily available and conclusive. More often the information available, as in the Tris controversy, is indefinite and uncertain. Occasionally, needed data are only theoretically obtainable, and not infrequently the most definitive data (on human exposure, for example) are both unavailable and unobtainable.

As much as these factors contribute to regulatory delay, they also

[78] See B. Boer, M. Bowers, D. Edleman, C. Cartwright, and H. Toin, *Phase II, Report of the Trade Regulation Rulemaking Procedures of the FTC 73–75* (Report to the Administrative Conference of the United States 1980); and see *Aqua Slide 'N' Dive Corp. v. Consumer Product Safety Commission*, 569 F.2d 831 (5th Cir. 1978); *D. D. Bean & Sons v. CPSC*, 574 F.2d 643 (1st Cir. 1978); and *Southland Mower Corp. v. CPSC*, 619 F.2d 499 (5th Cir. 1980).

[79] General Accounting Office, *Delays in Setting Workplace Standards for Cancer-Causing and Other Dangerous Substances* (Washington, D.C.: GAO, 1977); Office of Technology Assessment, supra note 44, at 205–208; General Accounting Office, *EPA Slow in Controlling PCBs* (Washington, D.C.: GAO, 1981); and General Accounting Office, *EPA Is Slow to Carry Out Its Responsibilities to Control Harmful Chemicals* (Washington, D.C.: GAO, 1980).

bear on agencies' spending vast resources to establish relatively high standards for a few substances, while leaving the overwhelming number unregulated. Because of the high information costs and the legal vulnerability of health-safety and environmental regulations, agencies devote their limited resources to a few suspected substances that they may regulate in legally defensible ways. Hence, the overregulation of a few toxic substances leads to the underregulation of many others.[80]

Delay and inefficiency in turn further widen debate over the benefits and cost-effectiveness of regulating risk. The cost of regulating health and environmental risks has been substantial. In large part, this is due to the procedural complexity of rulemaking and to the difficulties of achieving consensus on the basis for regulatory standards. OSHA and the EPA, for example, spent an estimated total of $2,132,800 on rulemaking in formulating their standards for vinyl chloride. The estimated cost for industrial compliance with the OSHA and EPA standards has been calculated at $102.6 million and $152.8 million, respectively. More generally, the Council on Environmental Quality estimates that in 1979 the nation spent $136.9 billion to comply with federal environmental protection regulations, or approximately 1.5 percent of the gross national product.

Debate over the wisdom of such regulation is further fueled by the costs of extensive formal rulemaking proceedings. The total cost of OSHA's initial seven carcinogen regulations, for instance, has been estimated at $96 million each. The average cost per cancer death averted by various OSHA standards, furthermore, has been estimated at $20.2 million for its arsenic standard, $18.9 million for benzene and $4.5 and $3.5 million, respectively, for coke-oven emissions and acrylonitrile. For many economists and regulatory reformers, the cost-effectiveness and the net benefits simply do not justify present regulatory strategies for setting relatively high standards for a few substances via a lengthy rulemaking process.[81]

Regulatory delay and inefficiency remain fundamentally related

[80] For a further discussion of this point, see J. Mendeloff, "Does Overregulation Cause Underregulation?," *Regulation* 47 (1981).

[81] See Commission on Federal Paperwork, supra note 15, at 85–110; Council on Environmental Quality, supra note 45, at 387–400; and P. Johnson, "The Perils of Risk Avoidance," *Regulation* 15 (1980).

to the dilemma of agencies—especially the OSHA, the EPA, and the CPSC—endeavoring to establish a record of scientific evidence that will survive judicial scrutiny. Adjudicatory-type proceedings prolong the rulemaking process and generate an extraordinary amount of paperwork. For instance, OSHA's rulemaking proceedings for the regulation of vinyl chloride generated over 600 written comments, with more than 200 separate oral and written submissions. The final record exceeded 4,000 pages; it was surpassed by the EPA's record for its vinyl chloride standard, which contained over 5,000 pages.[82]

More formalized and procedurally complex rulemaking, however, eliminates neither scientific uncertainties nor the normative-political choices inherent in health-safety and environmental regulation. What the attorney general's final report on the APA recognized in 1947, numerous independent and presidential study commissions have since come to acknowledge, namely, that in the area of health-safety and environmental regulation, agencies should be permitted to use more flexible, less formal rulemaking procedures.[83]

Science-Policy Disputes and the Judicial/Administrative Partnership

The judicialization of the administrative process rests on the misconception that science-policy disputes center on purely scientific controversies. Only a small percentage of those disputes, however, actually appears to involve disagreements of a purely scientific nature. Those disputes, moreover, are exceedingly narrow and marginally related to determining the course of most regulatory strategies.

The principal source of contention involves essentially normative, political judgments that must be made in the absence of complete scientific evidence. Even when ostensibly adequate evidence exists, regulatory decisions inevitably register basic political judgments. Commentators such as Robert Crandall and Lester Lave of the Brookings Institution correctly point out that scientific evidence itself

[82] Commission on Federal Paperwork, supra note 15, at 91.
[83] See Commission of Federal Paperwork, supra note 15.

cannot be the determining factor in health-safety and environmental regulation. They nonetheless misleadingly suggest that scientific uncertainties necessarily undermine the legitimacy of agency regulations. "The difficulty," in their words, "is not that science has nothing to offer; rather it is that science is not perceived as helpful because it is inconclusive."[84] Yet, most regulations do not depend on (and it would be unrealistic to expect) complete scientific certainty.

Regulatory decisions are political decisions, based on agency expertise, negotiations, and compromises. As the Court of Appeals for the District of Columbia Circuit put it, "a rulemaking agency necessarily deals less with 'evidentiary' disputes than with normative conflicts, projections, differing assessments of possible risks, and the like."[85] Steven Jellnick, a former assistant administrator for toxic substances at the EPA, likewise observes that most regulations "must be established without direct evidence linking the substance with its potential victims: in other words, in the absence of certainty."[86] Richard Cooper, chief counsel for the FDA, similarly notes that "agencies have no alternative but to make fundamental value judgments as best they can," even when there are ample data on the effects of different levels of carcinogenic exposure.[87]

If the actual number of purely scientific factual disputes is relatively small, and health-safety and environmental regulations register fundamentally political decisions based on imperfect scientific evidence, then the trends toward greater procedural complexity and heightened judicial review of agency rulemaking are problematic and paradoxical. In precisely these areas of regulation there exists a greater need for flexibility and deference to agency discretion and expertise in developing, negotiating, and setting regulatory standards.

[84] R. Crandall and L. Lave, eds., *The Scientific Basis of Health and Safety Regulation* (Washington, D.C.: Brookings Institution, 1981), at 14–17.

[85] *Amoco Oil Co. v. EPA*, 501 F.2d 722, 735 (D.C. Cir. 1974).

[86] S. Jellnick, "Risk/Benefit Regulation: A Necessary Luxury" (Address at Syracuse University, Summer Lecturers, 1981). See also S. Jellnick, "Toxic Substances: The 'Raucous Truth' About Uncertainty," 1 *Toxic Substances* 3 (1979).

[87] R. Cooper, "The Role of Regulatory Agencies in Risk-Benefit Decision-Making," 33 *Food/Drug/Cosmetic Law Journal* 755, 766 (1978).

The movement away from traditional patterns of judicial review displaces agency expertise and the bargaining central to regulatory politics, substituting instead judicial supervision. From the perspective of *Marbury*, the judiciary's self-proclaimed role of "constructive cooperation with the agency involved in the furtherance of the public interest" is paradoxical. The new era in administrative law presumes that agencies cannot be trusted to carry out their congressionally delegated responsibilities, and that judicial judgment and competence are superior not only to those of agencies but also to those of other political branches.

An Elusive Senior Partner

When considering the trends toward greater judicialization of regulatory politics in earlier chapters, I gave particular attention to the role
of state and federal district courts. Here, we will focus on the role of
federal appellate courts in reviewing lower court decisions and federal agencies' regulations of health-safety and environmental risks.

The reason for doing so is that the problems that science-policy
disputes pose for appellate courts are different from those facing trial
courts, whether in the state or in the federal judiciary. Trial court
judges such as Judge Miles Lord, as we saw in Chapter 3, sit and
decide cases alone. They confront, often for the first time, scientific
uncertainties and intense value conflicts as well as pressures of local
communities and bureaucratic politics.

Federal appellate court judges sit on three-judge panels. Occasionally, in important cases on which the judges in the circuit or on
other circuit courts are divided, all of the judges on an appellate court
sit together, or *en banc*. Appellate court decisions are thus collegial
and reflect the interaction of three or more judges and their law
clerks. The necessity for reasoning and bargaining with others in

reaching a ruling works to moderate final decisions and to lessen the influence of outside political pressures that trial court judges may confront when deciding especially controversial cases.

No less important, appellate courts do not decide issues for the first time. They have the benefit of the records and decisions of a lower court or administrative agency. As Judge Frank Coffin of the Court of Appeals for the First Circuit emphasizes:

> Deciding an appeal is not a matter of approaching a problem as if for the first time. It is determining whether another, earlier, carefully structured decision should be upheld. That earlier decision, if by a court, is already the full-bodied product of a formal adversary hearing, held with all the garnishments of due process; if by an agency, it is the product of either such an adversary hearing or a rule-making proceeding in which the responsible official must invite and respond to public comments.[1]

With the benefit of a record of the factual disagreements and value conflicts, appellate courts are spared prolonged trials and share responsibility for a final decision with their colleagues.

Still, many appellate judges find reviewing the records of science-policy disputes vexing and divisive. The Court of Appeals for the District of Columbia Circuit in particular became polarized over responses to disputes surrounding agency regulation of health-safety and environmental risks.

The battle over two seemingly alternative approaches, championed, respectively, by Judges David Bazelon and Harold Leventhal, remains instructive about the role of appellate courts in the politics of regulating risk. This is so not merely because it mirrors the larger controversy over the judicialization of regulatory politics discussed in the last chapter but because the battle within the D.C. Circuit was more apparent than real. Both Bazelon and Leventhal agreed on the need for greater judicial oversight of federal regulation. What they disagreed on was the means by which to ensure greater judicial super-

---

[1] F. Coffin, "Reflections from the Appellate Bench," in M. Cannon and D. M. O'Brien, eds., *Views from the Bench: The Judiciary and Constitutional Politics* (Chatham, N.J.: Chatham House, 1985), at 55.

vision. The Supreme Court eventually ended their debate and endorsed what has come to be known as the "hard look" approach to
reviewing agency regulations.

From a discussion of that debate, we move to two case studies—
involving the regulation of benzene and cotton dust—that illustrate
the problems with heightened judicial scrutiny of agency regulations.
I argue, however, that this pattern will persist even in the era of
deregulation. Indeed, the chapter concludes with two further studies
involving the regulation and deregulation of the Environmental Protection Agency's "bubble policy" and the Department of Transportation's requirements for passive restraints in automobiles. They show
the persistence of the "hard look" doctrine and indicate why the
judiciary will remain a key player in the politics of regulating health-
safety and environmental risks.

More Process or More Reason?

The Court of Appeals for the District of Columbia Circuit confronts
science-policy disputes more than other federal appellate courts because it reviews the overwhelming majority of challenges to regulations. This role has come to the court because of its proximity to the
headquarters of federal agencies in Washington, D.C., and as a result
of congressional encouragement of suits in this court so as to discourage inconsistent rulings by the various circuit courts around the nation. Its rulings in turn provide guidance for other appellate and
federal district courts.

Because of its special role in regulatory politics, the D.C. Circuit
nicely illustrates the approaches that appellate judges have taken
when reviewing science-policy disputes. On the one hand, judges like
David Bazelon have been inclined to push greater procedural complexity on agencies in the belief that "strict procedures will ensure
correct results." On the other hand, Judge Leventhal argued that
courts should confine themselves to a searching examination of regulatory records and require agencies to articulate the basis and reasons
for regulating risks.

The Demand for Procedural Safeguards

Always a thoughtful and forceful advocate, Judge David Bazelon contends that judges have no "knowledge and training to assess the merits of competing scientific arguments" that form the basis for agency rulemaking. Their lack of professional training and competence necessitates self-restraint, he argues, and courts should not substitute their judgments for those of administrative experts.

"Courts are *not* the agency either to resolve the factual disputes, or to make the painful value choices," he insists.[2] That much of Bazelon's position is consistent with *Marbury*'s defense of the limited scope of judicial review. But, like other judges and advocates of interest-group pluralism, Bazelon maintains that regulatory agencies cannot be trusted—they often succumb to the pressures of special interest groups. He therefore argues that adherence to self-restraint in substantive review need not preclude heightened scrutiny of the process of agency decision making. "[T]he best way for courts to guard against unreasonable or erroneous administrative decisions is not for judges themselves to scrutinize the technical merits of each decision. Rather, it is to establish a decision-making process which assures a reasoned decision that can be held up to the scrutiny of the scientific community and the public."[3]

According to Bazelon, the judiciary has a major role in supervising the process of administrative decision making. When necessary, courts should even impose additional procedural requirements on agencies in order to ensure public participation, open discussion, and the reasoned elaboration of the basis for agency rulemaking. By forcing more procedural requirements on agencies, Bazelon contends, agencies "may then correct their own mistakes, thereby minimizing the number of times they must defend, in court, a decision they really

[2] D. Bazelon, "Coping with Technology Through the Legal Process," 62 *Cornell Law Review* 817 (1977).

[3] *International Harvester Co. v. Ruckelshaus*, 478 F.2d 615, 652 (D.C. Cir. 1973) (Bazelon, J., con. op.). See also *Natural Resources Defense Council, Inc., v. NRC*, 547 F.2d 633 (D.C. Cir. 1976); *Ethyl Corporation v. EPA*, 541 F.2d 1, 66 (D.C. Cir. 1976) (Bazelon, J., con. op.); and *Welford v. Ruckelshaus*, 439 F.2d 598 (D.C. Cir. 1971).

do not support."[4] Also, by forcing agencies to allow interested parties to give their views and contest those of others, and by requiring them to keep a record of that exchange, reviewing courts may ensure that agencies are not captured by regulated industries and businesses.

At bottom, Bazelon seeks to promote environmental values as set forth in congressional statutes by requiring agencies to show that they have seriously considered those values and have not treated them in a capricious manner, or in a way responsive to pressure from regulated industries.

The Demand for More Reasons

The late Judge Harold Leventhal was no less sympathetic to health-safety and environmental regulations. He looked for what he called "danger signals" of agencies giving into pressure for underregulation. However, he maintained that a reviewing court should engage in "enough steeping" in technical matters to permit an informed substantive review. Through a searching review of the basis for regulation, he argued, judges become "aware, especially from a combination of danger signals, that the agency has not genuinely engaged in reasoned decisionmaking." This kind of review "assumes that judges will acquire whatever technical knowledge is necessary as background for decision of the legal questions" underlying science-policy disputes.[5]

Federal judges, in other words, are capable and have a responsibility to develop technical expertise—or a "sufficient background orientation"—so that they may judge the soundness of agency decisions. For Leventhal, such substantive review was modest and less intrusive than the ad hoc imposition of procedural requirements on agencies. "On issues of substantive review," as he put it, "the judges must act with restraint. Restraint yes, abdication, no."[6]

---

[4] D. Bazelon, "The Impact of Courts on Public Administration," 52 *Indiana Law Journal* 101, 105 (1976).

[5] *Ethyl Corporation v. EPA*, 541 F.2d 1, 68 (D.C. Cir. 1976) (Leventhal, J., con. op.). See also H. Leventhal, "Environmental Decisionmaking and the Role of the Courts," 122 *University of Pennsylvania Law Review* 509 (1974); and H. Leventhal, "Principaled Fairness and Regulatory Urgency," 25 *Case Western Reserve Law Review* 66 (1974).

[6] Id. at 69.

The Policy Debate

With either approach, federal courts assume an activist role in regulatory politics. With either, agencies are not accorded the same deference as Congress in lawmaking despite the judiciary's sanctioning of a broad delegation of power to agencies. Heightened judicial review is, for both Bazelon and Leventhal, justifiable for a number of reasons. Unlike legislators, administrators are not popularly elected or accountable. Agencies have lower political visibility and a more specialized jurisdiction. Hence, there is less competition for influence among special interest groups than in the legislative arena, and those interests may capture agencies. According to Bazelon, judicial imposition of adjudicatory-type procedures on agencies is necessary to ensure the fairness and enhance the "accuracy" of final regulations. For the same reasons, Leventhal advanced the no less activist position that courts should engage in penetrating substantive review of the basis for agencies' decisions.

Either approach has its problems. Bazelon's position invites sharp criticism on a number of grounds. For one thing, his approach amounts to administrative common law and thus runs counter to the Administrative Procedure Act. Ad hoc imposition of additional procedural requirements on agencies not only defeats the purposes of the APA but, in the words of Bazelon's respected colleague on the bench, J. Skelly Wright, "convert[s] the reviewing court into a super-agency" and comes "at the cost of paralyzing agencies with procedures otherwise irrelevant to sound rulemaking. Surely the court's task," Wright adds, "can be rendered tolerable without rendering rulemaking a practical impossibility." Moreover, Wright points out that "the ad hoc approach mandates that the courts prescribe précise and formal methods for bureaucratic policymaking. This mandate assumes an expertise in administrative science which duty on the bench simply does not confer."[7]

Substantive review of the regulatory policies by courts may be necessary, but the scope of that review remains problematic. In an early environmental case, *Overton Park v. Volpe* (1971), the Supreme

[7] J. S. Wright, "Courts and the Rulemaking Process: The Limits of Judicial Review," 59 *Cornell Law Review* 375 (1974).

Court underscored that the judiciary "is not empowered to substitute its judgment for that of the agency."[8] But, that becomes a real possibility when courts embrace Leventhal's "hard look" approach. Indeed, the Achilles' heel of his approach is that it has no central core; it invites judicial differences over the soundness of regulations. The contours of the "hard look" approach are difficult to ascertain and predict because judges vary both in their technical mastery of agency decisions and in their own ideological orientations toward regulatory actions.

The disagreements between Bazelon and Leventhal, however, are ultimately over strategy rather than over objectives in reviewing agencies' regulation of risks. In other words, the "strict procedures ensure the correct results" and the "hard look" approaches are more compatible than they are at odds with each other. Both aim at getting agencies to elaborate the basis for their decisions and to make explicit their value choices in managing risks. The goal of each was to further "the broad public interest of enabling the public to repose confidence in the process as well as the judgments of its decision-makers."[9]

Together, Bazelon and Leventhal helped forge a majority on the appellate court that took an activist and generally pro-environmental position when reviewing agency regulations. Yet, Bazelon's approach remained hotly contested because it called for the imposition of additional requirements on agencies and thus went well beyond simply heightened scrutiny of regulations. Initially, the Court of Appeals for the D.C. Circuit justified the imposition of procedural requirements as following the congressional lead in mandating hybrid rulemaking procedures. But, the court gradually grew bolder and asserted its own power to impose additional procedural requirements on agencies.[10]

[8] *Overton Park v. Volpe*, 401 U.S. 402, 416 (1971).

[9] *Greater Boston Television Corporation v. FCC*, 444 F.2d 841, 850 (D.C. Cir. 1970), *cert. denied*, 403 U.S. 923 (1977).

[10] See, e.g., *Walter Holm & Co. v. Hardin*, 449 F.2d 1009, 1015 (D.C. Cir. 1971); *Kennecott Copper Corp. v. EPA*, 462 F.2d 846, 850 n.18 (D.C. Cir. 1972); *International Harvester Co. v. Ruckelshaus*, 478 F.2d 615 (D.C. Cir. 1973); *Mobil Oil Corp. v. FPC*, 483 F.2d 1238 (D.C. Cir. 1973); and *Friends of the Earth v. NRC*, 547 F.2d 633 (D.C. Cir. 1976); and compare *O'Donnell v. Shaffer*, 491 F.2d 59, 62 (D.C. Cir. 1974).

The Supreme Court Ends Debate

The appellate court's intervention in regulatory politics angered the more conservative majority of the Supreme Court no less than federal administrators. The Court finally brought the debate between Bazelon and Leventhal to an end in *Vermont Yankee Nuclear Power Corporation v. Natural Resources Defense Council, Inc.* (1978). There, the Court embraced Leventhal's "hard look" approach and sharply repudiated Bazelon's position and opinion for the lower court in *Natural Resources Defense Council, Inc. v. NRC* (1976).

The central issue in *Vermont Yankee* was the legitimacy of a rule by the Atomic Energy Commission, subsequently renamed the Nuclear Regulatory Commission (NRC). The rule assigned numerical values to the environmental effects of the nuclear fuel cycle, which then were factored into a cost-benefit analysis when licensing individual reactors. The Natural Resources Defense Council (NRDC), a non-profit environmental interest group, sought to overturn the rule because the quantification of environmental values basically rendered them "insignificant" for the NRC. In its rulemaking proceedings, the NRC had allowed oral comments from environmental and other interest groups, but had not permitted discovery proceedings or the cross-examination of witnesses. At dispute was evidence pertaining to the adequacy of waste disposal techniques. A twenty-page statement by the director of the agency's Division of Waste Management and Transportation was read during the oral hearings. Yet, the NRDC argued, and the appellate court agreed, that the statement was superficial and failed to consider such things as actual experience with the disposal of radioactive wastes.

When overturning portions of the NRC's rule, Bazelon emphasized that "a reviewing court is incapable of making a penetrating analysis of highly scientific or technical subject matter on its own, it must depend on the agency's expertise, as reflected in the statement of basis and purpose, to organize the record, to distill the major issues which were ventilated and to articulate its reasoning with regard to each of them."[11] The appellate court presumed a "hard look" at regulatory agencies' decisions.

[11] *Natural Resources Defense Council, Inc. v. NRC*, 547 F.2d 633, 642 (D.C. Cir. 1976).

But, Bazelon went on to argue that there was an inadequate record to enable the court's strict scrutiny, and therefore to support the NRC's ruling. The inadequacy of the record in turn led him to insist that the commission's rulemaking procedures were inadequate as well. To put the matter differently, inadequate (that is, not fully adversarial) procedures produce inadequate records—records that are not as detailed as those of trial courts and do not permit detailed judicial review of the substantive basis for agencies' decisions.

Bazelon left no doubt that the NRC was to adopt more rigorous procedures that would produce more detailed records of the basis for its decisions. When remanding the case back to the commission, he offered the following directions:

> Many procedural devices for creating a genuine dialogue on these is-
> sues were available to the agency—including informal conferences be-
> tween intervenors and staff, document discovery, interrogations, tech-
> nical advisory committees comprised of outside experts with differing
> perspectives, limited cross-examination, funding independent research
> by intervenors, detailed annotation of technical reports, surveys of ex-
> isting literature, memoranda explaining methodology. We do not pre-
> sume to intrude on the agency's province by dictating which, if any, of
> these devices it must adopt to flesh out the record. It may be that no
> combination of the procedures mentioned above will prove adequate,
> and the agency will be required to develop new procedures to accom-
> plish the innovative task of implementing NEPA through rulemaking.
> . . . Whatever techniques the Commission adopts, before it promulgates
> a rule limiting further consideration of waste disposal and reprocessing
> issues, it must in one way or another generate a record in which the
> factual issues are fully developed.[12]

Bazelon's opinion put into sharp relief the underlying political question of how far courts should go when reviewing regulatory decisions. Yet, in many ways, *Vermont Yankee* was a very poor vehicle for the Supreme Court's rejection of Bazelon's approach. Here, the appellate court had not actually mandated any specific additional procedures. Rather, it only ordered the NRC to employ such procedures as would guarantee a "ventilation of the issues" and permit a searching judicial scrutiny of the record.

[12] Id. at 653–654.

Writing for a unanimous Court (minus Justices Powell and Blackmun, who did not participate) in *Vermont Yankee*, Justice William Rehnquist went out of his way to reject Bazelon's "strict procedures ensure correct decisions" approach as judicial "Monday morning quarterbacking." Adjudicatory procedures do not per se assure the "correct" or the "best" regulatory decision, he correctly observed. Agencies might adopt them simply in the hope of avoiding judicial review and reversal of their decisions. But courts alone do not have the power to compel agencies to adopt them. Further emphasizing that such an activist exercise of judicial review "clearly runs the risk of 'propel[ling] the courts into the domain which Congress has set aside exclusively for the administrative agency,' " Rehnquist castigated the D.C. Circuit for thwarting the "very basic tenet of administrative law that agencies should be free to fashion their own rules of procedure."[13]

Vermont Yankee remains noteworthy in that the Court sought to stem the tide toward increasing procedural complexity in agency rulemaking and ever more intervention by federal courts when reviewing agency rules. The Court noted that when regulations affect "a very small number of persons," the constitutional guarantees for due process may require additional procedural safeguards. But, here, Rehnquist indicated, where there were no "constitutional constraints or extremely compelling circumstances the administrative agencies 'should be free to fashion their own rules of procedure and to pursue methods of inquiry capable of permitting them to discharge their multitudinous duties.' "[14] The issue of what process is due should be left to Congress and federal agencies.

Although the Supreme Court sought to put an end to lower courts' imposition of adversarial procedures on agency rulemaking, it did little to counter the other trend in regulatory politics, namely, that of more searching judicial oversight of regulatory decisions. Instead of reversing the D.C. Circuit's ruling in *Vermont Yankee*, the Court

---

[13] *Vermont Yankee Nuclear Power Corp. v. Natural Resources Defense Council, Inc.*, 435 U.S. 519 (1978) at 547 and 545, quoting *SEC v. Chenery Corp.*, 332 U.S. 194, 196 (1947).

[14] Id. at 542 and 543, quoting *FCC v. Schreiber*, 381 U.S. 279, 290 (1965), which was quoting *FCC v. Pottsville Broadcasting Co.* 309 U.S. 134, 143 (1940).

remanded the case back to the appellate court so that it might again "review the [Commission's] rule as the Administrative Procedure Act provides." In effect, the Court endorsed the position of Judge Edward Tamm, who had concurred in the lower court's initial decision but who wanted it to "remand [the] case to the Commission to insure that it has taken a hard look at the waste storage issue."[15]

Unresolved Issues

Vermont Yankee stands for less judicial imposition of procedural complexity on agencies but also for greater scutiny of the reasons offered by agencies for their regulations. The "hard look" approach, however, remains no less interventionist than that advanced by Bazelon and rejected in *Vermont Yankee*. Rather than presuming the "reasonableness" of regulation, or limiting judicial review of agencies to the APA's standard of "arbitrary, capricious, an abuse of discretion," *Vermont Yankee* sanctioned heightened scrutiny of the basis for regulations.

Heightened judicial scrutiny of the basis for agencies' decisions, as we saw in the last chapter, is basically ill-defined; often excessive; and problematic in a number of ways for the efficiency, effectiveness, and legitimacy of agency regulation of health-safety and environmental risks. The ill-defined nature of the "hard look" approach and the inevitable problems of judges' differing views of the adequacy of the reasons for regulation are well illustrated by the Supreme Court's review of challenges to the OSHA's regulation of benzene and cotton dust.

When Reasons Are Not Enough: Regulating Benzene

When have agencies reasoned enough? When does the judicial demand for the reasoned elaboration of regulations come to an end? Even when there is a full record setting forth the reasons for regulating health-safety or environmental risks, what is to stop courts from substituting their own risk assessments and policy judgments?

[15] *Natural Resources Defense Council, Inc. v. United States Nuclear Regulatory Commission*, 547 F.2d 633, 658 (D.C. Cir. 1976) (Tamm, J., con. op.).

These are the hard questions left unanswered by the Court's embrace of the "hard look" approach. The problematic nature of that approach is revealed in the rulings of the lower courts and the Supreme Court on reviewing challenges to regulations governing the risks of exposure to benzene, in *Industrial Union Department, AFL-CIO v. American Petroleum Institute* (1980), and to cotton dust, in *American Textile Manufacturers Institute, Inc. v. Donovan* (1981).

OSHA's Regulation of Benzene

For more than eighty years, exposure to high levels of benzene was associated with adverse health affects. Not until the 1970s, though, did studies reveal that low levels of exposure—at levels of less than 100 ppm (parts per million)—might be linked to leukemia, nonmalignant blood disorders, and chromosomal damage. During those years, the production and use of benzene, a transparent colorless liquid, rapidly increased. As a raw material for other synthetic-organic chemicals, benzene was widely used in detergents, gasoline, and rubber tires. By 1976, approximately 11 billion pounds of benzene were produced annually for use by petrochemical and refining industries in the United States. According to the OSHA, almost 200,000 workers were exposed to benzene in the workplace.[16]

As the possible health risks of occupational exposure to benzene became of greater concern to the scientific community, labor unions mounted pressure on the OSHA to regulate the levels of benzene exposure in the workplace. In the Occupational Safety and Health Act, Congress delegated the power to regulate carcinogenic and toxic substances by authorizing the OSHA to set standards that "most adequately assure, to the extent feasible, on the basis of the best available evidence, that no employee will suffer material impairment of health or functional capacity."[17]

In 1971, the OSHA responded initially by adopting a "consensus standard" from the American National Standards Institute, prescribing that during an eight-hour day workers not be exposed to an

[16] U.S. Department of Labor, Occupational Safety and Health Administration, *Economic Impact Statement: Benzene*, 2 vols. (Washington, D.C.: OSHA, 1977), at vol. 1, 5-2.

[17] Occupational Safety and Health Act, Section 6(b)(5).

average of more than 10 ppm, with the highest concentration of no more than 25 ppm and peak exposures of 50 ppm for no more than ten minutes during an eight-hour shift.

Further studies of low levels of exposure to benzene led the National Institute for Occupational Safety and Health (NIOSH), the research arm of the OSHA, to designate benzene a suspected carcinogen in 1974. Labor unions, particularly the rubberworkers' union, then intensified efforts to get the OSHA to revise its benzene standard. But, the OSHA resisted because it viewed available scientific evidence as still insufficient to justify a lower standard. Two years later, however, the NIOSH revised its earlier position, finding benzene to be a leukenogen and recommending that workers not be exposed to more than 1 ppm.[18]

Coincidentally, Democratic President Jimmy Carter won election in 1976. His administration quickly moved to regain what it considered lost ground in health-safety and environmental protection during the Republican Nixon and Ford administrations. The OSHA in particular had been widely criticized for not moving fast enough in regulating carcinogens. Its new director, Eula Bingham, a toxicologist familiar with the benzene controversy, immediately pressed for a new standard in order to show that the agency now meant business in regulating risks.

On May 3, 1977, the OSHA issued a temporary emergency standard for occupational exposure to benzene at 1 ppm. The secretary of labor had gathered more than fifty volumes of exhibits and testimony in deciding that exposure to benzene, even at the level of 1 ppm, creates risks of leukemia, cancer, chromosomal damage, and a variety of nonmalignant but potentially fatal blood disorders. The OSHA, however, based the benzene standard largely on its general policy for regulating carcinogens.

Like other regulatory agencies, the OSHA maintained that there is no safe threshold level of carcinogenic exposure and that the present state of science renders it impossible to calculate the number of lives that would be saved by a 1 ppm benzene standard. Central to the dispute, thus, was whether the OSHA could justify its regulation of benzene at the lower level of exposure based on its general carcinogen

---

[18] See 43 *Fed. Reg.* 5919 (1978).

policy, or whether it had to give concrete evidence of the risks, costs, and benefits of lowering the standard for benzene exposure.

The benzene standard was immediately attacked by the American Petroleum Institute and other industry groups. They succeeded in getting the Fifth Circuit Court of Appeals to issue a restraining order on the enforcement of the standard, and it never went into effect. Subsequently, the OSHA announced a proposed permanent standard for exposures at the level of 1 ppm and published an environmental impact statement for the standard.[19] During the summer of 1977, the OSHA held a full month of hearings and gathered testimony from other agencies, unions, industrial groups, and interested parties. The final standard, basically the same as that originally proposed, was announced on February 10, 1978.

Industry groups continued their attack. Central to their assault was the scientific basis for lowering the standard. Although there was evidence that benzene is toxic at high levels, the risks at low levels of exposure remained impossible to quantify. "It is not clear," the agency admitted when announcing its rule, "what adverse health effects occur below 20 ppm."[20] At very low levels of exposure, it is hard to show that benzene causes leukemia. The long latency between exposure and the onset of diseases further complicates matters. In addition, benzene appears to affect animals differently than it does humans, and so animal bioassays are not helpful. As with other regulation of carcinogens and toxins, there were large scientific uncertainties about the effects of different levels of exposure and no hard evidence to justify the regulation of benzene at the level of 1 ppm.

The OSHA's rationale for the benzene regulation ultimately rested on its policy for regulating carcinogens—its "generic carcinogen policy," as it became known.[21] That policy in turn was based on the no-safe-threshold theory of carcinogenesis, discussed in Chapter 1. Under the policy, once a substance is found to be a carcinogen (at any level of exposure), all levels of exposure are deemed to

[19] 42 *Fed. Reg.* 27452, 27455 (1977).

[20] 43 *Fed. Reg.* 5918 (February 10, 1978).

[21] 45 *Fed. Reg.* 5001–5296 (January 22, 1980).

put workers at risk and to justify regulation. The only limitation in setting standards, in the view of the agency, was its congressional mandate (in Section 6(b)(5)) requiring that they be as protective as feasible. Economic and administrative feasibility was the only limitation on regulating the levels of exposure to carcinogens. The OSHA could set a standard at zero exposure if that were deemed feasible. The 1 ppm standard set for benzene was not the lowest feasible standard but, in the view of the OSHA, one that was workable administratively and for the industry.

The Fifth Circuit's Ruling

In a challenge brought by the American Petroleum Institute and a coalition of other benzene producers and users, the Court of Appeals for the Fifth Circuit struck the standard down. In *American Petroleum Institute v. Occupational Safety and Health Administration* (1978), the appellate court accepted the OSHA's estimates of the costs of its standard and that it was feasible. But, it ruled that there was insufficient support for the estimated benefits of the standard. Although agency estimates were supported by scientific and economic analysis, in the court's view, they were not sufficient evidence.

Basically, the Fifth Circuit found that the OSHA had not given concrete evidence for its regulation of benzene. In this, the court departed from other federal courts holding that regulations may be upheld, even when there remain scientific uncertainties, so long as agencies comply with their congressional mandates and set forth their reasons for particular standards.[22]

The Fifth Circuit followed one of its own earlier rulings, in *Aqua Slide 'N' Dive Corporation v. Consumer Product Safety Commission* (1978). There, the CPSC's safety standard for pool slides was overturned due to a failure to undertake a cost-benefit analysis. Although the congressional mandates for regulating health-safety risks by the CPSC and the OSHA are different (as discussed in Chapter 4 and shown in Appendix B), the Fifth Circuit found them "precisely similar." The

[22] See *American Iron & Steel Institute v. OSHA*, 577 F.2d 825 (3d Cir. 1978) (regulating coke ovens); *Society of the Plastics Industry v. OSHA*, 509 F.2d 1301 (2d Cir. 1975) (regulating vinyl chloride); and *Industrial Union Department, AFL-CIO v. Hodgson*, 499 F.2d 467 (D.C. Cir. 1974) (regulating asbestos dust).

agency had estimated the costs of complying with its benzene standard and determined that they were feasible, which the industry did not contest. But, the court ruled that it failed to show that "the relationship between the benefits and costs of the benzene standard is reasonable." The court therefore concluded that the benzene regulation was not supported by sufficient analysis and concrete evidence of "the expected benefits in light of the burdens to be imposed by the standard."[23]

Divisions Within the Supreme Court on Review

What should be judicially considered sufficient analysis and concrete evidence? That proved no less divisive for the Justices of the Supreme Court. When deciding an appeal of the Fifth Circuit's ruling on the benzene standard, in *Industrial Union Department, AFL-CIO v. Marshall* (1980), the Court was badly divided. A bare majority affirmed the lower court's ruling, though on different grounds. The majority, furthermore, could not agree on how far to go when scrutinizing the agency's justification for the benzene standard. Justice John Paul Stevens's opinion announcing the decision was joined (and joined only in part) by Chief Justice Burger and Justices Potter Stewart and Lewis F. Powell. Rehnquist provided the crucial fifth vote but issued his own separate opinion, as did Chief Justice Burger and Justice Powell, even though they joined parts of the plurality opinion accompanying the Court's ruling. The various positions taken by the Justices show how widely judges may differ in their responses to agency regulations.

Stevens struck down the standard on the ground that the OSHA failed to show a significant risk at or below the level of 10 ppm. He did so by rejecting the agency's view both of its congressional mandate for regulating occupational risks and of the substantive basis for regulating benzene.

According to Stevens, Section 3(8) of the OSH Act, authorizing the regulation of health and safety risks as "reasonably necessary," modifies the agency's mandate (in Section 6(b)(5)) for setting standards as protective as "feasible." The government had contended that

---

[23] *American Petroleum Institute v. Occupational Safety and Health Administration*, 581 F.2d 493, 502 and 503 (5th Cir. 1978).

Section 3(8) was basically meaningless as a limitation on regulations. But, Stevens held that under Section 3(8) the agency must make a "finding" that particular workplaces are not safe, and then quantify a "certain" level of risk showing that the risks are indeed "significant," as well as demonstrate that a new standard will bring identifiable benefits at feasible costs for regulated industries.

Stevens's opinion strongly implied that the OSHA should undertake a cost/benefit analysis, yet he also held that the basis for even the old benzene standard at the level of 10 ppm was insufficient. Hence, he did not further scrutinize the basis for the 1 ppm standard. The OSHA had not made a showing (or rather had asserted that it was scientifically impossible to show) that there are "significant health risks" at low levels of exposure. Stevens accordingly rejected its regulation as unsupported by evidence, and as resting simply on the assumption that the risks of leukemia will decrease as exposure levels decrease.[24] The presumption of significant risks, however, was based on the OSHA's carcinogen policy, which had been developed in light of the practical difficulties of getting hard evidence and risk assessments of low levels of exposure to carcinogens. For Stevens that policy was an inadequate basis for setting standards. More than reasoned explanations of agency policy were required: there must be hard evidence of significant risks and a showing that regulation will in fact reduce those risks.

What should count as a justification for regulation split not only the Court but also those Justices who agreed on overturning the benzene standard. In particular, Powell departed from Stevens's view of the OSHA's burden of proof. He likewise rejected the agency's "carcinogen policy" as a substitute for hard evidence. But, since the OSHA had reduced the previous limit on exposures by a factor of 10 at the cost of hundreds of millions of dollars, Powell thought that the agency had implicitly shown that benzene posed significant risks. According to him, the agency still failed to provide substantial evidence for its regulation. It was not enough to assert that the quantification of risks was impossible, and that the OSHA's standard was supported by the "best available evidence" as well as its generic "carcinogen policy." For Powell, the agency also had to formally show substantial evidence

____

[24] *Industrial Union Department, AFL-CIO v. Marshall,* 448 U.S. 607 (1980).

for its "carcinogen policy" and the lack of empirical data on the risks of low levels of benzene exposure.

The difference between Stevens and Powell might be put this way: For the former, hard evidence was needed, rather than the agency's "carcinogen policy" (which had been developed because of the absence of hard evidence on carcinogenic risks at low levels). The latter was willing to allow the agency to regulate risks when there was little or no hard evidence, but he wanted the agency to document the lack of reliable data and the impossibility of predicting low-level risks on the basis of high-level data.

Rehnquist provided the crucial fifth vote in the case, but he took an entirely different approach. Like the four dissenters, he did not think that Section 3(8) of the OSH Act modified the feasibility requirement in Section 6(b)(5). But unlike them and Stevens's plurality, he thought that Section 6(b)(5) was unconstitutionally vague. It simply gave the agency too much discretion in regulating occupational risks. Rehnquist alone would resurrect the long-discarded nondelegation doctrine to invalidate the OSH Act as too broad. It is up to Congress to provide more precise regulatory standards.

Not surprisingly, the four dissenters sharply criticized the majority for substituting its view for that of the agency. Thurgood Marshall, joined by William Brennan, Byron White, and Harry Blackmun, characterized the majority's ruling as insensitive to the high level of scientific complexity and uncertainty in regulating carcinogens. Marshall reminded them that so often in science-policy disputes "the factual finger points, it does not conclude," and hence agencies must make fundamental policy choices.

The dissenters agreed that courts should take a "hard look" at the basis for regulations. But, here, the majority went too far. What the majority had done was impose its own philosophy of regulating risk for that of the agency. Just "as the Constitution 'does not enact Mr. Herbert Spenser's *Social Statics*,' " Marshall concluded, "so the responsibility to scrutinize federal administrative action does not authorize this Court to strike its own balance between the costs and benefits of occupational safety standards."[25]

[25] Id. at 696 n. 9.

As the dissenters pointed out, under the "hard look" approach reviewing courts may be tempted to substitute their own philosophy of risk regulation for that of agencies. Stevens's opinion certainly gives that impression. What united the majority was the perception that "safe" is not the same as "risk-free." But, when Stevens explained that observation, he unwittingly revealed the problematic nature of extensive judicial scrutiny of the basis for health-safety and environmental regulation.

Stevens cited driving an automobile as one example of an activity generally recognized as "safe." Yet, in the United States roughly 50,000 persons die each year in automobile accidents, while only about 15,000 die in the workplace.[26] Applying the kind of risk/cost/benefit analysis that Stevens suggested was necessary, there would be comparatively speaking no need for any health and safety legislation in the first place. Congress, however, had already deemed the health-safety risks of the workplace to be serious and a "significant risk" when it passed the OSH Act. Moreover, five years after the ruling in *American Petroleum Institute*, and after the more conservative administration of President Ronald Reagan imposed greater oversight on agencies by the Office of Management and Budget (OMB) and required by executive order a cost/benefit analysis for all new regulations, the OSHA announced in 1985 that it would reissue its standard for limiting benzene exposure at the level of 1 ppm.[27]

[26] See U.S. Congress, 91st Cong., 2d Sess., Senate, Sen. Rept. No. 1282, *Legislative History of the Occupational Safety and Health Act* (Washington, D.C.: Government Printing Office, 1970).

[27] See P. Perl, "OSHA Offers New Rules on Workers' Exposure to Benzene, Formaldehyde," *The Washington Post* A25 (December 4, 1985). As one of his first official acts, President Reagan issued in 1981 Executive Order 12291 mandating that all federal agencies undertake a cost-benefit analysis when promulgating new regulations. That order in 1985 was supplemented by another, Executive Order 12498, which further extended the OMB's oversight of new regulations. For a critical discussion, see U.S. Congress, 97th Cong., 1st Sess., House of Representatives, Committee on Energy and Commerce, *Presidential Control of Agency Rulemaking* (Washington, D.C.: Government Printing Office, 1981). See also General Accounting Office, *Cost-Benefit Analysis Can Be Useful in Assessing Environmental Regulations, Despite Limitations* (General Accounting Office, April 6, 1984).

Toward Clarity: Regulating Cotton Dust

The Court's ruling in *American Petroleum Institute* generated considerable confusion. In particular, it remained unclear whether the OSHA had to undertake a cost-benefit analysis in support of the "feasibility" of its regulations. More generally, it was unclear how much reasoned elaboration for regulation courts would demand. The Supreme Court sought clarity a year later when reviewing the OSHA's cotton dust standard.

OSHA Regulates Cotton Dust

For more than a century, a number of respiratory diseases have been associated with the inhalation of cotton dust. Cotton dust is the residue of fibers that result from the processing of cotton. Workers may suffer from byssinosis, a pulmonary condition that ranges in severity from a cough to the disease known as "brown lung," which is a disabling breathlessness and tightness of the chest. About 35,000 workers currently suffer from "brown lung" disease and another 100,000 suffer some degree of byssinosis. There are between 250,000 and 800,000 workers at risk in the cotton industry.[28]

It was not until 1964 that cotton dust was first regulated under the Walsh-Healey Public Contracts Act of 1936. At that time, the standard for ambient cotton dust was set at 1,000 micrograms per cubic meter (1,000 $\mu g/m^3$). In 1974, in light of further studies, the American Conference of Governmental Industrial Hygienists revised its standard, which had been the basis for the 1964 regulation, to limit exposures at the level of 200 $\mu g/m^3$.

In response to these developments, the OSHA initiated rulemaking proceedings in 1974 and four years later promulgated a new standard for cotton dust.[29] The standard limited exposure levels in an

[28] See National Institute for Occupational Safety and Health, Center for Disease Control, *Criteria for a Recommended Standard for Occupational Exposure to Cotton Dust* (HEW Publication No. 75-118), at 28–33; and U.S. Department of Labor, *Report to Congress: Cotton Dust—Review of Alternative Technological Standards and Control Technologies* (U.S. Department of Labor, May 14, 1978).

[29] See Advance Notice of Proposed Rule Making, 39 *Fed. Reg.* 44769 (December 27, 1974); Notice of Proposed Rule Making, 41 *Fed. Reg.* 56498 (December 28, 1976); and Notice of Final Rule, 43 *Fed. Reg.* 27350 (June 23, 1978).

eight-hour period to 200 $\mu g/m^3$ for yarn manufacturing, 750 $\mu g/m^3$ for slashing and weaving operations, and 500 $\mu g/m^3$ for all other processing activities.[30] Since cotton dust is not considered a carcinogen, it did not fall under the OSHA's generic carcinogen policy. The agency nonetheless interpreted its mandate to require the most protective standard feasible. But, the agency did not undertake a cost-benefit analysis.

The new cotton dust standard was immediately challenged by the American Textile Manufacturers Institute and the National Cotton Council of America, among other industry groups. At dispute was whether the new standard would yield significant benefits for workers. Attorneys for the cotton industry argued that the agency failed to demonstrate that the benefits of the new standard outweighed the cost of compliance. In their view, a cost-benefit analysis was implicitly required by Section 6(b)(5) of the OSH Act. This, of course, was one of the arguments that the petroleum industry had asserted when attacking the benzene standard, and also one that a majority of the Supreme Court appeared to view favorably in *American Petroleum Institute*.[31]

The D.C. Circuit Rules One Way

On appeal initially in the Court of Appeals for the D.C. Circuit, the cotton dust standard was upheld by a three-judge panel in *AFL-CIO v. Marshall* (1979). Bazelon, writing for the panel, rejected the argument that a cost-benefit analysis was necessary, and held that the OSH Act requires simply that standards be as protective as feasible. The agency need not support its regulations by a cost-benefit analysis, Bazelon reasoned, because Congress had not mandated such an analysis. To the contrary, Congress recognized that occupational safety standards would be costly. In addition, Bazelon argued, cost-benefit analysis would not necessarily improve regulations. As the National Academy of Sciences and others have concluded, there are severe problems in quantifying many costs and benefits—particularly in valuing human life and health given the difficulties of interpersonal and intergenerational comparisons.

[30] 29 C.F.R. Section 1910.1043.

[31] Brief for the Petitioners, *American Textile Manufacturers Institute v. Donovan*, at 22 and 51.

After deciding that the agency need not undertake a cost-benefit analysis, Bazelon turned to whether there was a sufficient basis for the regulation. That task after the Court's ruling in *Vermont Yankee*, he claimed, is confined to determining "whether the agency sufficiently supported its feasibility determination with material in the record." Here, the record exceeded 105,000 pages, including comments from 263 interested parties and testimony from 109 participants heard during fourteen days of public hearings. He concluded that the agency "had fairly considered and took account of objections to its assessments of technological feasibility for the textile industry."[32]

The Fifth Circuit Rules the Other Way

Although the cotton dust regulation survived review by the Court of Appeals for the District of Columbia Circuit, it was subsequently attacked by other industry groups in the Court of Appeals for the Fifth Circuit. They challenged the standards for exposure to cotton dust during the ginning process—the process by which cotton lint and seed are separated so that the former may be processed by textile mills, and the latter used by cottonseed oil mills. Four gin employee organizations later intervened and countered that the standards actually did not adequately protect workers' health.

In *Texas Independent Ginners Association v. Marshall* (1980), a three-judge panel in the Fifth Circuit struck down the regulations. In contrast to the D.C. Circuit, the Fifth Circuit ruled that cost-benefit analysis was required. The court did so based on its own earlier holdings and the Supreme Court's opinions in the benzene case.[33]

The issue of cost-benefit analysis in support of occupational health and safety standards was clearly before the Supreme Court when it granted an appeal from the D.C. Circuit's ruling on the cotton dust standard in *American Textile Manufacturers Institute v. Donovan* (1980). The Court's ambiguous ruling in the benzene case had invited confusion, and circuit courts were divided over whether a cost-benefit analysis was necessary to support occupational health and safety regulations.

---

[32] *AFL-CIO v. Marshall*, 617 F.2d 636, 656 and 658 (D.C. Cir. 1979).

[33] *Texas Independent Ginners Association v. Marshall*, 630 F.2d 398, 409–412 (5th Cir. 1980).

The controversy over cotton dust further escalated when the Reagan administration, which had just come into office, asked the Court not to decide the central question. It wanted the Court to remand the case back to the OSHA for further consideration. Under President Reagan's 1981 executive order, requiring a cost-benefit analysis for all new federal regulations, the OSHA would have to undertake a cost-benefit analysis in support of its cotton dust standard. This, of course, is precisely what the agency during the years of the Carter administration had maintained it was not required to do.

The Supreme Court Remains Divided

A bare majority of the Supreme Court in *American Textile Manufacturers Institute* ruled that the agency was not required to undertake a cost-benefit analysis, and indicated that it was improper for courts to require such an analysis. Brennan wrote the opinion for the majority, which included his three fellow dissenters from the benzene ruling. They were joined by Stevens, the author of the benzene decision. Stewart and Rehnquist, along with Burger, dissented. Powell did not participate in the consideration of the case.

Besides the central question of whether Section 6(b)(5) of the OSH Act requires a cost-benefit analysis, two other related issues were decided. The majority affirmed the D.C. Circuit's holding that the agency had marshalled substantial evidence to justify its finding of a significant risk and one that would be alleviated by its new standard. But, the Court struck down one part of the regulation—requiring a guarantee of the wages of employees who are transferred to other jobs within a company because they are unable to wear the required respirators in the workplace—because it was not sufficiently related to the achievement of the agency's health and safety goals.

When turning to the issue of whether a cost-benefit analysis is required, the majority followed the lower court's interpretation of the congressional history of the OSH Act. In addition, Brennan relied on dictionary definitions of "feasible" to conclude that the word means "capable of being done." That basically settled the matter for the majority, though it also pointed out that under other statutes Congress had specifically required a cost-benefit analysis but not here.

The Court's holding in the cotton dust case remains significant in that the OSH Act does not, and a reviewing court cannot, require a cost-benefit analysis in support of occupational health-safety regulations. Congress, as it were, already struck a balance in Section 6(b)(5) by requiring regulations that are "feasible." The standard of "feasibility" was the result of political compromise within Congress. Despite dissenting Justice Rehnquist's view that the Court should have struck down the standard as unconstitutionally vague and should require Congress to enact more specific guidelines, the process of coalition-building usually works against achieving greater precision in congressional legislation. Moreover, the "feasibility" standard permits different administrations to differ in their interpretations of what should count as "feasible."

Changes in the electorate and shifts in public perceptions of risks are registered by changes in the White House. The majority in the cotton dust case appeared sensitive to the need to preserve that measure of democratic control over regulation. Brennan's opinion accepted the position, advanced in the benzene case by Stevens, that Section 3(8) modifies Section 6(b)(5) of the OSH Act. Brennan also suggested that that section may be interpreted, as the Reagan administration contends, to require a cost-benefit analysis.

The cotton dust ruling thus does not preclude the OSHA from undertaking cost-benefit analysis. Rather, just as the Court in *Vermont Yankee* signaled the end to courts imposing more procedural complexity on agency rulemaking, the Court in the cotton dust case appeared to warn lower courts that they may not on their own require agencies to undertake more rigorous analysis than clearly required by Congress or mandated by the White House.

Judicial Review and Deregulation

Under the "hard look" doctrine, federal appellate courts will remain an elusive senior partner in regulatory politics. This is precisely because of the ill-defined and open-ended nature of judicial demands for agency reasons.

Appellate courts may demand more reasons than agencies have (or can give) for regulating particular risks. They may also, as in the benzene and cotton dust controversies, differ in their views of the kinds of reasons that agencies must give in support of regulations.

The judicial demand for more reasons may therefore serve to under-cut or enhance the regulation of risks. The Fifth Circuit, as we saw, tends to demand more from agencies in order to strike down regula-tions. By contrast, at least in the 1970s, the D.C. Circuit generally tended to be more supportive of health-safety and environmental regulations. The regional differences among the circuits thus invite conflicts among appellate courts when reviewing agencies' regula-tions.

Courts will continue to have a role in supervising the regulation of health-safety and environmental risks. This is so both because of the "hard look" doctrine and because of the Reagan administration's push for deregulation.

Consider, first, appellate courts' demands for the reasoned elab-oration of the basis for regulating health-safety and environmental risks. Under the "hard look" doctrine, federal courts in the 1970s elevated the threshold for administrative rationality. At a minimum, agencies must state clearly their scientific and technological assump-tions; reveal the data, methodology, and literature on which they rely; explain their rejection of alternative theories and technological op-tions; and, finally, articulate their rationales for setting particular standards in a manner that permits public comment and judicial scrutiny.[34]

By the early 1980s, the Supreme Court was clearly trying to stem the trend toward demanding more and more reasons for agencies' regulatory standards. Following the ruling in the cotton dust case, for example, the Court rejected the D.C. Circuit's view that the Nuclear Regulatory Commission (NRC) had to weigh the psychological effects on local residents before allowing the start-up of the undamaged nuclear reactor at Three Mile Island in Pennsylvania.[35]

---

[34] See, e.g., *Portland Cement Association v. Ruckelshaus*, 468 F.2d 375, 393 (D.C. Cir. 1973); *International Harvester Co. v. Ruckelshaus*, 478 F.2d 615, 651 (D.C. Cir. 1973); *Amoco Oil Co. v. EPA*, 501 F.2d 722, 738 (D.C. Cir. 1974); *American Petroleum Institute v. Costle*, 609 F.2d 20 (D.C. Cir. 1981); *Lead Indus-tries Association v. EPA*, 627 F.2d 416 (D.C. Cir. 1980); and *National Lime Association v. EPA*, 627 F.2d 416 (D.C. Cir. 1980).

[35] *People Against Nuclear Energy v. U.S. Nuclear Regulatory Commission*, 678 F.2d 222 (D.C. Cir. 1982), overruled in *Metropolitan Edison Co. v. People Against Nuclear Energy*, 460 U.S. 752 (1983).

For a unanimous Court in *Metropolitan Edison Co. v. People Against Nuclear Energy* (1983), Rehnquist rejected the lower court's contention that the NRC had to consider the psychological effects of local residents of the plant in a required "environmental impact statement" under the National Environmental Protection Act (NEPA). He did so for two reasons. Courts alone have no power to demand such considerations, and the language of NEPA does not suggest that Congress intended agencies to consider such psychological effects. In addition, he noted that it "would be extraordinarily difficult for agencies to differentiate between 'genuine' claims of psychological health damage and claims that are grounded solely in disagreement with a democratically adopted policy."

The tone of the Three Mile Island ruling underscores the Court's striving to limit how far courts go when demanding reasons for regulatory decisions. The Court sent a signal to lower courts to accord agencies greater deference in regulation. At least to Judge Patricia Wald of the Court of Appeals for the District of Columbia, that means a less rigorous application of the "hard look" doctrine and some retrenchment from Leventhal's vision of a "constructive partnership" between courts and agencies in regulatory politics.[36]

Reviewing EPA's "Bubble Policy"

The Court indeed appears to be calling for more deference to federal agencies. In *Chevron v. Natural Resources Defense Council* (1984), for example, the Court unanimously overturned a decision by the D.C. Circuit that had struck down the controversial "bubble policy" of the EPA in regulating air pollution.[37]

The dispute centered on whether the EPA could revise an earlier policy, requiring each emission source within a plant to be assessed independently. The agency substituted a policy giving a plantwide or "bubble" definition of a polluting "stationary" source under the Clean

---

[36] See P. Wald, "Negotiation of Environmental Disputes: A New Role for the Courts?" 10 *Columbia Journal of Environmental Law* 1 (1985).

[37] *Natural Resources Defense Council, Inc. v. Gorsuch*, 685 F.2d 718 (D.C. Cir. 1982), overturned in *Chevron v. Natural Resources Defense Council*, 467 U.S. 837 (1984). Justices O'Connor, Marshall, and Rehnquist did not participate in the decision.

Air Act. The policy was supported by industry, some states, and the Reagan administration as a more cost-effective means of achieving air pollution control. At the same time, environmental groups criticized it for being less protective. The "bubble policy" allows particular pollution-emitting sources to exceed air pollution control standards, so long as the emissions on a plantwide basis are at or below federal air quality standards.

Neither the legislative history nor the applicable definitions of the "stationary source" in the Clean Air Act address this issue.[38] The D.C. Circuit ruled that the bubble policy ran counter to the purposes of the Clean Air Act. On appeal, the Supreme Court rejected that conclusion for being "a static judicial definition of the term 'stationary source.' " As Stevens explained, "if the statute is silent or ambiguous with respect to the specific issue, the question for the courts is whether the agency's answer is based on a permissible construction of the statute."

To an even greater degree than in the cotton dust controversy, the majority in the bubble-policy case went out of its way to emphasize that judges should defer to agencies and agencies to the directives of the White House. Stevens's explanation merits quoting:

> Judges are not experts in the field, and are not part of either political branch of the government. Courts must, in some cases, reconcile competing political interests, but not on the basis of the judges' personal policy preferences. In contrast, an agency to which Congress had delegated policymaking responsibilities may, within the limits of that delegation, properly rely upon the incumbent administration's views of wise policy to inform its judgments. While agencies are not directly accountable to the people, the Chief Executive is, and it is entirely appropriate for this political branch of the Government to make such policy choices—resolving the competing interests which Congress itself either inadvertently did not resolve, or intentionally left to be resolved by the agency charged with the administration of the statute in light of everyday realities.[39]

[38] 42 U.S.C. Section 7441l(a)(3)(1982).
[39] *Chevron v. Natural Resources Defense Council,* 467 U.S.837, 865 (1984).

This language reinforces the push in earlier rulings toward greater judicial deference to the regulatory policies set by agencies. When upholding the cotton dust standard, promulgated during the Carter administration and attacked by the Reagan administration, Brennan's majority opinion thus suggested that agencies should follow the directives of the White House when interpreting congressional mandates. In the Three Mile Island case, a unanimous Court rejected an expansive reading of congressional language that would force agencies (against the wishes of the White House) to consider more factors and more data than clearly mandated by Congress in support of regulatory decisions. And in the bubble-policy case, a unanimous Court again expressly underscored that courts and agencies should defer to the White House when congressional mandates are ambiguous.

Reviewing the Regulation and Deregulation of Passive Restraints

These rulings suggest a change toward a more deferential relationship between reviewing courts and regulatory agencies, but they actually signal a more important shift from congressional to presidential influence in the regulatory politics. Whereas in the 1970s federal courts largely sought to ensure that agencies complied with (rather than thwarted) the health-safety and environmental goals set by Congress, those courts are now legitimating the power of the White House to reinterpret congressional mandates (within certain bounds). Federal appellate courts are becoming more sensitive to their limitations and to the limits of law in resolving science-policy disputes while also becoming more receptive to the demands of democratic politics, and specifically to shifts in the electorate.

It would be wrong, however, to conclude that the Court has signaled the end of the "hard look" doctrine or uncritically embraced deregulation. To the contrary, appellate courts and the Supreme Court have adapted the "hard look" approach to challenges to deregulation by the Reagan administration. Since deregulation often involves the reversal of an agency's former regulatory policy, in the words of the D.C. Circuit, it may "constitute 'danger signals' that the will of Congress is being ignored."[40]

---

[40] *State Farm Mutual Automobile Insurance Co. v. Department of Transporta-*

When Congress enacts new legislation authorizing deregulation—as it did, for example, with the Airline Deregulation Act of 1978—courts have not questioned regulatory policy changes.[41] But, when deregulation proceeds without congressional authorization, federal courts take a hard look at whether the reversal in policy is irrational, simply politically motivated, or contrary to congressional mandates.

Within the first three years of the Reagan administration, seventy-six regulatory rules inherited from earlier administrations were revised or eliminated. In thirty-four challenges to agencies' deregulation policies, federal courts struck down twenty-two.[42] One of the

---

tion, 680 F.2d 206, 221 (D.C. Cir. 1982). For further discussion, see M. Garland, "Deregulation and Judicial Review," 98 *Harvard Law Review* 507 (1985); and, for a different view, L. Smith, "Judicialization: The Twilight of Administrative Law," 1985 *Duke Law Journal* 427 (1985).

[41] See *North American Van Lines v. ICC*, 666 F.2d 1087 (7th Cir. 1980); *American Trucking Associates v. ICC*, 656 F.2d 1115 (5th Cir. 1981); and *National Small Shipments Traffic Conference, Inc. v. Civil Aeronautics Board*, 618 F.2d 819 (D.C. Cir. 1980).

[42] Agencies' deregulation was struck down in *Office of Communication of the United Church of Christ v. FCC*, 560 F.2d 529 (2d Cir. 1977); *American Trucking Association v. ICC*, 656 F.2d 1115 (5th Cir. 1981); *McGinness v. ICC*, 662 F.2d 853 (D.C. Cir. 1982); *Wheaton Van Lines v. ICC*, 671 F.2d 520 (D.C. Cir. 1982); *State Farm Mutual Automobile Insurance Co. v. Department of Transportation*, 680 F.2d 206 (D.C. Cir. 1982); *Natural Resources Defense Council v. EPA*, 683 F.2d 752 (3d Cir. 1982); *Environmental Defense Fund, Inc. v. Gorsuch*, 713 F.2d 802 (3d Cir. 1982); *Center for Science in the Public Interest v. Department of the Treasury*, 573 F. Supp. 1168 (D.D.C. 1983); *ILGWU v. Donovan*, 772 F.2d 795 (D.C. Cir. 1983); *Office of Communication of the United Church of Christ v. FCC*, 770 F.2d 1413 (D.C. Cir. 1983); *Action on Smoking & Health v. Civil Aeronautics Board*, 699 F.2d 1209 (D.C. Cir. 1983); *Detroit, T. & I.R.R. v. United States*, 725 F.2d 47 (4th Cir. 1984); *Motor Vehicle Manufacturers Association of the United States, Inc. v. State Farm Mutual Automobile Insurance Co.*, 463 U.S. 29 (1983); *Arizona Public Services Co. v. United States*, 742 F.2d 644 (D.C. Cir. 1984); *Brae Corp. v. United States*, 740 F.2d 1023 (D.C. Cir. 1984); *International Brotherhood of Teamsters v. United States*, 735 F.2d 1525 (D.C. Cir. 1984); *New England Coalition on Nuclear Pollution v. Nuclear Regulatory Commission*, 727 F.2d 1127 (D.C. Cir. 1984); *National Association of Broadcasters v. FCC*, 740 F.2d 1190 (D.C. Cir. 1984); and *Coal Exporters Association v. United States*, 745 F.2d 76 (D.C. Cir. 1984).

Federal courts have also upheld deregulation in *Office of Communication of the United Church of Christ v. FCC*, 590 F.2d 1067 (D.C. Cir. 1978); *FCC v. WNCN Listeners Guild*, 450 U.S. 582, 598–599 (1981); *Malrite TV v. FCC*, 693 F.2d 198 (D.C. Cir. 1982); *Computer & Communications Industries Association v. FCC*, 693 F.2d 198 (D.C. Cir. 1982); *Telocator Network of America v. FCC*, 691

most controversial of these deregulation cases led to the Supreme Court's affirmation, in *Motor Vehicle Manufacturers Association v. State Farm Mutual Automobile Insurance Co.* (1983), that courts continue to have a major role in supervising the basis for deregulation, no less than for regulation.

State Farm involved a challenge to the rescission of a safety regulation requiring automobile manufacturers to install automatic crash protection devices in all cars manufactured after September 1982. But like most regulatory controversies, *State Farm* was rooted in a long history of disagreements over the costs and benefits of regulatory policy.

The National Traffic and Motor Vehicle Safety Act of 1966 directed the secretary of the Department of Transportation (DOT) to establish, upon "relevant available motor vehicle safety data," standards that are "reasonable, practicable and appropriate" for motor vehicles. The secretary of DOT delegated to the National Highway Traffic Safety Administration (NHTSA) the responsibility for developing standards for drivers' safety. Initially, in 1967 the NHTSA required under Standard 208 the installation of seatbelts in all automobiles. But it was soon evident that drivers tended not to use seatbelts. Thus the agency considered requiring the installation of "passive restraints"—devices that do not depend for their effectiveness on actions taken by the occupants of a vehicle.

Attention was primarily given to two types of passive restraints—automatic seatbelts and airbags. The first is a traditional seatbelt that is deployed automatically when a passenger enters a vehicle. The second, more expensive device is concealed in the dashboard and steering column and automatically inflates upon impact. After a series of studies, the NHTSA estimated that these passive restraints could

---

F.2d 525 (D.C. Cir. 1982); *NAACP v. FCC,* 682 F.2d 993 (D.C. Cir. 1982); *Western Union Telegram Co. v. FCC,* 674 F.2d 160 (2d Cir. 1982); *Building & Construction Trades Department v. Donovan,* 712 F.2d 611 (D.C. Cir. 1983); *Black Citizens for a Fair Media v. FCC,* 719 F.2d 407 (D.C. Cir. 1983); *National Black Media Coalition v. FCC,* 706 F.2d 1224 (D.C. Cir. 1983); and *World Communications, Inc. v. FCC,* 735 F.2d 1465 (D.C. Cir. 1984).

prevent approximately 12,000 deaths and over 100,000 serious injuries annually.

The agency's rulemaking process began in 1969, when DOT initially proposed a standard requiring the installation of passive restraints. The following year the agency revised Standard 208, and in 1972 it further amended the standard to include passive protection for all cars manufactured after August 1975. To meet the standard, automobile manufacturers at first chose an "ignition interlock" system—which prevented the ignition of a car unless the seatbelts were locked. But that proved highly unpopular with consumers. Opposition was so intense that Congress amended the National Traffic and Motor Vehicle Safety Act to prohibit any vehicle safety standard that requires or permits such a system, as well as to provide for a congressional veto of any driver's safety standard that it found objectionable. The effective date for the installation of passive restraints was also extended until 1976.

President Gerald Ford's secretary of transportation, William Coleman, initiated new rulemaking proceedings. That reexamination concluded that passive restraints would be widely unpopular. To educate the public about the risks of automobile accidents and the need for improved driver's safety, Coleman proposed a demonstration project involving 500,000 cars installed with passive restraints.

The 1976 presidential elections brought another change in policies. President Jimmy Carter named Brock Adams as Coleman's successor. Adams decided that the demonstration project was unnecessary. In 1977, he issued what became known as Modified Standard 208, mandating the phasing-in of passive restraints (either automatic seatbelts or airbags) beginning with large cars in 1982 and extending to all cars by 1984. A conservative "public interest" law firm and a coalition of automobile manufacturers attacked the new standard. But it survived scrutiny in *Pacific Legal Foundation v. Department of Transportation* (1979), as well as a subsequent congressional oversight hearing.

Automobile manufacturers and advocates of deregulation nevertheless continued their attack on passive restraints. They had little success until after the next presidential election. The 1980 election of Ronald Reagan brought in an administration more sympathetic to claims that passive restraints are not cost-effective. Shortly after

Reagan's inauguration, DOT Secretary Drew Lewis reopened the rulemaking process in order to reexamine the cost-effectiveness of Modified Standard 208. Within two months, DOT ordered a one-year delay in the application of the standard to large cars and proposed the possible rescission of the standard. After holding public hearings on October 29, 1981, the NHTSA rescinded the standard for passive restraints.

The NHTSA based its rescission not on new data on the effectiveness of passive restraints but on changes in the automobile industry. In 1977, the NHTSA explained, it had assumed that airbags would be installed in 60 percent of all new cars and automatic seatbelts in 40 percent. But by 1981 it learned that, due to economic difficulties in the industry, manufacturers were going to install automatic seatbelts in 99 percent of all new cars. The life-safety potential of airbags would thus not be realized. The overwhelming majority of passive seatbelts to be installed could be detached and left that way permanently by car owners. The agency accordingly reasoned that there was no longer any basis for reliably predicting whether the standard would lead to any significant increased usage of restraints and lives saved. Since the standard would have cost about $1 billion to implement, the agency concluded that it was no longer cost-effective.

State Farm Mutual Automobile Insurance Company and the National Association of Independent Insurers successfully challenged the rescission of the regulation in the D.C. Circuit. That court held that the rescission was arbitrary and capricious for basically three reasons. First, the agency had not shown that there was an insufficient basis for predicting a decrease in the use of seatbelts. Second, it had inadequately considered the possibility of having automakers install nondetachable passive seatbelts. And, finally, the agency failed to consider the option of requiring the installation of airbags in all cars. The court suggested that the basis for deregulation was not only unreasonable but reflected a political bias. The court noted that the White House Press Office had announced the rescission as part of a package of "Actions to Help the U.S. Auto Industry." "It is difficult to avoid the conclusion," the court observed, "that [the agency's] analysis . . . has been distorted by solicitude for the economically depressed automobile industry—which is not the agency's mandate—at the expense of consideration for traffic safety, which is."[43]

When the Motor Vehicle Manufacturers Association of the United States appealed the ruling, it found a largely unsympathetic high bench. Byron White delivered the Court's opinion upholding the lower court's decision. While emphasizing that its review is "narrow and a court is not to substitute its judgement for that of the agency," the Court took a hard look at the basis for the rescission. For basically the same reasons as those of the D.C. Circuit, it found inconsistency in the reasoning behind rescinding the regulation. As White put it, "the agency's explanation for rescission of the passive restraint requirement is *not* sufficient to enable us to conclude that the rescission was the product of reasoned decisionmaking."[44]

Even the most conservative members of the Court agreed that the rescission of the standard governing airbags was arbitrary. In a separate opinion, Rehnquist conceded that "the agency gave no explanation at all" for rescinding that part of the regulation. But, along with Chief Justice Burger and Justice Powell, he thought that the agency had adequately explained its basis for rescinding the requirement for automatic seatbelts.

Subsequently, the Department of Transportation suspended the requirement for passive restraints for one year and, after further study, issued a final rule in July 1984 calling for the "installation of automatic restraints in all new cars beginning with the model year 1990 (September 1, 1989) unless, prior to that time, state mandatory belt usage laws are enacted that cover at least two-thirds of the U.S. population."[45]

Conclusion

The Supreme Court's ruling in *State Farm* underscores both the persistence of the hard look approach and the elusive senior status of

[43] *State Farm Mutual Automobile Insurance Co. v. Department of Transportation*, 680 F.2d 206 (D.C. Cir. 1982).

[44] *Motor Vehicle Manufacturers Association of the United States v. State Farm Mutual Automobile Insurance Company*, 463 U.S. 29, 43 and 52 (1983).

[45] 48 *Fed. Reg.* 39908 (1983), and 49 *Fed. Reg.* 28962 (1984).

appellate courts in the politics of regulation and deregulation.[46] More than that, the controversy over passive restraints was a classic example of democratic politics and changing political responses to regulating risk. Within that political context *State Farm* remains a prime example of how courts limit the impact of democratic politics in determining the outcome of disputes over regulating risk. Courts no longer simply adjudicate disputes between individuals or interest groups and regulatory agencies. They have and will continue to have a major role in resolving conflicts among agencies and between Congress and the executive branch over the direction of regulatory policy.

[46] Some federal courts have also responded to challenges to agencies' refusal to act or regulate health, safety, and environmental risks. See *Illinois v. Gorsuch*, 530 F. Supp. 340 (D.C.C. 1981); *Allison v. Block*, 723 F.2d 631 (8th Cir. 1983); *Environmental Defense Fund v. EPA*, 716 F.2d 915 (D.C. Cir. 1983); and *Chaney v. Heckler*, 718 F.2d 1174 (D.C. Cir. 1983), reversed in *Heckler v. Chaney*, 105 S.Ct. 1649 (1985). See, generally, P. Cooper, "Conflict or Constructive Tension: The Changing Relationship of Judges and Administrators," in *Law and Public Affairs, Special Issue*, 45 *Public Administration Review* 643 (1985), ed. C. Wise and D. M. O'Brien.

Reconsidering Courts and Science-Policy Litigation

Controversy over courts and science-policy disputes is often misdirected. Courts and the judicial process have an important role in resolving disputes over the regulation of health-safety and environmental risks. Such disputes are not new to courts, though their nature changes with technological advances and social forces. Like other kinds of social conflict, science-policy disputes tend to come to the courts because of expectations about conflict resolution that are deeply rooted in our cultures of science, law, and democratic politics.

Science cannot dictate responses to the perceived risks of industrial society. Indeed, science is often part of the problem. Uncertainties, and the evolution of scientific knowledge, as well as the basic choices in models and modes of risk assessment usually only serve to heighten the clash among special interest groups over whether and how to regulate health, safety, and the environment. But, even if science could provide a firm uncontestable foundation for regulating risks, democratic politics would not let it entirely dictate regulatory responses (just as it forbids human experimentation that would give science a firm basis for assessing risks).

Democratic politics by itself does not provide a complete solution either. In regulating risks in an industrial society it would be irrational and imprudent to rest public policy solely on bargains struck through political compromise—compromises that are not reasonably informed by scientific evidence. Yet that, of course, leads us back to the difficulties of how we determine what is a "sufficient scientific basis" for regulation. Even though political compromise is valued, it becomes difficult if not impossible to achieve on the most divisive issues of regulatory policy in a pluralistic society.

When political compromises are achieved in Congress or in state legislatures, they may come at the cost of disregarding or distorting scientific evidence, as in the controversies over saccharin and cyclamates. In any event, legislation cannot solve the problems of assessing and managing risks, any more than science can dictate regulatory policies. For the most part, Congress delegates broad regulatory powers to federal agencies, which only serves to focus political conflict at the level of agencies and reviewing courts. Agencies, moreover, cannot resolve underlying scientific disagreements any more than can Congress. And their regulations—like the ban on Tris—typically rest on data that remain subject to considerable scientific debate. Even in situations of greater scientific certainty, agency regulations—such as OSHA's standards for benzene and cotton dust—generate political conflict that finds its way to the courts.

Because of the underlying scientific uncertainties and the difficulties of accommodating all interests and achieving political compromises on the regulation of perceived risks, science-policy disputes tend to be judicialized and forced into the courts. This is fundamentally a cultural response of a society that places great premium on preserving the perception, if not a measure, of fairness in the resolution of social conflict.

Not surprisingly, then, science-policy disputes are hardly new to courts. Courts have historically handled scientifically complex disputes over trespass, nuisance, negligence, and the like. When doing so they perform an important regulatory role in assessing risks and responsibilities, as well as in responding in a more discriminating way than other kinds of governmental regulation to new-found risks and injuries, like those revealed in the DES litigation. In short, through private law litigation courts respond to demands for simple compensatory justice and further the expansion of social justice.

Have courts gone too far in recognizing new claims and in award-ing damages? They have indeed refashioned traditional common law doctrines in light of new science-policy disputes and pushed private law litigation in the direction of a public law of toxic torts. But it would be hard to say that they have gone too far. Although judges and juries occasionally make extraordinarily large awards and their rulings may have broad socioeconomic impact, courts are generally modest and moderate, relying on precedents and ruling on a case-by-case basis. They rarely fashion policy on a grand scale and appear ill-suited to resolve disputes involving massive tort claims, such as those over air and water pollution. In addition, science-policy litigation is costly, cumbersome, time-consuming, and haphazard. It may prove distributively uneven and unfair for victims and industries alike. Only a small fraction of those injured actually initiate lawsuits and even fewer win awards for health and environmental damages, and those awards are usually modest.

Like other forms of governmental regulation, science-policy liti-gation involves tradeoffs. On the one hand, courts are neither struc-turally nor situationally predisposed to resolve but a modest number of disputes over the impact of technological developments. Judges lack the resources, opportunity, and training of administrative agen-cies to assess the impact of advancing technologies. On the other hand, courts are not as likely as agencies to be captured by the inter-ests that they are supposed to regulate. Agencies, moreover, cannot screen and regulate all of the thousands of suspected toxins, let alone manage all of the risks in society. Courts can and do respond when injuries occur. And in some ways private law litigation is a more democratic and more representative response to managing risks than administrative regulation. It allows individuals who have the most at stake to help forge regulatory policy. Still, there are limitations to what courts and the system of tort liability may accomplish. At best, courts and private law litigation are one means of forging changes in public policy. Through the imposition of tort liability, courts can prompt other governmental responses, and historically our demo-cratic society has relied on private law litigation to settle science-policy disputes, compensate victims, and stimulate regulatory changes. But by themselves, it seems fair to conclude, courts have limited utility in regulating risks through private law litigation.

Are judges competent to decide science-policy disputes and is the judicial process amenable to resolving them? People are not likely to agree on this; it is often a matter of whose ox dies, or whose backyard is polluted. Yet, judges do decide disputes over matters on the frontiers of science, and they are no more or less competent to do so than when they decide equally vexing and complex disputes over social and regulatory policies involving, for example, abortion, reapportionment, or antitrust. What remains crucial is that judges do not purport to resolve scientific questions but the underlying normative conflicts.

The role of judges is basically no different in science-policy disputes than in settling other kinds of social conflicts. The adjudicatory process is an imperfect method of fact-finding, particularly from a scientific perspective. But it does not aim at a resolution of underlying scientific disagreements and uncertainties. Like administrative agencies, trial courts must make fundamental value choices based on inconclusive scientific evidence and opinion. State and federal trial courts often cannot escape making those hard value judgments. They are forced to do so, as in the Reserve Mining controversy, because of the failure of political processes to settle the underlying social conflict.

The role of courts—particularly federal courts—has grown enormously in the politics of regulating health-safety and environmental risks. Still, that is not because courts have set out to usurp the power of other governmental branches. Rather, they respond to social forces; courts are not self-starters but reactive agents of social change. The growth in congressional legislation and federal regulation dealing with health, safety, and the environment; the lack of consensus on the scientific basis for that regulation; and the inevitable clashes of interest groups over whether and how much regulation is needed all contributed to propelling courts into a larger role in overseeing the regulation of health-safety and environmental risks. Quite simply, this is a function of the disputes that arise from scientific, technological, and economic progress in an increasingly pluralistic and litigious society.

Finally, it bears repeating that much of the controversy over the role of courts in regulatory politics and the judicialization of the administrative process rests on the misconception that science-policy disputes revolve around purely scientific controversies over the factual basis for regulation. Only a small percentage actually appears to involve disagreements of a purely scientific nature. Those disputes are exceedingly narrow and marginally related to determining the course of most regulatory decisions.

The principal source of contention in science-policy litigation involves essentially normative, political judgments that must be made in the absence of complete scientific evidence. Because this is so, courts will remain a forum for resolving conflicts between individuals or interest groups and regulatory agencies as well as between Congress and the executive branch over the direction of regulatory policy. Courts and the rule of law constrain democratic politics no less than the latter conditions the influence of science on regulatory responses to health-safety and environmental risks.

Appendix A

Chronology of Major Federal Laws Relating to Environmental Quality and Health

Year	Title	Administering Agency	Mandate
1877	Dangerous Cargo Act (amended 1901, 1905, 1913, 1914, 1918, 1925, 1940, 1946, 1952, 1975)	Department of Transportation	Prohibition of certain hazardous substances
1899	Rivers and Harbors Appropriation Act	Environmental Protection Agency	Regulation of use of waterways
1906	Federal Meat Inspection Act	Department of Agriculture	Prevention of contaminated meat
1906	Federal Food, Drug, and Cosmetic Act (amended 1938, 1958, 1960, 1962, 1968, 1976)	Food and Drug Administration	Regulation of food, drugs, cosmetics, and medical devices
1934	Fish and Wildlife Coordination Act	Fish and Wildlife Service	Regulation of wildlife habitats
1948	Federal Water Pollution Control Act (1948, amended by Clean Water Act, 1978)	Environmental Protection Agency	Regulation of disposal of hazardous substances in waterways
1954	Atomic Energy Act (amended 1974, 1977)	Nuclear Regulatory Commission	Regulates use and disposal of radioactive wastes
1957	Poultry Products Inspection Act	Department of Agriculture	Prevention of contaminated poultry

Year	Act	Agency	Description
1960	Federal Hazardous Substances Act (15 U.S.C. 1261–1273)	Consumer Product Safety Commission	Regulates consumer product hazards and toxic, corrosive, flammable, combustible, or irritation substances
1963	Clean Air Act (42 U.S.C. 1857 et seq.)	Environmental Protection Agency	Established federal enforcement in interstate air pollution and the development of air quality criteria
1965	Clean Air Act Amendment	Environmental Protection Agency	Title I: Motor Vehicle Air Pollution Control Act—directs federal regulation of motor vehicle exhaust
1965	Solid Waste Disposal Act (42 U.S.C. 3251 et seq.)	Environmental Protection Agency	Established program of federal research and grants-in-aid in solid waste disposal
1967	Air Quality Act (42 U.S.C. 1957 et seq.)	Environmental Protection Agency	Established criteria and standards for control of air pollution; set up air quality regions
1969	National Environmental Policy Act (NEPA) (42 U.S.C. 4321 et seq.)	Council on Environmental Quality	Created the Council on Environmental Quality; requires environmental impact statements before major actions—"balancing analysis" in which economic and social benefits are weighed against environment costs
1969	Federal Coal Mine Health and Safety Act (15 U.S.C. 633, 636; 30 U.S.C. 801 et seq.), and 1977	Department of Labor	Promulgated and revised mandatory health and safety standards

Appendix A

(*continued*)

Year	Title	Administrative Agency	Mandate
1970	Clean Air Act Amendment	Environmental Protection Agency	Strengthened and expanded air pollution control activities; placed board regulatory responsibility in new Environmental Protection Agency
1970	Resource Recovery Act (42 U.S.C. 3251 et seq.)	Environmental Protection Agency	Shifted emphasis from solid waste disposal to overall problems of control, recovery, recycling of wastes
1970	Occupational Safety and Health Act (29 U.S.C. 651 et seq.)	Occupational Safety and Health Administration	Provided federal program of research standard-setting and enforcement to assure safe and healthful conditions for workers
1970	Poison Prevention Packaging Act	Consumer Product Safety Commission	Regulation of packaging and labeling of poisonous substances
1971	Lead-Based Paint Poisoning Prevention Act (amended 1978)	Department of Health and Human Services	Prevents use of lead-based paint in consumer products
1971	Noise Control Act (42 U.S.C. 4501 et seq.)	Environmental Protection Agency	Authorized broad federal program to coordinate noise research and control activities; established standards

1972	Consumer Product Safety Act and Major Amendments in 1976, 1977, and 1978 (15 U.S.C. 2051 et seq.)	Consumer Product Safety Commission	Expanded and strengthened federal role in safety and prevention, transferred enforcement of hazardous substances, flammable fabrics, Poison Prevention Packaging Acts to Consumer Product Safety Commission
1972	Federal Insecticide, Fungicide, and Rodenticide Act (amended 1975, 1978)	Environmental Protection Agency	Regulation of use and labeling of pesticides
1972	Black Lung Benefits Act (30 U.S.C. 801 et seq.)	Department of Labor	Provides benefits and other assistance for miners suffering from black lung disease (pneumoconiosis)
1972	Federal Environmental Pesticide Control Act (7 U.S.C. 136–136y)	Environmental Protection Agency	Expanded and strengthened provisions on product regulation, labeling, environmental production, registration of manufacturers, and national monitoring of pesticide residues in food and water
1972	Marine Protection, Research and Sanctuaries Act of 1972 (33 U.S.C. 1401 et seq.)	Environmental Protection Agency	Designate marine areas as sanctuaries for conservation, recreation, or ecological purposes
1972	Coastal Zone Management Act (16 U.S.C. 1451 et seq.)	Office of Coastal Zone Management, Department of Commerce	Requires states to adopt acceptable coastal plans as condition for continued federal assistance; plans generally designate permissible uses of coastal lands

Appendix A
(continued)

Year	Title	Administrative Agency	Mandate
1972	Noise Control Act (1972)		
1973	Endangered Species Act, amended in 1974 (16 U.S.C. 1531 et seq.)	Fish and Wildlife Service, Department of the Interior	Requires "protection of the critical habitat" of an endangered species in any project with federal involvement
1974	Energy Supply and Environment Coordination Act (15 U.S.C. 791–798)	Environmental Protection Agency	Among other things, directs the National Institute of Environmental Health Sciences to study the effects of chronic exposure to sulfur oxides
1974	Safe Drinking Water Act, amended in 1977 (42 U.S.C. 300 et seq.)	Environmental Protection Agency	Requires EPA to set national drinking water standards and to aid states and localities in enforcement
1975	Transportation Safety Act (49 U.S.C. 1801–1812)	Department of Transportation	Regulates any aspect of the transportation of such "hazardous materials" as is deemed necessary or appropriate

1976	Toxic Substances Control Act (15 U.S.C. 2601 et seq.)	Environmental Protection Agency	Authorizes federal government to collect any formation of chemicals that may damage human health or the environment and control them when necessary. Federal government given authority to require screening of chemicals before they reach the marketplace. EPA required to publish inventory of existing chemical substances. Requires industry to keep records and to report information relevant to determining potential risk, requires industry to develop data on health and environmental effects of chemicals they manufacture if they seem to present any environmental risk, or if few data are available
1976	Resource Conservation and Recovery Act (42 U.S.C. 3251 et seq.)	Environmental Protection Agency	Control of waste disposal and hazardous wastes
1976	Solid Waste Disposal Act, amended 1978	Environmental Protection Agency	Governs collection, transportation, and treatment of hazardous solid waste

Appendix A
(continued)

Year	Title	Administrative Agency	Mandate
1977	Clean Air Act Amendments (42 U.S.C. 7401 et seq.)	Environmental Protection Agency	Established more stringent new-source-performance standards (NSPS); institutionalized and toughened EPA's prevention of significant deterioration policy. EPA directed to review ambient air-quality standards for five basic "criteria" pollutants—ozone, nitrogen dioxide, carbon monoxide, sulfur dioxide, and total suspended particulates
1977	Clean Water Act (91 Stat. 1566; 33 U.S.C.A. 1324)	Environmental Protection Agency; U.S. Army Corps of Engineers	Reduce water pollution and the discharge of toxic waste materials into all waters. Altered requirements of 1972 Federal Water Pollution Control Act by extending the 1983 deadline to July 1, 1984 (EPA required to set technology-based effluent control limits for all industries discharging wastes into U.S. waters) and by establishing three categories of pollutant discharges: conventional, toxic, and nonconventional

Year	Act	Agency	Description
1977	Federal Mine Safety and Health Amendments Act (30 U.S.C.A. 801)	Mine Safety and Health Administration, Department of Labor	Extended federal mine safety activities. Required new or revised safety and health regulations for mining activities. Mandatory training of miners, mine rescue, and control of harmful physical agents. Underground mines inspected four times per year; surface mines inspected at least two times per year
1978	Federal Pesticide Act (7 U.S.C. 136 et seq.)	Environmental Protection Agency	Strengthened export safeguards and notification procedures. Simplified registration of pesticides
1979	Hazardous Liquid Pipeline Safety Act	Department of Transportation	Regulation of transportation of hazardous liquids
1980	Comprehensive Environmental Response, Compensation and Liability Act	Environmental Protection Agency	Established fund for compensation of victims of hazardous substances
1980	Solid Waste Disposal Act Amendments	Environmental Protection Agency	Regulates disposal of solid wastes

Appendix B

Bases for Health, Safety, and Environmental Regulation

A. IMPLICIT, VAGUE BALANCING REQUIREMENTS

1. National Environmental Policy Act — consideration of unquantified environmental values along with economic and technology considerations

2. Safe Drinking Water Act — protection of health "to the extent feasible . . . (taking costs into consideration). . ."

3. Resource Conservation and Recovery Act — "as may be necessary to protect human health and the environment"

4. Solid Waste Disposal Act

5. Federal Food, Drug and Cosmetic Act
   a. Provisions for food contaminants — "necessary for the protection of public health"

   b. Drugs — cancer risk balances with health benefits

   c. Cosmetics — no consideration of health benefits; based on risk assessment (if health benefits claimed, treated as a drug)

   d. Medical devices — balancing of risk of adulteration and consideration of safety and efficacy

6. Atomic Energy Act 42 U.S. §2201 (b) — "necessary to . . . promote the common defense and security or to protect health . . ."

7. Federal Inspection Act — "acceptable risk"

8.	Poultry Products Inspection Act	"acceptable risk"
9.	Federal Hazardous Substances Act	"establish such reasonable variations or additional label requirements . . . necessary for the protection of public health and safety"
10.	Federal Mine Safety and Health Act	standards for "the protection of life and prevention of injuries in coal and other mines"
11.	Ports and Waterways Safety and Health Act	lists factors to be considered, but regulations "shall consider fully the wide variety of interests which may be affected"
12.	Dangerous Cargo Act	"regulations as may be necessary"
13.	Federal Railroad Safety Act	"appropriate" standards
14.	Hazardous Liquid Pipeline Safety Act	"reasonable" standards contributing to public safety
15.	Marine Protection, Research and Conservation Act	"necessary and reasonable" regulations
16.	Surface Mining Control and Reclamation Act	"balance between protection of the environment and agricultural productivity and the Nation's need for coal"
17.	Endangered Species Act	"necessary and advisable" regulations to protect listed species

201

Appendix B
(*continued*)

B. BALANCING BASED ON HEALTH RISKS AND TECHNOLOGICAL FEASIBILITY

1. Clean Air Act, Sec. 202 (vehicles)

"greatest degree of emission reduction achievable through . . . technology . . . available"

2. Federal Water Pollution Control Act

"best practicable control technology"; "best available technology economically achievable"

3. Poison Prevention Packaging Act

regulations to protect children from "serious personal injury or serious illness"; the packaging should be "technologically feasible, practicable, and appropriate for such substance"

4. Occupational Safety and Health Act

"reasonably necessary and appropriate" standards that "adequately assure to the extent feasible that no employee will suffer material impairment of health or functional incapacity"

C. BALANCING BASED ON "UNREASONABLE RISK"

1. Federal Insecticide, Fungicide, and Rodenticide Act

registration based on "reasonable adverse effects"; "reasonable risk to man or the environment taking into account the economic, social, and environmental costs and benefits"

2. Toxic Substances Control Act, 15 U.S.C. §2603 — "may present unreasonable risk of injury to health or the environment"

   a. Sec. 4 (require testing of substances)

   b. Sec. 6 (regulation of substances)

   c. Sec. 7 (commence civil action against imminent hazards) — "an imminent and unreasonable risk of serious or widespread injury"

3. Marine Protection Research and Sanctuaries Act — "unreasonably degrade or endanger human health, welfare, or amenities, or the marine environment, ecological systems, or economic potentialities"

4. Consumer Product Safety Act — "reasonably necessary" regulations to reduce an "unreasonable risk of injury"

5. Hazardous Materials Transportation Act — "necessary or appropriate" standards for materials which pose an "unreasonable risk" to health and safety

D. BALANCING PROHIBITED: NO ACCEPTABLE RISK

1. Federal Food, Drug and Cosmetic Act Delaney Clause (food additives) — no acceptable risk of carcinogens

2. Lead-Based Paint Poisoning Prevention Act — prohibition of lead-based paint on cooking utensils, housing, toys, and furniture

203

Appendix C

Substances Regulated as Carcinogens Under Federal Legislation

Evaluation by — NCI: A	IARC: H	IARC: A	Chemical	Statutes — CAA	CWA 307	CWA 311	SDWA	FIFRA	OSHA	FDCA	CPSA
—	—	—	2-acetylaminofluorene (2-AAF)	—	—	—	—	—	—	—	—
—	PC	S	Acrylonitrile	C	RR	L	—	V	R	—	—
—	PC	S	Aflatoxin	—	—	L	—	—	—	R	—
L	—	L	Aldrin	—	RR	L	—	V	R	—	—
—	C	S	4-aminobiphenyl	—	—	—	—	—	R	—	—
—	—	S	Aramite	P	RR	—	—	V	—	—	—
—	C	I	Arsenic	—	RR	L	R[a]	R	R	—	—
—	C	I	Arsenic compounds	—	RR	—	—	R	R	—	—
—	C	S	Asbestos	R	RR	—	—	—	R[a]	—	R
—	—	S	Benz(a)anthracene	—	RR	—	—	—	—	—	—
—	C	I	Benzene	P	RR	L	—	—	R	—	R
—	C	S	Benzidine	—	RR	L	—	—	R	—	R
—	—	S	Benzo(b)fluoranthene	—	RR	—	—	—	—	—	—
—	—	S	Benzo(a)pyrene	C	RR	—	—	—	—	—	—
—	PC	S	Beryllium	R	RR	—	—	—	—	—	—
—	PC	S	Beryllium compounds	—	RR	L	—	—	—	—	—
—	—	L	Bis(2-chloroethyl)ether (BCEE)	—	RR	L	—	—	—	—	—
—	C	S	Bis(chloromethyl)ether (BCME)	—	RR	—	—	—	R	—	—
—	PC	S	Cadmium	C	RR	—	R[a]	R	—	—	—
—	I	S	Cadmium compounds	—	RR	L	—	R	—	—	—

204

					Compound							
—	I	C	—	S	Carbon tetrachloride	RR	L	—	—	—	—	—
S	I	—	S	L	Chlordane	RR	L	—	R	—	—	—
S	—	C	L	L	Chlorobenzilate	—	L	—	R	—	—	—
S	C	—	L	S	Chloroform (a trihalomethane, THM)	RR	—	R	—	R	—	—
—	C	—	S	S	Chloromethyl ether	—	L	—	—	—	—	—
—	C	—	—	S	Chromium compounds (hexavalent)	RR	—	—	R	—	—	—
—	—	C	—	S	Coal tar and soot	—	—	—	R	—	—	—
—	—	—	—	N	Coke oven emissions (polycyclic organic matter; "POM")	—	—	—	R	—	—	—
—	—	—	—	N	Creosote	—	—	—	—	R	—	—
—	—	—	—	N	Cyclamates	—	—	—	—	—	—	—
—	—	—	—	N	D&C Blue No. 6	—	—	—	—	—	R	—
—	—	—	—	N	D&C Red No. 10	—	—	—	—	—	R	—
—	—	—	—	N	D&C Red No. 11	—	—	—	—	—	R	—
—	—	—	—	N	D&C Red No. 12	—	—	—	—	—	R	—
—	—	—	—	N	D&C Red No. 13	—	—	—	—	—	R	—
—	—	—	—	N	D&C Yellow No. 1	—	—	—	—	R	R	—
—	—	—	—	N	D&C Yellow No. 9	—	—	—	—	—	R	—
—	—	—	—	N	D&C Yellow No. 10	—	—	—	—	R	R	—
—	S	—	—	L	DDT (dichlorodiphenyltrichloroethane)	RR	—	—	—	—	—	—
—	—	—	—	S	Dibenz(a,h)anthracene	RR	—	—	R[a]	—	—	—
S	S	C	S	S	1,2-dibromo-3-chloropropane	—	—	—	—	—	—	—
—	—	—	—	N	1,2 dibromoethane	—	L	—	—	—	—	—
S	—	C	—	S	3,3'-dichlorobenzidine	RR	—	—	R	—	—	—
S	S	C	L	S	1,2-dichloroethane	RR	L	—	R	—	—	—
—	I	—	L	L	Dieldrin	RR	L	—	R	—	—	—
—	—	—	—	N	Diethylpyrocarbonate	—	—	—	—	—	R	—

205

Appendix C
(continued)

NCI A	IARC H	A	Chemical	CAA	CWA 307	CWA 311	SDWA	FIFRA	OSHA	FDCA	CPSA
—	C	S	Diethylstilbestrol (DES)	—	—	—	—	—	—	R	—
—	—	S	4-dimethylaminoazobenzene	—	—	—	—	—	R	—	—
L	—	N	2,4-dinitrotoluene	C	RR	L	—	—	—	—	—
S	—	S	1,4-dioxane	—	—	—	—	—	—	—	—
—	—	N	1,2-diphenylhydrazine	—	RR	L	—	—	—	R	—
—	L	L	Dulcin	C	—	L	—	—	—	—	—
—	I	L	Epichlorohydrin	C	—	L	—	R	—	—	—
—	—	N	Ethylene bis dithiocarbamate	—	—	—	—	R	—	—	—
—	PC	I	Ethylene oxide	C	—	—	—	—	—	R	—
—	—	N	FD&C Red No. 2	—	—	—	—	—	—	R	—
—	—	N	FD&C Violet No. 1	—	—	—	—	—	—	R	—
—	—	N	Formaldehyde	C	—	L	—	—	—	—	—
—	—	N	Graphite	—	—	L	—	R	—	—	—
(S)	—	L	Heptachlor	—	RR	L	—	R	—	—	—
—	—	S	Hexachlorobenzene	—	RR	L	—	—	—	—	—
—	—	N	Hexachlorobutadiene	—	RR	L	—	—	—	—	—
—	I	L	Hexachlorocyclohexane	—	—	L	—	—	—	—	—
—	—	N	α-hexachlorocyclohexane	—	RR	L	—	—	—	—	—
—	—	N	β-hexachlorocyclohexane	—	RR	L	—	—	—	—	—
(S)	—	N	Hexachloroethane	—	RR	L	—	—	—	—	—
—	—	S	Ideno(1,2,3-cd)pyrene	—	RR	—	—	—	—	—	—
S	—	S	Kepone (chlordecone)	—	—	L	—	V	—	—	—

							Substance			
—	—	R	R^a	L	RR	—	Lindane	L	—	—
R	—	—	—	—	—	—	Mercaptoimidazoline	N	—	—
R	R	—	—	—	—	—	4,4′ methylene bis (2-chloroaniline)	S	—	—
—	R	—	—	—	—	—	α-naphthylamine	L	C	—
—	R	—	—	—	RR	C	2-naphthylamine	S	PC	—
—	R	—	—	L	RR	—	Nickel	S	PC	—
—	R	—	—	—	—	—	Nickel compounds	S	—	—
R	—	—	—	—	—	—	Nitrosamines	N	—	—
—	R	—	—	L	—	—	4-nitrobiphenyl	L	—	—
—	—	—	—	L	RR	—	N-nitrosodi-n-butylamine	S	—	—
—	R	—	—	L	—	—	N-nitrosodiethylamine (DENA)	S	—	—
—	R	—	—	—	RR	C	N-nitrosodimethylamine (DMNA)	S	—	—
—	—	—	—	—	RR	—	N-nitrosodi-n-propylamine	S	—	—
R	—	—	—	—	—	C	N-nitroso-N-ethylurea (NEU)	S	—	—
R	—	—	—	—	—	C	N-nitroso-N-methylurea (NMU)	S	—	—
—	—	—	—	—	—	—	Oil of calamus	N	—	—
R	—	—	—	—	RR	—	P-4000	N	—	—
—	—	R	—	—	—	—	Pentachloronitrobenzene (PCNB)	N	I	I
R	—	—	—	—	—	—	Polychlorinated biphenyls (PCBs; Toxic Substances Control Act-RR)	S	I	—
—	—	—	—	L	RR	C	β-propiolactone	S	—	—
—	—	V	—	—	—	—	Safrole	S	—	—
—	R	—	—	—	RR	C	2,3,7,8-tetrachlorodibenzo-p-dioxin (TCDD, "dioxin")	N	—	—
R	—	—	—	L	RR	C	1,1,2,2-tetrachlorethane	N	—	(S)
R	—	—	—	L	RR	C	Tetrachloroethylene (perchloroethylene)	N	—	(S)
R	—	R	R^a	L	—	—	Thiourea	S	—	—
—	—	—	—	L	RR	—	Toxaphene	S	—	s
—	—	—	—	L	RR	—	1,1,2-trichloroethane	N	—	(S)

Appendix C
(continued)

| Evaluation by | | | | Statutes | | | | | | | |
| NCI | IARC | | | | | | | | | | |
A	H	A	Chemical	CAA	CWA 307	CWA 311	SDWA	FIFRA	OSHA	FDCA	CPSA
(S)	I	L	Trichloroethylene	C	RR	L	—	—	—	—	—
S	—	N	2,4,6-trichlorophenol	—	RR	—	—	—	—	—	—
—	—	N	Trihalomethanes (THM)	—	—	—	R	—	—	—	—
—	—	N	"Tris"(flame retardant)	R	RR	—	—	—	R	—	R
—	C	S	Vinyl chloride	R	RR	—	—	—	—	—	R
—	—	N	Vinylidene chloride	C	RR	L	—	—	—	—	—
—	—	N	Radionuclides	R	—	—	—	—	—	—	—

Abbreviations

NCI   National Cancer Institute data (146)
IARC International Agency for Research on Cancer evaluation (185, 186)
    A = animal evidence
    S = sufficient evidence for carcinogenicity (for more description see Chapter 4, Appendix A)
    (S) = Class 3 of NCI; very strong evidence is 1 species; no evidence in 2nd species
    L = limited evidence for carcinogenicity
    I = inadequate evidence for carcinogenicity
    H = human evidence
    C = identified as a carcinogen from human studies
    PC = identified as a probable carcinogen from human studies
    I = inadequate evidence to reach a conclusion about carcinogenicity from human studies
    N = not evaluated

CAA   Clean Air Act
CWA 307   Clean Water Act §307
CWA 311   Clean Water Act §311
SDWA   Safe Drinking Water Act
FIFRA   Federal Insecticide, Fungicide, and Rodenticide Act
OSHA   Occupational Safety and Health Act
FDCA   Food, Drug, and Cosmetic Act
CPSA   Consumer Product Safety Act

C = being considered for regulation
P = regulation proposed
R = regulated
RR = regulation required by Act
L = discharge levels restricted
V = voluntarily withdrawn from market

[a]Regulation based on non-carcinogenic toxicity (in addition to those indicated, many other listed substances encountered in the workplace are regulated because of toxicities other than carcinogenicity).

Source: Office of Technology Assessment, *Assessment of Technologies for Determining Cancer Risks from the Environment* (Washington, D.C.: U.S. Government Printing Office, 1981).

Selected Bibliography

Abel, Richard, "A Critique of American Tort Law," 8 *British Journal of Law & Society* 199 (1981).

Abelson, Philip H., "The Tris Controversy," 197 *Science* 113 (July 8, 1977).

Ackerman, Bruce A., and Hassler, William T., "Beyond the New Deal: Coal and the Clean Air Act," 89 *Yale Law Journal* 1466 (1980).

———, *Clean Coal/Dirty Air* (New Haven, Conn.: Yale University Press, 1981).

Ackerman, Bruce A., Susan Rose-Ackerman, James Sawyer, and Dale Henderson, *The Uncertain Search for Environmental Quality* (New York: Free Press, 1974).

Administrative Conference of the United States, *A Guide to Federal Agency Rulemaking* (Washington, D.C.: Office of the Chairman, Administrative Conference of the United States, 1983).

Albert, Roy, *Toward a More Uniform Federal Strategy for the Assessment and Regulation of Carcinogens* (Unpublished paper prepared for the Office of Technology Assessment, 1980).

Alston, Philip, "International Regulation of Toxic Chemicals," 7 *Ecology Law Quarterly* 397 (1979).

American Bar Association, Commission on Law and Economy, *Federal Regulation: Roads to Reform* (Washington, D.C.: American Bar Association, 1979).

American Cancer Society, *Cancer Facts and Figures: 1982* (New York: American Cancer Society, 1980).

American Industrial Health Council, *Recommended Alternative to OSHA's Generic Carcinogen Proposal* (Scarsdale, N.Y.: American Industrial Health Council, 1978).

———, *Comments on: A Report of the Interagency Regulatory Liaison Group (IRLG) Work Group on Risk Assessment Entitled "Scientific Bases for Identifying Potential Carcinogens and Estimating Their Risks"* (Scarsdale, N.Y.: American Industrial Health Council, 1979).

American Society for Testing and Materials, *The Voluntary Standards System of the United States of America* (Philadelphia: American Society for Testing and Materials, 1975).

Ames, Bruce, "Identifying Environmental Chemicals Causing Mutations and Cancer," 204 *Science* 587 (1979).

Ames, Charles, and Steven McCracken, "Framing Regulatory Standards to Avoid Formal Adjudication: The FDA as a Case Study," 64 *California Law Review* 14 (1976).

Baram, Michael S., *Alternatives to Regulation* (Lexington, Mass.: Lexington Books, 1982).

————, "Cost-Benefit Analysis: An Inadequate Basis for Health, Safety and Environmental Regulatory Decisionmaking," 8 *Ecology Law Quarterly* 473 (1980).

————, and J. Raymond Miyares, "The Legal Framework for Determining Unreasonable Risk from Carcinogenic Chemicals" (Unpublished paper prepared for the Office of Technology Assessment, 1980).

————, "Social Control of Science and Technology," 172 *Science* 535 (1971).

Bardach, Eugene, and Lucian Pugliaresi, "The Environmental-Impact Statement vs. The Real World," 47 *The Public Interest* 22 (1977).

Bardach, Eugene, and Robert Kagan, eds., *Social Regulation: Strategies for Reform* (San Francisco: Institute for Contemporary Studies, 1982).

Barth, Peter S., and H. Alan Hunt, *Workers' Compensation and Work-Related Illnesses and Diseases* (Cambridge, Mass.: Massachusetts Institute of Technology, 1980).

Bartlett, Robert V., *The Reserve Mining Controversy: A Case Study of Science, Technology, and Values* (Bloomington: Indiana University Press, 1979).

Baxter, William F., "The SST: From Harlem to Watts in Two Hours," 21 *Stanford Law Review* 1 (1968).

Bazelon, David, "Coping with Technology Through the Legal Process," 62 *Cornell Law Review* 817 (1977).

————, "The Impact of the Courts on Public Administration," 52 *Indiana Law Journal* 101 (1976).

Berger, Jeffrey, and Steven Riskin, "Economic and Technology Feasibility in Regulating Toxic Substances Under Occupational Safety and Health Act," 7 *Ecology Law Quarterly* 285 (1978).

Berman, Daniel M., *Death on the Job* (New York: Monthly Review Press, 1978).

Birnbaum, Sheila, *Toxic Substances: Problems in Litigation* (New York: Practising Law Institute, 1981).

————, and Paul D. Rheingold, eds., *Toxic Substances Litigation* (New York: Practising Law Institute, 1980).

Blank, Charles H., "The Delaney Clause: Technical Naivete and Scientific Advocacy in the Formulation of Public Health Policies," 62 *California Law Review* 1084 (1974).

Blum, Arlene, and Bruce Ames, "Flame-Retardant Additives as Possible Cancer Hazards," 195 *Science* 17 (January 7, 1977).

Boyer, Barry, "Alternatives to Administrative Trial-Type Hearings for Resolving Complex Scientific, Economic, and Social Issues," 71 *Michigan Law Review* 111 (1972).

Breyer, Stephen, *Regulation and Its Reform* (Cambridge, Mass.: Harvard University Press, 1982).

————, *"Vermont Yankee* and the Court's Role in the Nuclear Energy Controversy," 91 *Harvard Law Review* 1833 (1978).

————, "Analyzing Regulatory Failure: Mismatches, Less Restrictive Alternatives, and Reform," 92 *Harvard Law Review* 547 (1979).

Brodeur, Paul, *Expendable Americans* (New York: Viking Press, 1974).

Brown, Michael, *Laying Waste* (New York: Pantheon Books, 1980).

Buchanan, James, and W. Craig Stubblebine, "Externality," *Economica* 371 (1962).

Byse, Clark, *"Vermont Yankee* and the Evolution of Administrative Procedure: A Somewhat Different View," 91 *Harvard Law Review* 1823 (1978).

Calabresi, Guido, *Costs of Accidents* (New Haven: Yale University Press, 1970).

————, "Some Thoughts on Risk Distribution and the Law of Torts," 70 *Yale Law Journal* 499 (1961).

————, and Philip Bobbitt, *Tragic Choices* (New York: W. W. Norton, 1978).

Calabresi, Guido, and Jon T. Hirshoff, "Toward a Test for Strict Liability in Torts," 81 *Yale Law Journal* 1055 (1972).

Caldwell, Lynton K., *Science and the National Environmental Policy Act* (University: University of Alabama Press, 1982).

Carson, Rachel, *Silent Spring* (Greenwich, Conn.: Fawcett-Crest, 1962).

Chamber of Commerce of the United States, *Analysis of Workers' Compensation Laws* (Washington D.C.: Chamber of Commerce of the United States, 1981).

Chen, Edwin, *PBB: An American Tragedy* (Englewood Cliffs, N.J.: Prentice-Hall, 1979).

Clones, Julia P., *Preliminary Environmental Assessment of a Ban on the Use of TRIS (2,3, Dibromoprophyl) Phosphate as a Flame Retardant for Wearing Apparel* (Washington, D.C.: Consumer Product Safety Commission, Bureau of Economic Analysis, 1977).

Coase, R. H., "The Problem of Social Cost," 3 *Journal of Law and Economics* 1 (1960).

Commission on Federal Paperwork, *Rulemaking: A Report of the Commission on Federal Paperwork* (Washington, D.C.: Government Printing Office, 1977).

Consumer Product Safety Commission, *Final Report: Economic and Environmental Analysis of Proposed Amendments to Children's Sleepwear Flammability Standards* (Washington, D.C.: Consumer Product Safety Commission, 1977).

Cooper, Richard, "The Role of Regulatory Agencies in Risk-Benefit Decision-Making," 33 *Food/Drug/Cosmetic Law Journal* 755 (1978).

———, "Scientists and Lawyers in the Legal Process," 36 *Food/Drug/Cosmetic Law Journal* 9 (1981).

Cornfield, Jerome, "Carcinogenic Risk Assessment," 198 *Science* 693 (1977).

Cramton, Roger C., "The Why, Where and How of Broadened Public Participation in the Administrative Process," 60 *Georgetown Law Journal* 525 (1972).

Crandall, Robert, and Lester Lave, eds., *The Scientific Basis of Health and Safety Regulation* (Washington, D.C.: Brookings Institution, 1981).

Cutler, Lloyd, and David Johnson, "Regulation and the Political Process," 84 *Yale Law Journal* 1395 (1975).

Darling-Hammond, L., and T. Kniesner, *The Law and Economics of Workers' Compensation* (Santa Monica, Cal.: Rand, 1980).

Davies, J. C., S. Gusman, and F. Irvin, *Determining Unreasonable Risk Under the Toxic Substances Control Act* (Washington, D.C.: The Conservation Foundation, 1979).

Davis, Devra Lee, "The 'Shotgun Wedding' of Science and Law: Risk Assessment and Judicial Review," 10 *Columbia Journal of Environmental Law* 67 (1985).

———, "Cancer in the Workplace: The Case for Prevention," 23 *Environment* 25 (1981).

———, and Brian Magee, "Cancer and Industrial Chemical Production," 206 *Science* 1356 (1979).

Davis, Devra Lee, Kenneth Bridbord, and Marvin Schneiderman, "Estimating Cancer Causes: Problems in Methodology, Production and Trends," *Branbury Report 9: Quantification of Occupational Cancer* 285 (Cold Spring, N.Y.: Cold Spring Harbor Laboratory, 1981).

Davis, E. W., *Pioneering with Taconite* (St. Paul, Minn.: Minnesota Historical Society, 1964).

DeLong, James V., "Informal Rulemaking and the Integration of Law and Policy," 65 *Virginia Law Review* 257 (1979).

DeMuth, Christopher, "The Regulatory Budget," *Regulation* 29 (March/April, 1980).

Department of Health and Human Services, *First Annual Report on Carcinogens* (Bethesda, Md.: National Cancer Institute, 1980).

Department of Health, Education and Welfare, Public Health Service and National Institutes of Health, *Vinyl Chloride: An Information Resource* (Bethesda, Md.: National Cancer Institute, 1978).

Department of Labor, *An Interim Report to Congress on Occupational Diseases* (Washington, D.C.: GPO, 1980).

Derthick, Martha, and Paul Quirk, *The Politics of Deregulation* (Washington, D.C.: Brookings Institution, 1985).

Diver, Colin S., "Policymaking Paradigms in Administrative Law," 95 *Harvard Law Review* 393 (1981).

———, "A Theory of Regulatory Enforcement," 28 *Public Policy* 257 (1980).

Doniger, David, *Law and Policy of Toxic Substances Control: A Case Study of Vinyl Chloride* (Baltimore, Md.: Johns Hopkins University Press, 1979).

———, "Federal Regulation of Vinyl Chloride: A Short Course in the Law and Policy of Toxic Substances Control," 7 *Ecology Law Quarterly* 497 (1978).

Douglas, Mary, and Aaron Wildavsky, *Risk and Culture* (Berkeley: University of California Press, 1982).

Dupree, A. Hunter, *Science in the Federal Government: A History of Policies and Activities to 1940* (Cambridge, Mass.: Harvard University Press, 1957).

Efron, Edith, *The Apocalyptics: Cancer and the Big Lie* (New York: Simon & Schuster, 1984).

Egginton, Joyce, *The Poisoning of Michigan* (New York: W. W. Norton, 1980).

Environmental Defense Fund, *Troubled Waters: Toxic Chemicals in the Hudson River* (Washington, D.C.: Environmental Defense Fund, 1977).

———, *Malignant Neglect* (New York: Alfred A. Knopf, 1979).

Environmental Law Institute, *An Analysis of Past Federal Efforts to Control Toxic Substances* (Washington, D.C.: Environmental Law Institute, 1978).

Environmental Protection Agency, *PCBs in the United States Industrial Use and Environmental Distribution* (Washington, D.C.: Environmental Protection Agency, 1976).

———, *National Conference on Polychlorinated Biphenyls, November 19–21, 1975* (Washington, D.C.: Environmental Protection Agency, 1976).

Epstein, Richard, "The Social Consequences of Common Law Rules," 95 *Harvard Law Review* 17171 (1982).

———, "A Theory of Strict Liability," 2 *Journal of Legal Studies* 151 (1973).

———, "Manville: The Bankruptcy of Product," *Regulation* 14 (Sept./Oct., 1982).

———, "Products Liability—The Gathering Storm," *Regulation* 18 (Sept./Oct., 1977).

Epstein, Samuel, *The Politics of Cancer* (Garden City, N.Y.: Anchor Books, 1979).

———, Letter to Editor, 289 *Nature* 115 (January 15, 1981).

———, and Richard Gruny, eds., *The Legislation of Product Safety* (Cambridge, Mass.: Massachusetts Institute of Technology Press, 1974).

Epstein, Samuel, and Joel Swartz, "Fallacies of Lifestyle Cancer Theories," 289 *Nature* 127 (January 15, 1981).

Estreicher, Samuel, "Pragmatic Justice: The Contributions of Judge Harold Leventhal to Administrative Law," 80 *Columbia Law Review* 894 (1980).

Fletcher, George, "Fairness and Utility in Tort Theory," 85 *Harvard Law Review* 537 (1972).

Food Safety Council, Scientific Committee, *Proposed System for Food Safety Assessment* (Washington, D.C.: Food Safety Council, 1980).

Freedman, James, *Crisis and Legitimacy: The Administrative Process and American Government* (New York: Cambridge University Press, 1978).

———, "Expertise and the Administrative Process," 28 *Administrative Law Review* 363 (1976).

Friendly, Henry, *The Federal Administrative Agencies* (Cambridge, Mass.: Harvard University Press, 1962).

———, "The Courts and Social Policy," 33 *University of Miami Law Review* 21 (1978).

———, "Some Kind of Hearing," 123 *University of Pennsylvania Law Review* 1267 (1975).

Fuchs, Ralph, "Development and Diversification in Administrative Rulemaking," 72 *Northwestern University Law Review* 83 (1977).

Fuller, Lon, "The Forms and Limits of Adjudication," 92 *Harvard Law Review* 353 (1978).

Gardner, Warner, and Michael Greenberger, "Judicial Review of Administrative Action and Responsible Government," 63 *Georgetown Law Journal* 7 (1974).

Gellhorn, Ernest, "Public Participation in Administrative Proceedings," 81 *Yale Law Journal* 334 (1972).

Gelpe, Marcia, and Dan Tarlock, "The Uses of Scientific Information in Environmental Decisionmaking," 48 *Southern California Law Review* 371 (1974).

General Accounting Office, *Delays in Setting Workplace Standards for Cancer-Causing and Other Dangerous Substances* (Washington, D.C.: GAO, 1977).

———, *Environmental Protection Issues Facing the Nation* (Washington, D.C.: GAO, 1977).

———, *Improvements Needed in Administering the Flammable Fabrics Act* (Washington, D.C.: GAO, 1978).

————, *The Consumer Product Safety Commission Should Act More Promptly to Protect the Public from Hazardous Products* (Washington, D.C.: GAO, 1978).

————, *EPA Is Slow to Carry Out Its Responsibilities to Control Harmful Chemicals* (Washington, D.C.: GAO, 1980).

————, *The Consumer Product Safety Commission Has No Assurance that Product Defects Are Being Reported and Corrected* (Washington, D.C.: GAO, 1978).

————, *Sugar and Other Sweeteners* (Washington, D.C.: GAO, 1979).

Gori, Gio Batta, "The Regulation of Carcinogenic Hazards," 208 *Science* 256 (April 18, 1980).

Grabowski, Henry, *Drug Regulation and Innovation* (Washington, D.C.: American Enterprise Institute, 1976).

————, and John Vernon, "Consumer Product Safety Regulation," 68 *American Economic Review* 284 (1978).

————, *FDA Regulation of Pharmaceuticals* (Washington, D.C.: American Enterprise Institute, 1981).

Graham, Loren, *Between Science and Values* (New York: Columbia University Press, 1981).

Green, Harold, "The Role of Law and Lawyers in Technology Assessment," 13 *Atomic Energy Law Journal* 246 (1971).

————, "Limitations on Implementation of Technology Assessment," 14 *Atomic Energy Law Journal* 59 (1972).

————, "The Risk-Benefit Calculus in Safety Determinations," 43 *George Washington Law Review* 791 (1975).

————, "Cost-Risk-Benefit Assessment and the Law," 45 *George Washington Law Review* 901 (1977).

Green, Mark, and Norman Waitzman, *Business War on the Law* (Washington, D.C.: Corporate Accountability Research Group, 1981).

Haberer, Joseph, ed., *Science and Technology Policy* (Lexington, Mass.: Lexington Books, 1977).

Handler, Philip, "The Need for a Sufficient Scientific Base for Government Regulation," 43 *George Washington Law Review* 808 (1975).

Harris, Robert, "The Tris Ban," 197 *Science* 1132 (September 16, 1977).

Haveman, Robert, and Burton Weisbrod, "Defining Benefits of Public Programs: Some Guidance for Policy Analysts," 1 *Policy Analysis* 169 (1975).

Havender, William, "Ruminations on a Rat: Saccharin and Human Risk," *Regulation* 17 (March/April, 1979).

Havighurst, Clark, and Glenn Hackbarth, "Competition and Health Care," *Regulation* 39 (May/June, 1980).

Hiatt, Howard, James Watson, and Jay Winston, eds., *Origins of Human Cancer* (Cold Spring Harbor, N.Y.: Cold Spring Harbor Laboratory, 1977).

Higginson, John, "Cancer and Environment: Higginson Speaks Out," 205 *Science* 1363 (September 28, 1979).

Huber, Peter, "Exorcists vs. Gatekeepers in Risk Regulation," *Regulation* 23 (Nov./Dec., 1983).

Hutt, Peter, "Public Policy Issues in Regulating Carcinogens in Food," 33 *Food/Drug/Cosmetic Law Journal* 541 (1978).

Jaffe, Louis, "The Illusion of the Ideal Administration," 86 *Harvard Law Review* 1183 (1973).

_____, "The Citizen as Litigant in Public Actions: The Non-Hohfeldian or Ideological Plaintiff," 116 *University of Pennsylvania Law Review* 1033 (1968).

_____, and Laurence Tribe, *Environmental Protection* (Chicago: Bracton Press, 1971).

Jasanoff, Sheila, and Dorothy Nelkin, "Science, Technology and the Limits of Judicial Competence," 22 *Jurimetrics Journal* 266 (1982).

Juergensmeyer, Julian, "Control of Air Pollution Through the Assertion of Private Rights," 1967 *Duke Law Journal* 1126 (1967).

Kakalik, J., P. Ebener, W. Felstiner, G. Haggstrom, and M. Shanley, *Variation in Asbestos Litigation Compensation and Expenses* (Santa Monica, Cal.: Rand, 1984).

Kamlet, K. S., *Toxic Substances Programs in U.S. States and Territories: How Well Do They Work?* (Washington, D.C.: National Wildlife Federation, 1980).

Kantrowitz, Arthur, "The Science Court Experiment," *Trial* 48 (1977).

Karstadt, Myra, "Protecting Public Health from Hazardous Substances: Federal Regulation of Environmental Contaminants," 5 *Environmental Law Reporter* 50165 (1975).

Katz, Milton, "Decision-Making in the Production of Power," 223 *Scientific American* 191 (1971).

_____, "The Function of Tort Liability in Technology Assessment," 38 *Cincinnati Law Review* 587 (1969).

Kelman, Steven, *Regulating America, Regulating Sweden: A Comparative Study of Occupational Safety and Health Policy* (Cambridge: Massachusetts Institute of Technology Press, 1981).

Kennedy, Duncan, "Form and Substance in Private Law Adjudication," 89 *Harvard Law Review* 1685 (1976).

Kneese, Allen, and Charles Schultze, *Pollution, Prices and Public Policy* (Washington, D.C.: Brookings Institution, 1975).

Kuhn, Thomas, *The Essential Tension: Selected Studies in Scientific Tradition and Change* (Chicago: University of Chicago Press, 1977).

Lambright, Henry, *Governing Science and Technology* (New York: Oxford University Press, 1976).

Lave, Lester, *The Strategy of Social Regulation* (Washington, D.C.: Brookings Institution, 1981).

_____, ed., *Quantitative Risk Assessment in Regulation* (Washington, D.C.: Brookings Institution, 1982).

Lazarus, Simon, and Joseph Onek, "The Regulators and the People," 57 *Virginia Law Review* 1069 (1971).

Lederberg, Joshua, "The Freedoms and the Control of Science: Notes from the Ivory Tower," 45 *Southern California Law Review* 596 (1972).

Leventhal, Harold, "Environmental Decisionmaking and the Role of the Courts," 122 *University of Pennsylvania Law Review* 509 (1974).

_____, "Principled Fairness and Regulatory Urgency," 25 *Case Western Reserve Law Review* 66 (1974).

Levinson, L. Harold, "Elements of the Administrative Process: Formal, Semi-Formal, and Free-Form Models," 26 *American University Law Review* 872 (1977).

Lieberman, Jethro, *The Litigious Society* (New York: Basic Books, 1981).

McGarity, Thomas O., "Substantive and Procedural Discretion in Administrative Resolution of Science Policy Questions: Regulating Carcinogens in EPA and OSHA," 67 *Georgetown Law Journal* 729 (1979).

_____, "Courts, the Agencies, and NEPA Threshold Issues," 55 *Texas Law Review* 801 (1977).

McGowan, Carl, "Congress, Court, and Control of Delegated Power," 77 *Columbia Law Review* 1119 (1977).

Markey, Howard, "A Forum for Technology?" 60 *Judicature* 365 (1977).

Martin, James, "The Proposed 'Science Court.' " 75 *Michigan Law Review* 1058 (1977).

_____, "The Delaney Clause and Zero Risk Tolerance," 34 *Food/Drug/ Cosmetic Law Journal* 43 (1979).

Martin, Jeffrey, "Procedures for Decisionmaking Under Conditions of Scientific Uncertainty: The Science Court Proposal," 16 *Harvard Journal on Legislation* 2 (1979).

Mashaw, Jerry, "Regulation, Logic and Ideology," *Regulation* 44 (November/December, 1979).

_____, "The Management Side of Due Process: Some Theoretical and Litigation Notes on the Assurance of Accuracy, Fairness, and Timeliness in the Adjudication of Social Welfare Claims," 59 *Cornell Law Review* 772 (1974).

_____, "The Supreme Court's Due Process Calculus for Administrative Adjudication in *Mathews v. Eldridge*: Three Factors in Search of a Theory of Value," 44 *University of Chicago Law Review* 28 (1976).

Melnick, R. Shep, *Regulation and the Courts* (Washington, D.C.: Brookings Institution, 1983).

Mendeloff, John, *Regulating Safety* (Cambridge: Massachusetts Institute of Technology Press, 1979).

_____, "Does Overregulation Cause Underregulation? The Case of Toxic Substances," *Regulation* 47 (September/October, 1981).

Merrill, Richard, "FDA and the Effects of Substantive Rules," 35 *Food/ Drug/Cosmetic Law Journal* 270 (1980).

————, "Risk-Benefit Decision Making by the Food and Drug Administration," 45 *George Washington Law Review* 994 (1977).

————, and Michael Schewel, "FDA Regulation of Environmental Contaminants of Food," 66 *Virginia Law Review* 1357 (1980).

Merton, Robert, and Norman Storer, eds., *The Sociology of Science* (Chicago: University of Chicago Press, 1973).

————, "The Normative Structure of Science," 1 *Journal of Legal and Political Sociology* 115 (1942).

Nader, Ralph, Ronald Brownstein, and John Richard, *Who's Poisoning America* (San Francisco: Sierra Club Books, 1981).

National Academy of Sciences, *Principles for Evaluating Chemicals in the Environment* (Washington, D.C.: National Academy of Sciences, 1975).

————, *Decision Making for Regulating Chemicals in the Environment* (Washington, D.C.: National Academy of Sciences, 1975).

National Research Council, Institute of Medicine, *Food Safety Policy: Scientific and Societal Considerations* (Washington, D.C.: National Academy of Sciences, 1979).

National Wildlife Federation, *The Toxic Substances Dilemma* (Washington, D.C.: National Wildlife Federation, 1980).

Nelkin, Dorothy, *Controversy: Politics of Technical Decisions* (Beverly Hills, Cal.: Sage Publications, 1979).

————, "Scientific Knowledge, Public Policy and Democracy," 1 *Knowledge* 106 (1979).

————, and Michael Brown, *Workers at Risk* (Chicago: University of Chicago Press, 1984).

Nicholson, W., ed., *Management of Assessed Risk for Carcinogens* (New York: New York Academy of Science, 1981).

Noll, Roger, "The Economics and Politics of Regulation," 57 *Virginia Law Review* 1016 (1971).

Norwood, Christopher, *At Highest Risk* (New York: McGraw-Hill, 1980).

Nyhart, J. D., and Milton Carrow, *Law and Science in Collaboration* (Lexington, Mass.: Lexington Books, 1983).

O'Brien, David M., "*Marbury*, the APA, and Science-Policy Disputes: The Alluring and Elusive Judicial/Administrative Partnership," 7 *Harvard Journal of Law and Public Policy* 445 (1984).

————, " 'The Imperial Judiciary': Of Paper Tigers and Socio-Legal Indicators," 2 *Journal of Law & Politics* 1 (1985).

————, "The Courts and Science-Policy Disputes: A Review and Commentary on the Role of the Judiciary in Regulatory Politics," 4 *Journal of Energy Law and Policy* 81 (1983).

————, "The Seduction of the Judiciary: Social Science and the Courts," 64 *Judicature* 8 (1980).

————, and Donald Marchand, eds., *The Politics of Technology Assessment: Institutions, Processes, and Policy Disputes* (Lexington, Mass.: Lexington Books, 1982).

O'Connell, Jeffrey, *The Lawsuit Lottery* (New York: Free Press, 1979).

Office of Management and Budget, *Improving Government Regulation: Current Status and Future Directions* (Washington, D.C.: Executive Office of the President, 1980).

Office of Science and Technology, *Identification, Characterization, and Control of Potential Human Carcinogens: A Framework for Federal Decision-Making* (Washington, D.C.: Executive Office of the President, 1979).

Owen, Bruce, and Ronald Breutigam, *The Regulation Game: Strategic Use of the Administrative Process* (Cambridge, Mass.: Ballinger Publishing Co., 1978).

Page, Joseph, and Mary-Win O'Brien, *Bitter Wages* (New York: Grossman, 1973).

————, and Kathleen Blackburn, "Behind the Looking Glass: Administrative, Legislative and Private Approaches to Cosmetic Safety Substantiation," 24 *UCLA Law Review* 795 (1977).

————, and Peter Munsing, "Occupational Health and the Federal Government: The Wages Are Still Bitter," 38 *Law & Contemporary Problems* 651 (1974).

Page, Talbot, "A Generic View of Toxic Chemicals and Similar Risks," 7 *Ecology Law Quarterly* 207 (1978).

Penick, James, Carroll Pursell, Morgan Sherwood, and Donald Swain, eds., *The Politics of American Science: 1939 to the Present* (Chicago: Rand McNally, 1965).

Peskin, Henry, Paul Portney, and Allen Kneese, eds., *Environmental Regulation and the U.S. Economy* (Washington, D.C.: Resources for the Future, 1981).

Petro, Richard, "Distorting the Epidemiology of Cancer: The Need for a More Balanced Overview," 284 *Nature* 297 (March 27, 1980).

Polanyi, Michael, *The Logic of Liberty* (Chicago: University of Chicago Press, 1951).

Posner, Richard, "A Theory of Negligence," 1 *Journal of Legal Studies* 29 (1972).

————, "Strict Liability—A Comment," 2 *Journal of Legal Studies* 205 (1973).

Prest, A. R., and R. Turvey, "Cost-Benefit Analysis: A Survey," 75 *The Economic Journal* 683 (1965).

Price, Don, *America's Unwritten Constitution: Science, Religion and Political Responsibility* (Baton Rouge: Louisiana University Press, 1983).

————, *Scientific Estate* (Cambridge, Mass.: Harvard University Press, 1965).

Primack, Joel, and Frank Von Hippel, *Advice and Dissent: Scientists in the Political Arena* (New York: Basic Books, 1974).

Regulatory Council, *Regulation of Chemical Carcinogens* (Washington, D.C.: Regulatory Council, 1979).

Rheingold, Paul, "Civil Cause of Action for Lung Damage Due to Pollution of Urban Atmosphere," 33 *Brooklyn Law Review* 17 (1966).

———, Norman Landau and Michael Canavan, eds., *Toxic Torts* (Washington, D.C.: Association of Trial Lawyers, 1977).

Ricci, Paolo, and Lawrence Molton, "Risk and Benefit in Environmental Law," 214 *Science* 1096 (1981).

Robinson, Glen, "Multiple Causation in Tort Law: Reflections on the *DES* Cases," 68 *Virginia Law Review* 713 (1982).

———, "Making of Administrative Policy: Another Look at Rulemaking and Adjudication and Administrative Procedure Reform," 118 *University of Pennsylvania Law Review* 485 (1970).

Rodgers, William, Jr., "Judicial Review of Risk Assessments: The Role of Decision Theory in Unscrambling the Benzene Decision," 11 *Environmental Law* 301 (1981).

———, "Benefits, Costs, and Risks: Oversight of Health and Environmental Decisionmaking," 4 *Harvard Environmental Law Review* 191 (1980).

———, "A Hard Look at *Vermont Yankee:* Environmental Law Under Close Scrutiny," 67 *Georgetown Law Journal* 699 (1979).

Rosenberg, David, "The Causal Connection in Mass Exposure Cases: A 'Public Law' Vision of the Tort System," 97 *Harvard Law Review* 851 (1984).

Rosenberg, Maurice, "Let's Everybody Litigate," 50 *Texas Law Review* 1349 (1972).

Rosenberg, Ronald, and Allen Olson, "Federal Environmental Review Requirements Other Than NEPA: The Emerging Challenge," 27 *Cleveland State Law Review* 195 (1978).

Ruckelshaus, William, "Risk in a Free Society," 14 *Environmental Law Reporter* 10190 (1984).

Sabatier, Paul, "Regulatory Policy-Making: Toward a Framework of Analysis," 17 *Natural Resources Journal* 415 (1977).

Sachs, Joel, *Environmental Law and Practice* (New York: Practising Law Institute, 1981).

Sagoff, Mark, "Economic Theory and Environmental Law," 79 *Michigan Law Review* 1393 (1981).

Salsburg, David, and Andrew Heath, "When Science Progresses and Bureaucracies Lag—The Case of Cancer Research," 65 *The Public Interest* 30 (1981).

Scalia, Antonin, "A Note on the Benzene Case," *Regulation* 25 (July/August, 1980).

———, "Vermont Yankee: The APA, the D.C. Circuit, and the Supreme Court," 1978 *Supreme Court Review* 345.

Schuck, Peter, "Litigation, Bargaining and Regulation," *Regulation* 26 (July/August, 1979).

——, "Regulation: Asking the Right Questions," 11 *National Journal* 711 (1979).

Schultze, Charles, *The Public Use of Private Interest* (Washington, D.C.: Brookings Institution, 1977).

——, "The Public Use of Private Interest," *Regulation* 10 (1977).

Shapiro, David, "The Choice of Rulemaking or Adjudication in the Development of Administrative Policy," 78 *Harvard Law Review* 1601 (1965).

Shapiro, Martin, *The Supreme Court and Administrative Agencies* (New York: Free Press, 1968).

Shapo, Marshall, *A Nation of Guinea Pigs: The Unknown Risks of Chemical Technology* (New York: Free Press, 1979).

Shils, Edward, ed., *Criteria for Scientific Development: Public Policy and National Goals* (Cambridge: Massachusetts Institute of Technology Press, 1968).

Sive, David, "Environmental Decisionmaking: Judicial and Political Review," 10 *Land Use & Environmental Law Review* 3 (1979).

Slesin, Louis, and Ross Sanders, "Categorization of Chemicals Under the Toxic Substances Control Act," 7 *Ecology Law Quarterly* 359 (1979).

Soble, Stephen, "A Proposal for the Administrative Compensation of Victims of Toxic Substances Pollution: A Model Act," 14 *Harvard Journal on Legislation* 683 (1977).

Sofaer, Abraham, "Judicial Control of Informal Discretionary Adjudication and Enforcement," 72 *Columbia Law Review* 1293 (1972).

Stewart, Richard, "The Development of Administrative and Quasi-Constitutional Law in Judicial Review of Environmental Decisionmaking," 62 *Iowa Law Review* 713 (1977).

——, "Paradoxes of Liberty, Integrity, and Fraternity: The Collective Nature of Environmental Quality and Judicial Review of Administrative Action," 7 *Environmental Law* 463 (1977).

——, "*Vermont Yankee* and the Evolution of Administrative Procedure," 91 *Harvard Law Review* 1804 (1978).

——, "The Reformation of American Administrative Law," 88 *Harvard Law Review* 1669 (1975).

Stone, Christopher, "Should Trees Have Standing?—Toward Legal Rights for Natural Objects," 45 *Southern California Law Review* 450 (1972).

Susskind, Lawrence, and Alan Weinstein, "Towards a Theory of Environmental Dispute Settlement," 9 *Boston College Environmental Affairs Law Review* 311 (1980–1981).

Thibaut, John and Laurens Walker, "A Theory of Procedure," 66 *California Law Review* 54 (1978).

Thompson, Frank, *Health Policy and the Bureaucracy: Politics and Implementation* (Cambridge: Massachusetts Institute of Technology Press, 1981).

Trauberman, Jeffrey, "Compensating Victims of Toxic Substances: Existing Federal Mechanisms," 5 *Harvard Environmental Law Review* 1 (1981).

Tribe, Laurence, *Channeling Technology Through Law* (Chicago: Bracton Press, 1973).

Turvey, Ralph, "On Divergences between Social Cost and Private Cost," *Economica* 309 (1963).

U. S. Congress, Congressional Research Service, *Toxic Substances Control Act: Testing Issues* (Washington, D.C.: Library of Congress, 1979).

_____, House of Representatives, Committee on Government Operations, 95th Cong., 2d Sess., *Performance of the Occupational Safety Health Administration* (Washington, D.C.: GPO, 1977).

_____, Committee on Interstate and Foreign Commerce, 95th Cong., 2d Sess., *Consumer Product Safety Commission's Regulation of TRIS: The Need for an Effective Chronic Hazards Program* (Washington, D.C.: GPO, 1978).

_____, Committee on Energy and Commerce, *Presidential Control of Agency Rulemaking: An Analysis of Constitutional Issues That May Be Raised by Executive Order 12291* (Washington, D.C.: GPO, 1981).

_____, Committee on Interstate and Foreign Commerce, 94th Cong., 2d Sess., *Toxic Substances Control Act: Report Together with Supplemental and Minority Views* (Washington, D.C.: GPO, 1976).

_____, Office of Technology Assessment, *Assessment of Technologies for Determining Cancer Risks from the Environment* (Washington, D.C.: GPO, 1981).

_____, Senate, Committee on Governmental Affairs, 95th Cong., 1st Sess., *Public Participation in Regulatory Agency Proceedings* (Washington, D.C.: GPO, 1977).

_____, *Delay in the Regulatory Process*, Vol. 4 (Washington, D.C.: GPO, 1977).

_____, Committee on Environment and Public Works, 96th Cong., 2d Sess., *Six Case Studies of Compensation for Toxic Substances Pollution: Alabama, California, Michigan, Missouri, New Jersey, and Texas* (Washington, D.C.: GPO, 1980).

Viscusi, W. Kip, *Risk by Choice* (Cambridge, Mass.: Harvard University Press, 1983).

Weidenbaum, Murray, "On Estimating Regulatory Costs," *Regulation* 14 (May/June, 1978).

Weisburger, John, and Gary Williams, "Carcinogen Testing: Current Problems and New Approaches," 214 *Science* 401 (1981).

Wessel, Milton, "Science, Technology and the Law in America: A Plea for Creditibility in Dispute Resolution," 22 *Jurimetrics* 245 (1982).

White, Lynn, Jr., "The Historical Roots of Our Ecologic Crisis," 155 *Science* 1203 (March 10, 1967).

Whiteside, Thomas, *The Pendulum and the Toxic Cloud* (New Haven, Conn.: Yale University Press, 1979).

Wilkey, Malcolm, "Agency Problems in Light of Environmental Problems," 26 *Administrative Law Review* 143 (1974).

Williams, Stephen, " 'Hybrid Rulemaking' Under the Administrative Procedure Act: A Legal and Empirical Analysis," 42 *University of Chicago Law Review* 401 (1975).

Wilson, James Q., ed., *The Politics of Regulation* (New York: Basic Books, 1980).

Wilson, Richard, and Edmond Crouch, *Risk-Benefit Analysis* (Cambridge, Mass.: Ballinger Publishing Co., 1982).

Wright, J. Skelly, "Beyond Discretionary Justice," 81 *Yale Law Journal* 575 (1972).

————, "Courts and the Rulemaking Process: The Limits of Judicial Review," 59 *Cornell Law Review* 375 (1974).

————, "New Judicial Requisites for Informal Rulemaking: Implications for the Environmental Impact Statement Process," 29 *Administrative Law Review* 59 (1977).

————. "Rulemaking and Judicial Review," 30 *Administrative Law Review* 461 (1978).

Yellin, Joel, "High Technology and the Courts: Nuclear Power and the Need for Institutional Reform," 94 *Harvard Law Review* 489 (1981).

————, "Judicial Review and Nuclear Power: Assessing the Risks of Environmental Catastrophe," 45 *George Washington Law Review* 969 (1977).

List of Cases

Page references included when available.

Index